POWER/
RESISTANCE

POWER/ RESISTANCE

local politics and the chaotic state

Andrew Kirby

Indiana University Press
Bloomington and Indianapolis

The paper used in this publication meets the minimum requirements of American National Standard for Information Sciences—Permanence of Paper for Printed Library Materials, ANSI Z39.48-1984.

 ™

Manufactured in the United States of America

Library of Congress Cataloging-in-Publication Data

Kirby, Andrew.
    Power/resistance : local politics and the chaotic state / Andrew Kirby.
        p.   cm.
    Includes bibliographical references and index.
    ISBN 0-253-33144-7 (cloth)
    1. State, The.   2. Power (Social sciences)   3. Government, Resistance to.   4. Local government.   I. Title.
    JC325.K58   1993
    320.8—dc20   92-41702

1 2 3 4 5   97 96 95 94 93

To Sallie
without whom it wouldn't have been worth doing

CONTENTS

ACKNOWLEDGMENTS

This book has been a long time in the writing, and I have accumulated many debts. I'm not naive enough to think that all those who have helped me are desperate to see their names in print, but the convention of listing one's accomplices remains a good one. Besides, they know that they'll get a copy of the book as well.

I first sketched out the basics of the argument at lunch one day in Boulder in 1983, and I developed my ideas in a working paper in 1987. My colleagues in the Program for Political and Economic Change at the University of Colorado were always supportive, and I have missed their intellectual contributions since I left. They should all be able to see their influence on my work, especially Mike Ward, who was ever helpful in resolving crucial issues to do with power. I also want to thank Jim Caporaso, who used an early version of the argument developed here in his book *The Elusive State.* In passing, I should note that parts of chapter 6 were first published in *Urban Geography,* and I thank both Gordon Clark and Nick Blomley for their helpful comments on my ideas in putting that special issue together, and V. H. Winston and Sons for permission to reproduce that material.

This manuscript was written entirely in Arizona; I began it in the foothills looking down over Tucson during the heat of the summer of 1989, and I concluded it with the same view, in the same heat, in 1992. I am grateful to Fred and Mary for letting me use their home for my own purposes. In the interim, it was written during weekends and, as my administrative responsibilities got heavier, in the quiet hours before dawn. Once the book began to take shape, I was helped by a number of people who read the manuscript; Sallie Marston, Marv Waterstone, and Kevin Cox all get my thanks, as do several anonymous referees. All the comments were valuable, and I have incorporated as many as my skills permit. As usual, I would like to pretend that any inelegancies or inaccuracies are entirely the result of others, but that wouldn't be true.

This book is dedicated to Sallie Marston, who has been my most effective critic by the example that she sets.

Thank you all, in these very different ways, for your contributions.

PROLOGUE

Consider for a moment Mr. Palomar as he stands upon a beach. As his narrator Italo Calvino observes, he has decided to look at a wave. A simple enough task, we might assume. It is more complex than it seems, however, for

> you cannot observe a wave without bearing in mind the complex features that concur in shaping it and the other, equally complex ones that the wave itself originates. These aspects vary constantly, so each wave is different from another wave, even if not immediately adjacent or successive; in other words, there are some forms and sequences that are repeated, though irregularly distributed in time and space.[1]

Here lies the ultimate problem of observation, namely the level of resolution that we employ. By focusing upon the specific, we lose sight of the complex interactions that constitute reality. By searching for order, we lose the singularity that coexists. Mr. Palomar is never able to resolve this paradox, nor is he the first to face it. Nor does he lose heart:

> And at each moment he thinks he has managed to see everything to be seen from his observation point, but then something always crops up that he had not borne in mind. . . . Concentrating the attention on one aspect makes it leap into the foreground . . . just as, with certain drawings, you have only to close your eyes and when you open them the perspective has changed. . . . Is this perhaps the real result that Mr. Palomar is about to achieve? To make the waves run in the opposite direction, to overturn time, to perceive the true substance of the world beyond sensory and mental habits? No, he feels a slight dizziness, but it goes no further than that.[2]

The more he observes, the more it seems that reflection will elude him. He has to bear all he has observed in mind at once, in order to begin the second phase of his operation,

extending this knowledge to the entire universe. . . . It would suffice not to
lose patience, as he soon does. Mr. Palomar goes off along the beach, tense
and nervous as when he came, and even more unsure about everything.

Mr. Palomar's concerns may not be ours, but his dilemmas most certainly
are. He is, to use John Berger's phrase, experimenting with ways of seeing.[3]
Such experiments are necessary because reality can be viewed in many
ways, and each method of seeing opens—or closes—particular insights
into that reality. Now, this has little to do with some primitive humanism,
which insists that we can know the world only by penetrating the vision of
those who are represented within it. Clearly, this would be paralyzing.
Rather, it dictates that we, as observers and participants, mesh the jumble
of the world with a latticework that we can call "order." The challenge is
that we should neither impose order where none exists, nor become immo-
bilized by an apparent glut of chaotic information.

There are numerous paths that lead us away from chaos and toward
order. Typically, these are counterposed, as though they have little or nothing in common, whereas they are in many significant ways interchangeable.
Some marxists, to take an example, have more in common with those who
would answer to the epithet "positivist" than they would care to believe. In
other words, the way of seeing may be very similar for both groups; they
create complex taxonomies, deal in aggregate behavior, and search for
laws or general theory.[4] Of course, the terms may differ, and the intentions
may vary, but the outcomes are often surprisingly similar.[5]

For this reason, this book eschews explicit epistemological labels, on the
grounds that they may mask more than they reveal (unless, like postmodernism, they are still in the process of accumulating intellectual baggage).
Instead, the argument concentrates upon a particular way of seeing. As the
example of Mr. Palomar will have signaled, the concern is for the broad
patterns of reality, but in addition, some privilege is given to what Geertz
has called the "ineluctably local shapes of knowledge," and these are,
almost by definition, less open to generalization.[6] Where possible, I have
depended upon theory, by which I mean broad statements that identify the
significance of the events under examination. If a label were mandated, that
of ethnography would be attractive, for it captures the sense of bringing
together the concerns of theory and the specifics of time and place. Nonetheless, like all labels, ethnography too has its burdens of meaning, and in
this case it is the implication that the research will focus upon the distant
and the exotic, which is usually, if mistakenly, seen as the true locale of the
anthropologist.[7]

In short, this book is groping toward a way of thinking about the world, or at least some important bits of it, namely the growth of the state and the politics of resistance. I have consciously tried for a hybrid style, one that mixes the abstraction of much critical theory with more grounded knowledge and examples. My aim is to avoid becoming, like Palomar, even more unsure about everything, although there are no guarantees that either reader or author will avoid becoming tense or nervous.

The Argument

My choice of title contains a number of allusions. Most obviously, the coupling of *Power/Resistance* echoes the juxtaposition of *Power/Knowledge* in Michel Foucault's work.[8] As we shall see, he saw these phenomena as linked, but not in a mechanistic manner. As he once remarked, power does not *equal* knowledge, and in the same vein, we must distrust attempts to connect power and resistance too mechanistically.[9] The argument developed here in the later chapters is an exploration of the ways in which resistance to the state can emerge and the extent to which it can be successful. In addition, I refer to the "chaotic state" (indeed, for much of its life, this manuscript was entitled *A State of Chaos*). On one level, this alludes to one of the principal themes developed here, namely that we live in a fragmented, even a chaotic, world.[10] From a different perspective, this book argues that one of the key dynamics of state creation has been to impose some uniformity upon the multitudes of local practice that exist within what we recognize as the nation state.* In other words, the chaotic state is an apparatus that grapples with, and attempts to minimize, the difference extant within civil society.

With its recognition of variation, this argument differs markedly from the social scientist's usual response to complexity, which is an attempt to transcend disorder via universal statements. Of course, such statements are rarely the generalizations that they appear to be. For example, much American social science reflects a pervasive ideology of possessive individualism, and thus focuses upon isolated subjects and their behavior, while, in contrast, much European research reflects the prevalence of collective conflict, which it seeks to explore via structural analysis.[11] While researchers in both traditions seek universal insights, their inferences are inevitably colored by the specifics of particular moments and different locations.

---

*For clarity, the following convention is employed throughout the book; the lowercase version "state" represents the general category of national bureaucratic institutions, and the uppercase "State" relates to the now-fifty States within the USA.

The drive within social science toward law-like statements has necessitated that the specifics of time and place be reduced to the status of noise factors. Within formal, linear analyses, such factors may be incorporated as an error term. The generic technique of regression analysis, which has driven much of the progress made in sociology, political science, and other quantitative studies in recent decades, depends upon the reduction of a spread of data to some mean characteristics. In consequence, to many sociologists and political scientists, introducing temporal or spatial context into an analysis is frequently little more than an attempt to increase an R^2 value. Theory becomes the logical outcome of empirical analysis, rather than vice versa, and without theoretical statements, the methods of regression (and its many counterparts) destroy some of our information. The most important element within a data set may be its diversity, a richness that is destroyed in the creation of mean values, and the counterpoint of terms such as *richness* and *meanness* is intentional.

This book tries to face up to a complex reality on its own terms, and to explore some of the implications of a contextual analysis that does not try to force all events into methodological pigeonholes. Its object is the importance of understanding the complexity of state-society relations. Beginning from the premise that it is crucial to take the raw rubble of the world seriously, it becomes necessary to reinterpret the emergence of the state as a set of institutions created to stabilize this jumble, and to control the affairs that take place within a specific territory.

This conception of the state is sharply at odds with most interpretations. Without slavishly re-creating their taxonomies, we can agree with Alford and Friedland that there are three dominant views of the state within advanced societies.[12] By focusing upon the admitted differences between the pluralist, managerialist, and class-based perspectives on the state, they fail, however, to point out how fundamentally similar these sets of literature are. That is to say, each possesses a view of a number of interlocking institutions that they name the state. This much is not normally open to argument, as the point of divergence revolves around the interpretation of the nature of control, the loci of power, and the relations between the state and the political processes of government. In contrast, the argument developed here is that the state is not a monolith. It is, rather, to be viewed as a complicated political, legal, and administrative jigsaw puzzle that contains a vast number of pieces. Most important is the recognition that the state apparatus is not a bureaucracy confined to office buildings in a capital city. It is a fragmented hydra of institutions that cover the geographic extent of the nation state. These institutions are based in, and thus linked to, the locations within which people undertake their everyday lives and re-create their own cultural and political practices. Crucial to this view is the realization that clear tensions exist between the state and civil society. As much as control is exerted downward from the state, so too resistance is manifested within local jurisdictions, resistance that reflects a broad sweep of individual and collective interests. In certain instances, this collective action may increase in strength and begin to move back toward the state itself. This is a dialectical perspective which cannot, by definition, be viewed solely as state- or society-centered, for it conjoins both these partial views. Indeed, it assumes that any understanding of the historical evolution of the state must revolve around this crucial tension—between the bureaucratic and political necessity of standardization and control on the one hand, and the fragmentation of society on the other. As Lefebvre argued:

> The state's tendency to establish centres of decision armed with all the tools of power and subordinated to a single main centre, the capital, thus encounters stiff resistance. Local powers (municipalities, departments, regions) do not readily allow themselves to be absorbed.[13]

This then leads to an additional theme that runs through the book. To understand the state, we must understand the locality, what goes on within it, and how local practices vary from one locality to another. Here, it is argued that this tension—between fragmentation and control—remains crucial to the investigation of the state, and that the power of the state apparatus has consequently to be reinterpreted. Attempts to remove the lowest levels of social and political practice from consideration (in either the academic or indeed the political realm) are based upon an insupportable tendency to elevate the power of the state. Opposition to this prevalent view is not to opt for some pluralist view that strives to see the state as a mirror that society holds up to itself. Rather, it is an attempt to find some room for human action and human struggle within the crowded corridors of social theory—and in so doing, to question the trajectory of the society in which we live. This book argues that the proliferation of social practices in different localities continues within advanced societies, and it does so despite the efforts of the state—and the efforts of social theorists—to downplay what goes on within the local arena.

In scope, then, this book is not designed to reprise many of the extant interpretations of the state. It does, in fact, present a view of the world which departs quite explicitly from basic assumptions held within much of political science and sociology. The ontological categories employed in the analysis will be fleshed out in subsequent chapters; at this juncture, however, it will be useful to present a sketch of the book's development, in order to provide a simple map of its premises.

Background

In an inchoate way, my efforts to shape this argument can be traced back a decade and more to the publication of Cynthia Cockburn's *The Local State,* which was one of the first books that tried to apply some form of state theory to the practice of local government.[14] This was in contrast to much prevailing work in Britain, which had been, up to that point, focused upon the specifics of local administration: housing, health care, education, and so on. As aspects of a massive experiment in welfare statism, it was, however, important to integrate these sectors into broader social and political analyses. Many researchers, myself included, had begun to venture toward an understanding of managers, then bureaucracies, then class elites, until one was led, breathless, to the conclusion that a broad study of capitalism was the answer—if only we could identify the deep structures, then everything else would somehow fall into place. Cockburn's book was the apotheosis of this trend, invoking as it does an Althusserianism of grandiose proportions. For all that, it remains a pioneering work, in several respects. Not least of these reflects the fact that her terminology (notably the phrase "local state") has survived, and it does so because she was the first to subject the apparent trivia of the welfare state to the scrutiny that had been reserved until then for larger forms of government. Still, the book portrays the local political process as little more than the sharp end of state control, a caricature that reduces a creative arena of political struggle to an arcane sideshow, far from the madding crowds of real politics.[15] In short, while providing an analytical signpost, Cockburn pointed us in rather the wrong direction.

As I have already observed, it became clear that one could not look at slices of the welfare state in isolation, and in particular one could not say anything of great importance simply by examining empirical arrangements.[16] It was clear enough that one could not have any great expectations of a single premise—such as accessibility to services or the racial composition of neighborhoods—as a peg upon which to hang a study of something as potentially complex as public goods. And yet here one ran into a central problem. It was clearly necessary to ground such empirical work in a framework that threw social and political realities into sharp relief. However, the only available tools for such a task involved the local state literature, and as noted, and as we will see in detail below, this argued little more than that local government was a weapon in the fist of the state. In consequence, my focus shifted toward the redevelopment of local state theory.[17] This has been, predictably enough, shaped by a number of other experiences and influences, and these will be sketched in turn, again for methodological rather than solipsistic reasons.

Manuel Castells's book *The City and the Grassroots* appeared in 1983, offering an important interpretation of collective action. It received the C. Wright Mills Award from the American Sociological Association, but elsewhere Castells received an abusive response to his efforts to embrace human conflict, of all types, as significant.[18] While this was none too surprising vis-à-vis its political implications, the example serves to underscore another of the themes that will emerge throughout this argument, notably the difficulty of interpreting collective action in terms beyond the terrain of class conflict. European sociologists have historically marginalized a large number of other struggles relating to ethnicity, gender, and sexuality, a point that will emerge again in chapter 4. In consequence, the discourse within much social science can be dominated by a crude materialism which claims privilege over all other approaches to knowledge.[19] In addition, this example also points to one of the more pervasive problems within contemporary social science, namely the search for what Quentin Skinner has termed "timeless questions and answers."[20] It is ironic that much American scholarship has been directed toward explicit comparisons with such interpretations of the European experience, with the issue of "American exceptionalism" being a prime example. What an example of a nonquestion! Why we should suppose for a moment that one society should replicate any other—that the institutions and forms of struggle should be consistent—is as logical as the attempt to shoehorn the practices of the past into the models of the present.[21]

Despite the prevalence of this thinking, it is possible to break away from this sterile view of the world. A number of important studies have presented a more detailed effort to identify a postmarxist, perhaps even a postmodern, terrain. Central to these is Giddens's *Contemporary Critique of Historical Materialism*.[22] Again, I will take issue with many of his theses as they relate to the nature of the state, but his attempts to recast the way we look at the world provide a number of important pointers. In particular, one must be gratified that a social theorist of his stature has bothered to investigate the interworkings of space and time. On the other hand, the manner in which it has been done leaves something to be desired, specifically with regard to the way that time remains privileged before space (see page 62).[23] Conversely, Geertz's *Local Knowledge* deals explicitly with the settings of everyday life in the creation and re-creation of social structures; any mention of everyday life must also invoke mention of Fernand Braudel, whose evocation of a "total history" provides a compelling model of how massive doses of knowledge can be transformed into an exciting and meaningful narrative.[24] Braudel's work is also an important counterweight to that of Wallerstein, which has—inadvertently, I believe—done a great deal to devalue the importance of human struggle within contemporary social science. Despite his homage to Braudel, Wallerstein has given primacy to the world economy in a manner that leaves scant room for individual actors—an unfortunate reversal of the original *Annaliste* enterprise.

With the reader's indulgence, I will continue this list of influential authors who may serve to anchor the following chapters. The first of these is Charles Tilly, whose *The Contentious French* and its successor, *Coercion, Capital and European States,* unite in a masterful way a number of the themes that have been sketched here: the importance of collective action, the nature of political struggle, and in particular the fragmentation of society, whose study requires a finely tuned contextual sense.[25] A very different book is Stephen Skowronek's *Building a New American State,* which speaks to an entirely different literature.[26] This work is a response to calls to "bring the state back in," but it does so in a manner which is singular: the approach is historical, and its findings, as we shall see later, are of great importance, insofar as it shows how the state is formed—slowly, unpredictably, and frequently in the face of reverses.

A number of other authors could be invoked—Harré and Schorske would be two immediate possibilities—but I will mention by title only two more books.[27] Both are crucial insofar as they explore the interrelations between space and time, which are so central to a contextual understanding. The first is Stephen Kern's work *The Culture of Space and Time,* which deals with the discontinuities in the ways in which the basic material dimensions were viewed during the onset of modernity. A logical counterpart to Kern's work is that of Ed Soja, whose *Postmodern Geographies* investigates the role of spatial thinking in the postmodern urge. Both are important books, and both deserve to be discussed widely within the social sciences.[28] While noting the work of my own disciplinary colleagues, I should also give prominence to Allan Pred, whose studies of modernity have provided compelling blueprints for us all.[29]

These then constitute a sample of the works that have had some influence on this book.[30] In concluding the tally of my debts, I must also acknowledge the impact that Michel Foucault's writings have had on me. This has had less to do with method than with the presentation of a singular vision of the relation between the individual, society, and the state. In both his formal work and his interviews, Foucault has offered us crucial insights with regard to the nature of power, discipline, and the constitution of the individual, and these have moved my thoughts in very provocative directions. It is often argued that Foucault possessed a bleak view of the world, in which the individual had little hope of redemption. Yet I suspect that this comes from a reading of his early works and not his later studies, with their greater emphasis upon sexuality and the individual's ability to resist being turned into a political or psychiatric subject.[31] The reader will find numerous points in the text below where I have found Foucault to be instructive.

The present argument represents an attempt to bring these different strands together. The aim has been to evolve a perspective on human affairs that is at once contextual, yet also informed by general or theorized statements. The derivation of the latter has been guided by a number of premises, which have been implicit in the comments made above, but which are worthy of repetition:

1. Human affairs, grounded in place, cannot be understood without recourse to wider forces and events;

2. What goes on in localities is nonetheless singular and consequently important, and cannot solely be read off the actions of the state or evolution of the world economy;

3. The state does not develop in isolation; it exists within a social context, and consequently, one can neither privilege the state nor elevate state-centered approaches above broader interpretations of social actions;

4. State institutions cannot be seen as constituting a monolithic entity; the genesis of the state is in part a function of its historical evolution and concomitant relations of the local bases of political action;

5. The comprehension of these relations is to be understood only historically and geographically.

Organization

The book is constructed in the following way. Chapter 1 provides a general outline of the importance of state actions within the creation and re-creation of social relations. In addition, an overview is provided of the importance of understanding everyday life as the basis of political development and action. Chapter 2 builds on this latter theme, and explores the bases of political development within localities, examining the development of *common* sense within everyday life. Chapter 3 develops an understanding of the territorial state, to use Mann's phrase, exploring the historical evolution of state forms. Chapter 4 takes this further, by showing how the long-standing bases of political development, rooted in particular places, represent a dialectical tension within the state apparatus: the displacement of power from the locality to the national organization has not been completed, in other words. Chapter 5 builds on these insights and outlines a theory of the state that is new insofar as it incorporates the local state as a theoretical entity. Chapters 6 and 7 then provide an empirical exploration of this framework; the first is a study of the contemporary political struggles surrounding gun control, the second an analysis of the evolution of the Mexican-American borderlands. The last chapter is taken up with a discussion of the theoretical premises and their implications for our understanding of local politics and the nature of democracy within the modern state.

POWER/
RESISTANCE

ONE

TERRAINS OF DISCOURSE

The estate of political knowledge was the
"state" —*FARR*[1]

Introduction

Every era is marked by particular intellectual concerns, although these may be no great indicator of the events that surround them. From the American Civil War until the First World War, for example, the rival claims of heredity and culture were proposed both as fundamental questions and as fundamental opposites.[2] While the second half of the nineteenth century was a period of virtually unrestricted capitalism and imperialism, these were not debated solely in political-economic terms. To be sure, the confrontations of western civilization and supposedly primitive peoples generated some reflections on the economic systems that drove men and women across the globe, but contemporary science gave priority to the question why both primitive and advanced societies (as they were assumed to be) existed simultaneously.

This dissonance is reasserted within contemporary social science. This is an era of intervention by public institutions into private affairs on a more massive scale then ever before seen. As various commentators have argued, the master noun of political discourse is now the state—*that vertical structure of public authority with its message of public domination.*[3] Yet our fundamental concerns and debates revolve around the material bases of society, and not the political bases. The state has grown larger, and has involved itself more extensively in the affairs of the family and the neighborhood, and in the international arena; yet for two decades, critical interpretations of society have privileged the mechanisms of capitalism at the expense of the mechanisms of power and conflict. We have seen any number of studies that examine the "crisis" of late capitalism, while the crisis of the growth of state power has received, until very recently, only scant attention.[4] This stems less from the failure of Marx, Engels, Lenin, Trotsky, and Gramsci to provide definitive accounts of the state, than from the fact that they attempted to do so in what Jessop calls "inconsistent ways."[5] While marxist analysis has decelerated, other social scientists have responded to calls to "bring the state back in," although it is ironic that these emanate from sociologists and not political scientists. A century ago, the president of Yale could see the activities of the latter and the study of the state as synonymous, in an address entitled "Political Science; or, The State Theoretically and Practically Considered"; as Mitchell observes, now the rupture between the two is almost complete.[6]

Economy, Civil Society, and State

While this chapter takes as its starting point the proposition that disjunctures between academic discourse and social practice are not uncommon, its primary purpose is to emphasize the importance of the contemporary state. While it certainly does not argue that the material base of a society is without relevance, it is an attempt to redirect some of the attention currently given to economic restructuring.[7] Changes in the form of capitalist economic relations are both continual and of importance—as we shall see, there has been recent valuable discussion of the incorporation of flexible production systems into the manufacturing process, and the extent to which this has led to changes in city form and the national/international distribution of productive activities.[8] However, these developments have also implicated both civil society and the state, and these have received much less attention.[9]

This chapter will concentrate first upon the organization of industrial capitalism, indicating how this has changed over both time and space. I shall give a brief overview of ways that the structures of production have altered, particularly since 1945, with the important result that collective action defined by the workplace is no longer predominant. Indeed, as I shall show subsequently, there has occurred simultaneously a major increase in the activities of the institutions of the state, such that collective action has come to be defined much more frequently against the state itself.

Production, Everyday Life, and Collective Action

In this exploration of the relations between economic change, the state, and collective action, we will focus initially upon the relations of production as they existed at the emergence of the capitalist-industrialist phase.[10] Although there were obvious variations between the ways in which different productive processes evolved (e.g., textile production, shoe manufacture, iron and steel working), a common feature was the deliberate creation of a *space economy*. What this term reflects is the way in which the social relations at a location were molded by the productive institutions there, until a coherent and interlocking set of practices existed. The key component was a production site—a factory or mill. This naturally constituted an attraction for labor, and became a spatial and temporal focus. The domination of the factory was extended far beyond the factory gates, however. Capitalists sought to control the fine details of day-to-day existence, either directly, in terms of the long hours worked and the limited number of days of rest, or indirectly, in terms of the provision of lodging and the control of behavior. Because political practices were circumscribed so as to exclude all but the propertied, it is easy to see the ways in which nearly all social relations became predicated upon production relations. It is for this reason that we can term this situation a "coherent space economy."

Not all industries depended initially upon factory production, of course, but even in those contexts where there remained some workplace-home-place separation, the evidence suggests that capitalists intruded into many basic human relationships. To take a specific example, it has been shown in detail how women were pulled into the manufacture of shoes in Lowell, Massachusetts in the early nineteenth century by a falling rate of profit.[11] They were not given skilled tasks, nor were they paid; shoe buyers dealt with the male heads of individual families, and women's labor had to subsidize the family unit's production costs. Because individual entrepreneurs were able to pit one family production unit against another, they were able effectively to exclude women from the possibility of paid work, which would of course raise costs. When women went on strike to attempt to change their status, men were unable to break from their conditions of production, and consequently could not support the protest. In this way, production relations could intrude into nearly every family in the town, amplifying the traditional patriarchal role and driving a wedge between the sexes.

The coherence of these space economies has been incrementally destroyed by constant reorganizations in the workplace, leading to what Castells has described as "the abstraction of production."[12] One of the simplest—but most important—developments has been the growth of successful corporations at the expense of others. As Walker so succinctly puts it, today "the large firm is not coincident with the large factory."[13] Corporate growth has involved takeovers, relocations, specializations, and complex forms of integration, which may extend a single industry across a single city or a single continent. As David Harvey observes,

> The closer production approaches some spatial equilibrium condition (the equalization of profit rates across locations for example), the greater the competitive incentive for individual capitalists to disrupt the basis of that equilibrium through technological change. . . . In the absence of any restraining or countervailing forces, the individual search for excess profits would keep the space economy of capitalist production in a state that resembles an incoherent and frenetic game of musical chairs.[14]

While there are currently many restraining forces (not least the political control of the state), there is little to gainsay the proposition that capital is now mobile, in contrast to eras when banking was rudimentary and transportation costs were a major proportion of product costs, which made producers' locational decisions so critical.[15]

While discussion of the "global economy" has become a cliché, there continues to emerge a massive amount of important research dealing with the specific reconfigurations of capitalism. Under debate in this literature are a number of issues, including the typicality of certain well-studied industries (e.g., semiconductor producers); the representativeness of certain growth areas, such as Silicon Valley, Grenoble, or the Mexican-American border region; and even the qualitative differences between the present and former patterns of international investment.[16] Of central importance is the proposition that new "regional economies" or "territorial complexes" may be (re)emerging, with important implications for social relations.

Regional Economies?

It has been a conventional wisdom that the industrial terrain post-1945 is one of segmentation: labor has become highly fragmented, as the separate units of production have become integrated parts of a world economy, and dual labor markets have fueled the creation of divisions of skill, income, and unionization between workers.[17] In contrast, more recent studies point to the existence of regional economies or territorial complexes that display productive concentrations. Richard Walker, for example, notes that half the industrial output of all Latin America in 1981 was generated by the three cities of Buenos Aires, São Paulo, and Mexico City, and that Greater Los Angeles has a Gross Domestic Product greater than that of India. He argues that such concentration reflects advantages of propinquity (i.e., low transaction costs), while locational fixity and jurisdictional boundaries serve to sustain existing ties.[18]

The most celebrated example of this line of reasoning is the identification of the so-called Third Italy (the Northeastern and Central regions). It has been argued that this region displays an integrated and reinforcing industrial base, which can serve as a model for the pattern of new growth in the next century.[19] Even more important is the intimation that such territorial complexes will have implications for social relations. Storper and Scott indicate that there is emerging a "new post-Fordist politics of place," in which workers are "habituated" into the local productive culture—a scenario that is, of course, very reminiscent of the nineteenth-century space economies described above.[20]

This reinvention of early industrial capitalist forms should be treated with some skepticism. In the first instance, the conditions of development in the Third Italy hardly constitute the model for all "post-Fordist" enterprises, as Mingione emphasizes. Second, we require some clarification of the extent of a territorial complex (an issue that will be reprised below as we discuss other constructs such as locales). While it is the case that Greater Los Angeles possesses a massive GDP, it is more questionable whether it really constitutes a territorial complex. It is hard to see how there can be real interactive advantages for producers within an urban area that covers several thousand square miles, and in which there exist severe practical restrictions upon movement, overcrowding of phone capacity, and any number of environmental constraints; that is to say, the advantages of propinquity are more imagined than real. Third, it is also hard to fathom the extent of interactions between massive defense contractors, on the one hand, and tiny sweatshops run by recent immigrants, on the other. They are certainly both part of the same urban place, but they are, in reality, oblivious of each other's existence. Amin and Robins summarize these criticisms as follows, moving from the specific case (the Third Italy) to the general:

> It is only in the loosest possible sense that these areas constitute an articulated industrial system. The producers possess a restricted degree of freedom in the marketplace, and receive little support from the rest of the system. The firms tend to be isolated, highly dependent on a few buyers, and barely able to improve their market position. "Flexibility," here, tends to refer to an ability to survive . . . [and] to self-exploitation and the use of family labour, the evasion of tax and social security contributions, and the use of cheap female and young workers, especially for unskilled work. These conditions are also typical of the vast numbers of very small firms and artisans working in the traditional industries in many developing economies.[21]

Despite, then, the attention paid to certain territorial complexes, it remains important to argue that the centrality of production relations within the local area has weakened, at least within the industrialized nations. No single employer can normally maintain conditions of hegemony for a prolonged period of time, and those few examples of this still occurring have attracted some attention: Gaventa's study of quiescence in a mining valley in Appalachia indicates that the "company town" may still survive, but it requires many preconditions, such as a remote capitalist organization and a virtual lack of alternative economic prospects.[22] Elsewhere, even the largest corporate concentrations have faded, although they always leave a singular social and economic trace upon the landscape.[23]

This dissolution of the traditional space economy has had important consequences for the ways in which collective action unfolds. It was argued above that the nineteenth-century space economy was a setting in which relations of production were dominant, even if the analysis of Marx, Engels, Veblen, and others was necessary to expose the connections. The corollary of this is the emergence of canonical axes of organization as we move to the present. The struggles of labor remain, but are augmented (some say diluted) by other movements, defined well outside the workplace. It is still argued, of course, that the latter is central: "Feminists, neighborhood and civil rights groups stand to gain by collaborating . . . since the overwhelming majority of members in such groups are subordinate salary and wage earners."[24] However, the key point is that such activists do not choose to see themselves defined in that way. This has little, if anything, to do with supposed notions of "postindustrialization." It is obvious that a large service industry, dealing with magazine subscriptions or hotel bookings, is just as likely to involve labor exploitation as is a stockyard or dockyard. However, such a labor force has little demanded of it in terms of skills and is rarely permitted to unionize. Limited benefits, such as health care, may be enough to offset other disadvantages of the job and so produce workers who are inert so far as workplace issues are concerned. This does not preclude other forms of social action, of course.[25]

The Emergence of the Domestic State

Coincident with corporations relinquishing some of their tight control of the labor markets in which they operate has been an increase in the stature of the state throughout the industrialized nations. In order to refute any possibility of functionalism, I want to avoid the suggestion of direct causality, although such arguments exist.[26] For the moment, let us emphasize the shift from external state expenditure to internal spending, which first began to occur approximately a century ago.[27] The change is not a function of diminishing levels of conflict at the international level, but rather an increase in domestic projects. This has come about for a number of reasons: Skowronek has pointed to a series of crises (see chapter 3), while Mingione discusses the connections between Fordism as a form of production and welfare statism, itself extending from issues of social control (characterized as the Bismarckian model), through to the creation of welfare programs for populations unable to purchase them on the open market (a Keynesian model).[28]

Politics and the State

In contrast to early industrial capitalism, work intrudes less forcibly into the living space. Workplace-homeplace separation has increased, and leisure time has increased also. This does not imply, however, that a humanist view of a whole, independent being can be recouped. The opposite is true, as everyday existence is increasingly dictated by the actions of the state apparatus. At this juncture, this argument will not concentrate in detail upon the operation of the state, nor will it focus upon the coercive nature of much state action, including attacks on unions (see chapters 3 and 4).[29] For the moment, it is enough to examine the ways in which forms of the state's welfare activities intrude into civil society. For example, housing may be purchased via the state's underwriting of credit for homeowners, or may be rented, in many societies, directly from the state. Urban form is dictated by public road construction and facilitated by publicly underwritten rapid-transit systems.[30] The full impact of this cocoon was outlined by Michael Teitz some years ago, and his remarks are still apposite today (although many state apparatuses face endemic public spending crises that limit the quality of services,[31] and we should, of course, extend the argument to include women):

> Modern urban man is born in a publicly financed hospital, receives his education in a publicly supported school and university, spends a good part of his time travelling on publicly built transportation facilities, communicates through the post office or the quasi-public telephone system, drinks his public water, disposes of his garbage through the public removal system, reads his public library books, picnics in the public parks, is protected by his public police, fire and health systems; eventually he dies, again in a hospital, and may even be buried in a public cemetery.[32]

This penetration of the state into personal experience has numerous consequences. Most important of these is the fact that once the state has assumed responsibility for specific social spheres, it naturally becomes associated with the performance of its institutions. To invoke, in an illustrative manner, the structural terminology of Habermas, the state may be necessitated to intervene in order to deal with legitimation crises (e.g., in the context of urban poverty and regional economic imbalances). However, if such measures are unsuccessful, the failure of the economic development process becomes transformed into a failure of state intervention—a rationality crisis. In this manner, the components of the state increase their visibility and become, in turn, the focus of political action. In consequence, some commentators interpret the politics of the 1980s—Thatcherism and Reaganism in particular—as attempts to diminish the visibility of the state, and to recast social inequalities in the language of international liability ("the world economy is in recession"), or in terms of individual pathologies ("blaming the victim").

Political changes—in the form of, say, calls to get government off people's backs, or the apparent transfer of responsibilities between levels of government, both of which typified the 1980s—do not, however, remove or diminish the role of the public domain in the private realm of individuals and their affairs.[33] For that individual, consumption is a major determinant of well-being: the consumption of housing, the consumption of publicly underwritten infrastructure, the consumption of education. As Urry points out, it is right to regard these as "economistic issues." This does not, however, make them, by a process of reduction, class struggles. Class struggle—personified in its purest form by the skilled, male worker—diminishes in importance as new cycles of struggle emerge. These will reflect the achievement of basic worker rights (such as health and safety legislation), which then in turn highlight inequalities for others—such as women, homosexuals, the disabled, the elderly.[34]

These political contests may be regarded as "reactionary" (the term is, again, Urry's).[35] By this, Urry implies that such struggles have limited and highly selective goals, and are thus only on the periphery of social change. The same point is made by Harvey, who appears to argue that the social movements generated by 'others' are "regressive," whereas traditional class struggles that challenge capitalism are "progressive."[36] Here, we see a very traditional, masculinized conception of struggle. Men's actions are perceived to be universal (class conflict), while the struggles of gays or the handicapped are viewed as the politics of the self.

This is taken further by Parkin, in his discussion of social closure, by which he means the ways in which groups within a class may differentiate and exclude another group within the same class; typical and obvious examples relate to the closure displayed against people of color by Anglo males.[37] As he also shows, however, the nature of exclusion has changed, and now relates less frequently to employment and more often to social practices, such as education. Indeed, he might have added that a new form of geographical exclusion has emerged, which hinges upon the housing market and specific closed residential spaces.[38] This puts such struggles squarely within the realm of civil society, and focuses them in turn upon the state, which typically becomes involved in such contests through the legal system.[39] Although Parkin does not elaborate this process particularly successfully, his example is an interesting one, focusing as it does upon Protestant-Catholic antagonism within Northern Ireland. In recent decades, this has spilled out from the segregated shipyards of Belfast to become, once more, a wider and more visible conflict, at least in part directed at British political structures. As Parkin notes:

> Perhaps one of the more successful applications of solidaristic tendencies for exclusionary ends has been that conducted by Protestant workers in Ulster against the British government's insistence on the full inclusion of Catholics. The general strike . . . led to the collapse of the Northern Ireland parliament . . . one of the very few cases on record of workers in an advanced capitalist society bringing down a government by direct action.[40]

The apparent singularity of this example should not hide the fact that there are similarities to other, very different contests. Castells's discussions of specifically urban struggles suggest the gravity of politics expressed in the sphere of consumption.[41] His analysis of the Citizen Movement in Madrid at the end of the Franquist era is instructive, notably for the manner in which it shows the way that class struggle was stifled by repressive state institutions, which controlled most, if not all, aspects of the economy and civil society. Massive inequalities existed within a nation that had professed imperial ambitions but nurtured poverty, illiteracy, and poor daily conditions of existence. Active opposition did not develop through the repressed unions but via a Citizen Movement. This is, according to Castells's account, none too surprising, given the massive contradictions expressed within Madrid in the 1950s and 1960s. As a deliberately created growth pole and prestigious modern city, it nonetheless contained shanty towns, poor housing, and a minimum of infrastructure. It is to be emphasized, however, that the citizens' struggle was in explicit opposition to the state; indeed, any opposition to the governance and institutions of the nation's capital could be nothing else but a challenge to the state itself.

In terms of the theme being developed here, it is important to echo Castells's own analysis of the connections existing between the citizens' movement in Madrid and class struggle. His interpretation is unambiguous: "the experience in Madrid is clear: there was no connection."[42] By this, he means that labor struggles and urban (consumption) struggles were in solidarity but were taking place independently. As always, the figurative bottom line was the political-economic nature (of Spain, in this instance); this, however, influenced the political realm only in a tangential manner, as this lengthy quote indicates:

> It does not follow that the Citizen Movement had nothing to do with social classes. The interests it fought in opposing the consequences of a given model of urban development were ultimately class interests. Spanish finance capital . . . was the driving force behind accelerated metropolitan growth. . . . Banks, real estate firms, landowners and developers . . . were the agents of urban development based on speculation. . . . An authoritarian state . . . provided the class-dominated instrument of urban policy opposed by neighborhoods. Thus the Citizen Movement confronted class interests by arguing in favor of use value against exchange value, and by claiming local independence against centralized dictatorship. In weakening the capitalist domination over the city it also had a major impact on class struggle. But it was not a class-defined mobilization in terms of its social base, organization, and the issues in which it was involved. *The Movement was then a non-class, social movement challenging the structure of a class society* [my emphasis].[43]

The ways in which this challenge may be manifested are of course varied. As Castells indicates, there is a thin dividing line between consumption politics which are able to amplify political tensions, and situations in which the former are simply swamped and destroyed by existing power structures. Moreover, there have been many commentators who take issue with Castells's logic, and explicitly the autonomy of his actors.[44] Criticism notwithstanding, Castells has, in his identification of struggles between use value and exchange value, hit a particular nerve. Sociologists Molotch and Logan, for instance, have produced a persuasive interpretation of current urban struggles in the U.S., which they locate at the interface of development interests on the one hand, and community aspirations to control the quality of life within the locality on the other (see also chapter 5). Predictably, their work is not without critics, but their basic thesis—which can be reduced to the premise that communities can make a political difference to the way in which the development process operates—has attracted a good deal of sympathetic attention.

On a more formal level, there is also evidence that consumption issues can influence, in a consistent manner, the voting process. Research on consumption locations is about the ways in which housing and transportation issues cross-cut existing voting strategies, which in the British case have been based upon class positions.[45] Indeed, it would be possible to begin to analyze the dissolution of the British two-party system in terms of the way in which traditional Labour Party values, which revolved around the levels of wages and ways by which they could be improved, have ceased to attract many blue-collar voters; despite their apparent similarities with other working-class members, they are in fact crucially distanced by the ownership of property and their current commitment to exchange values, mortgage and interest rates, and the future of their investment.[46] Such voters were explicitly provided for within the ranks of the Conservative, and the short-lived Social Democratic, Party. In consequence, prosperity in the southern parts of Great Britain has produced a near-homogenous voting bloc that washes across more traditional class divisions, and which continually threatened to marginalize the Labour Party throughout the 1980s.[47] Some comparable studies have been undertaken in the United States, although the results seem less explicit. Electoral analysis done in the State of Washington on the links between electoral results and ballot initiatives on the one hand and sociocultural variables on the other suggests that voters do not vote along strict lines (e.g., blue-collar/white-collar); instead, votes indicate a mix of "inputs" that reflect production *and* consumption issues.[48]

In summary, then, in order to comprehend the nature of advanced societies, it is necessary to move beyond a materialist analysis that limits itself to the structures of production—a perspective which does, of course, place some priorities across our interpretations in a very specific manner—out to embrace the increasing salience of the state and its role in defining social action around issues of consumption.[49]

Locales, Localities, and Everyday Life

My goal here is to create some space for a discourse which includes consideration of, and acceptance of, the importance of everyday life, and struggles which, because they take place beyond the factory gates, have received less attention. This point cannot be emphasized too strongly, although it must be immediately qualified by reemphasizing that this is also not a matter of setting up or setting down straw dogs—the intention is not the affirmation of one mode of thought versus another, the reaffirmation of Weber, say, at the expense of Marx.[50] In important ways, both these perspectives (although they do not exhaust the possibilities, of course) are unhelpful. They are limited insofar as they take as their objects of inquiry categories which are vast aggregations of actors: this is true of classes, bureaucracies, and the processes that are associated with them. Human action is not contingent upon a Hegelian blueprint that sets out a path to be followed. Nor is it resolved at the scale of aggregates—the British working class, all African Americans, all Kenyan women. Instead, it reflects more localized and immediate demands, pressures, constraints, and tensions, the ways in which people set up coping strategies to deal with the events they encounter on a routine, and not so routine, basis. These strategies produce a particular result—each particular to a time and a place. This perspective sees "society" through a prism, a lens that breaks down the aggregate into its component parts.

Such a reconsideration has been attempted, and has produced some interesting but only partially successful ideas. Sociologists Urry and Giddens, for instance, have both emphasized the importance of what they variously describe as the "locality" or "locale." Urry focuses upon the locality as a setting within which particular forms of class struggle will emerge; that is, the locality is some form of unit—like a labor market—within which class practices may be subtly different from those exhibited elsewhere. In consequence, he notes that "social classes are spatially distributed."[51] Giddens's development of the term "locale" is characteristically a good deal more complex than that of the locality; he suggests that it is "a preferable term to that of 'place' . . . for it carries something of the connotation of place used as a setting for interaction."[52] As we would expect, Giddens's discovery of space-time constructs is closely involved with his elaboration of structuration and the manner in which social structures are re-created, with slight variations, from location to location. This notwithstanding, his use of examples is inordinately wide, ranging from the international division of labor through regional class concentrations and on to urban/rural differentiation and neighborhood formation.[53]

Work by Allan Pred has refined Giddens's own notions. Just as the latter has attempted to borrow from Pred's work on time-space, so Pred has extended the literature of structuration. He argues:

> The integration of time geography with the theory of structuration becomes possible when it is recognized that each of society's component institutions does not exist apart from the everyday and longer-term production, consumption and other projects for which it is responsible. If all of society's formal and informal institutions are project-bound, and if all projects require some human participation, then the following proposition may be stated: The detailed situations and material continuity of structuration are perpetually spelled out by the intersection of individual paths with institutional projects occurring at spe-

cific temporal and spatial locations. If this be the case, then place as histori-cally-contingent process—the becoming of place, all the humanly made elements of place, and all that takes place within a given area—is inseparable from the everyday unfolding of the structuration process in place(s).[54]

Pred's work (and the work of those closely in sympathy, such as Michael Watts) offers a glimpse of a powerful new regional geography, one in which all manner of connections can be grasped. We see, for example, an oppor-tunity to link individual biographies and social settings; human action and nature; and the evolution of social settings through time.[55] Interestingly, this is not at all alien to the creations of Castells, who has also evolved a view of social relations which is explicitly spatial. Of space, he writes:

> It is one of the fundamental material dimensions, and to consider it independ-ently from social relationships, even with the intention of studying their interac-tion, is actually to separate nature from culture and thus to destroy the first principle of any social science: that matter and consciousness are interre-lated and this fusion is what history and science are each about.[56]

Space thus becomes analogous to a chessboard upon which each and every person is located. The moves that the agent/pieces make take place within the constraints of the board and the social rules/directions that are permitted. Most important, if we remove the board, we can no longer under-stand the logic of the pieces that remain. This is, in fact, one of Castells's key thrusts, namely that swift changes within the capitalist mode of produc-tion are dissolving the current form of the chessboard, with the result that "the meaning of place in people's consciousness is being destroyed." He observes:

> Space is dissolved into flows; cities become shadows that explode or disap-pear. . . . The outer experience is cut off from the inner experience. The new attempted urban meaning is the spatial and cultural separation of people from their product and their history. It is the space of collective alienation and of individual violence. . . . Life is transformed into abstraction, cities into shadows.[57]

In short, places provide a setting within which individual behaviors mani-fest themselves, but they never do so in isolation. Places intersect with places and the styles of life represented there, and are subject to the con-trols and dictates of a wider social and economic structure. In conse-quence, relations "between places" are highly analogous to the relations between individual agents and some wider social totality.[58] Expressed a little differently, we can argue that locales or localities are themselves part of an existing social, economic, and political whole, and we must recognize that this totality has evolved, at least in part, as a result of the intersections between localities or locales. So, for example, it is clear that the shifts of investment from rustbelt locations in the 1960s and 1970s to sunbelt economies had a profound impact on the overall structure of the U.S. economy; it redefined the nature of work (from unionized male employment toward part-time and female labor), and it shifted the political balance of power (from the eastern seaboard to the west).

Places, Localities, Locales, and Cities

This argument demands some more specified definition of "place" and "locality." On one level, "local" might be viewed simply as the scale of social interaction below that of the nation state and, by definition, the world order. But what then constitutes the locality or the locale? Neighborhoods? Labor markets? Regions? If the notion of place is to be more than an ideal type, we require some specification of what kinds of setting are envisaged and what type of place is being considered. This problem is revealed historically—the notion of place used by Pred, for example, reflects a particular moment (more correctly, a durée) in the evolution of social, political, and economic relations, at which it was possible to see an integration of all these facets of activity. Place was more than a setting for interaction; it was the container for that activity, the sum of experience and the repository for experience. In short,

> in many traditional societies, localism had a particular economic base, in the system of agricultural and craft-manufacturing production. In particular, where the ownership and/or control of land was the crucial resource in the possession of power, then the hierarchical nature of society was always likely to be reflected in local terms, through the ownership of land over a finite geographical area.[59]

It can be argued—and such an argument will be presented below—that this localism remained important beyond the feudal and mercantile eras, and indeed into the period of early industrial capitalism. The factory, for example, was essentially a spatial device, an artificial creation designed to generate what we have termed a space economy. Within that place, there was an effort to unify timekeeping, discipline, and political behavior in the manner indicated by Foucault. These space economies became transformed, although in the American case this did not imply a collapse of localism. Political behavior remained rooted within the community, a tendency that is also well documented within European nations and Japan.[60] This notwithstanding, it must be emphasized that the notion of "place"—unspecified, undefined, but recognized—can no longer be utilized so simply once we transfer our attentions to the recent past and the present, typified by the interwoven nature of advanced capitalist production across highly discontinuous labor markets. This discussion inexorably brings us toward the ultimate problems of definition that face any spatial analysis.[61]

Cities, States, and the Level of Analysis

As an indication of these definitional problems, I want to explore one of the dimensions of the debate, which revolves around the existence of specifically *urban* society.[62] Of course, this question of sociological inquiry owes a major debt to the initial formulations produced by the Chicago ecological school in the 1920s, and has never really overcome the problems faced by that tradition. For the ecologists, the city was an a priori category with its own dynamics, tensions, and social relations, somehow apart from and indeed reshaping the social fabric as a whole.[63]

Unsurprisingly, there have been reactions against such a position, although they have not always produced compatible results. Castells's early work, written in French and not translated until later, explicitly posed the question "y-a-t-il un sociologie urbaine?"[64] His reformulation of the urban question was in a very specific mold—emphasizing the nature of collective consumption—but it represented a reemphasis upon the existence of the urban category as a distinct spatial unit with explicit functional characteristics. Saunders, to take another case, moved in a different direction, noting that there exists "a choice between sociological non-urban theories and urban non-sociological theories."[65] Saunders consequently accepts Giddens's position that the city has no social significance in societies that postdate the capitalist transformation, or put another way, that the urban category cannot be invoked in class societies:

> As Weber saw, as Durkheim saw, and as Giddens clearly sees, the smallest discrete spatial unit which can be taken as the basis for sociological analysis in contemporary capitalist societies is that defined by the territorial boundaries of the nation state.[66]

Giddens's propositions, which as Saunders notes are entirely consistent with the work of the "founding fathers" such as Weber, will be discussed again below in greater detail. I will argue that they are unsatisfactory on a series of levels: first, because they wish away large areas of the literature, such as Castells's assertion that "the city is society"; second, because they assume a total decline in the authoritative role exerted by cities in class societies; and third, because the nation state is elevated to a theoretical position that cannot be sustained as the smallest spatial unit that can be recognized and analyzed.

The detour of discussing urban society thus rewards us by bringing us to the suggestion that there can be no recognizable spatial unit below the nation state in a class society—which would certainly be one resolution of the question asked above, namely, What constitutes the locale or locality? That we cannot accept this assertion rests on the recognition that the nation state, as a realist category rather than an ideal type, has emerged through many iterations and as a result of many internal struggles. As already noted, then, the national unit *is* the sum of its constituent parts, and has emerged via the struggles of these smaller units. Again, it is to be stressed that this is not to elevate the relations between places to some pedestal, but is to recognize that everyday life varies from location to location, and that this segmentation produces conflict between economic interests, between political representatives, and between social actors who represent varied and frequently conflicting interests.

This argument has yet to spring us from the trap of asking, What is place? However, we can move forward here by a recognition that these tensions "between places" have become codified and indeed reified into political-geographic forms; i.e., conflict has produced identifiable forms of place, defined in terms of juridical units. These territorial forms therefore provide the missing link between the structurationist emphasis upon place and the recognition of the importance of the state. From this perspective, place becomes defined as a juridical unit, and it is the conflicts between these units, or more properly what they represent, that ultimately shape the national unit. This argument thus leads us to reject the state as the smallest spatial unit of analysis, and to insert instead the locality, or as we shall express it using different terminology, the local state.

Summary

The purpose of this chapter has been to introduce the rudiments of the argument to be developed below. A case has been made for the declining importance of the workplace as an influence in the terrain of collective action, and the consequent emergence of varied forms of social movement. There has also been a concomitant growth in importance of the state within domestic affairs, and in turn, the actions of the state's institutions have caused them to become the focus of much political action, most notably in the arena of public provision. The latter is typically organized and provided within local political jurisdictions, which underscores the importance of examining the local affairs in greater detail. This is the task to be attempted in the next chapter.

TWO

HERE AND
THE ELSEWHERE

The effects of habit   —DARWIN[1]

Preamble

In chapter 1, it was argued that there has occurred an increase in the activities of the institutions of the state, such that collective action has come to be defined much more frequently against the state itself. Implicit in this account is the assumption that the state is not a remote and monolithic entity but a large number of institutions that act, as do citizens, in recognizable settings, be they characterized as localities or locales, space economies or regional economies, local states or local jurisdictions. Such an interpretation involves a particular world view—indeed, it involves the replacement of a global view with a highly fragmented, localist consciousness. As this chapter will show, the localist perspective is not common within social science; consequently, this narrative will explore it in detail, beginning with the survival of places in an era of "real-time" interaction.

No Sense of Place?

It is the conventional wisdom within the field of communication, thanks to McLuhan, that the world has shrunk to the size of a medieval village. As a result of the proliferation of the electronic media of communication, with their instantaneous reach, the tyranny of distance has been overcome; indeed, some might assume that we are witnessing the progressive destruction of geography.[2] Joshua Meyrowitz states that these media are "of no place"; they reflect, he has argued, a world of shopping malls and ersatz food whose only characteristics are their very universality. In consequence, their flattening impact means that we find that places are increasingly like one another, and that the singularity of, and thus the importance of, the locality is consequently diminished. One of my tasks in this chapter is to argue that Meyrowitz is misguided in the emphasis that he gives to universality in his interpretations.[3] While it makes good sense to apply his analysis to interpersonal relations within the spaces of the home, it is not productive to extend this logic to the locality. Indeed, the electronic media exhibit all the contradictions that we have already begun to discuss in the context of the state. Below, I shall continue my dialogue with Meyrowitz, emphasizing that his behavioralist interpretations are poorly suited to the task of understanding collective issues. I then go on to examine just why spatial diversity has slipped from sight within American life. The third part of the chapter develops some examples to show how places function as social constructions, and particularly the ways in which political expressions develop.

Communication, Modernity, and Locality

In *No Sense of Place*, Meyrowitz indicates how the electronic media have increased greatly the influence that they exert. This leverage is to be understood via Grofman's concepts of front, middle, and back regions. In essence, the media, most noticeably television, have brought back-region behavior out into the open. Actions which were once manifested only in closed spaces, such as the bedroom or the locker room, are now in the public domain. Consequently, many of the spatial structures that have permitted both individuals and groups to maintain exclusivity have been eroded. Prisons, mental hospitals, operating and delivery rooms, even the British Houses of Parliament, have all experienced the glare·of the video camera.

No Sense of Place makes important points with respect to social interaction; there remain, however, lingering problems with the way that the argument is extended from individual spaces—such as the locker room—out toward places in their totality. On several occasions, Meyrowitz states that the singularity of place is disappearing because of the media: there exist "fewer distinctions among places" (p. 182), or "different places are still different, but they are not as different as they once were" (p. 145). Both radio and TV transmit mundane messages which are emphatically placeless. Don DeLillo captures this rather well in his book *White Noise*. The narrative is punctuated by the language of consumerism: significant phrases muttered during sleep turn out to be recitations such as "toyota corolla, toyota celica, toyota cressida"; as DeLillo observes, these are "supranational names, computer generated, more or less universally pronounceable."[4]

This recognition of the power of modernity to overcome the practices of different people in different places does not necessitate our acceptance of all that Meyrowitz indicates. It is plausible to argue that television has collapsed the internal organization of the home; it is not correct to argue the same for the locality.[5] For example, Meyrowitz suggests that there is a close link between communication and territoriality.[6] He submits that in medieval society, communication—which was essentially conversation—necessitated continual face-to-face interaction, with the result that there was little social segregation.[7] This is certainly true with respect to the home, which functioned as shop, factory, hospital, schoolroom, and occasional mortuary, but this logic cannot be extended to the medieval town as a whole. Residential segregation was quite marked, as families of the elite occupied the city center, close to the symbolic spaces that contained the loci of power, such as the court house and the cathedral. Beyond this core, poorer families dwelled in inferior homes; beyond them, in turn, were the indigent, who lived outside the city walls. In short, it is possible to argue that communication needs contributed to the lack of differentiation and segregation *within the home;* it is not possible to extend that argument to embrace the entire city.[8]

The steady erosion of the particularity of place, due to interaction based on warfare, trade, and publishing, should have undermined the importance of turf. As we share a common message, such as capitalism, so the symbols of territoriality collapse; the disappearance of the Berlin Wall comes readily to mind.[9] Once more, we must be cautious in making sweeping statements. While nations within the European Community, to take a salient example, may progressively lose their sovereignty, the physical segregation *within* countries is actually increasing, and regional movements continue to grow in importance. In the United States, there is a proliferation of exclusive residential spaces that take significant precautions to exclude those who do not belong: guards, gates, and guns all emphasize territoriality.[10] On a less exclusive note, the growth of adult or retirement communities, residential resorts based typically around a golf course, and gay neighborhoods (cf. chapter 4) all testify to a need to create explicit and exclusionary living spaces. Communication has an enabling role here, as electronic devices such as facsimile machines, modems, and cellular phones allow instantaneous transmission for both business and personal purposes, which makes face-to-face contact often irrelevant. However, the motivations are linked much more closely to the ties between the economics of real estate and exclusivity: as David Harvey observes, "The qualities of place stand thereby to be emphasized in the midst of the increasing abstractions of space."[11]

This argument can be extended to include the locality. Meyrowitz argues that TV is "of no place," while I would argue that it exhibits very much the same frictions that can be observed within the state—that is to say, a tension between national uniformity in terms of program planning and production on the one hand, and localist tendencies on the other. The network then is national, placeless, generic. Local, affiliated stations maintain their profitability by commodifying the locality. They do this in several ways: via local news programs, by selling cheap videotaped advertisement slots to local dealers, and by offering the reruns that viewers want to see. The local TV or radio station sells the locality back to itself, using the identification of place as a bond between consumer and producer.

The content of programs, too, has implications for our understanding of place and image. Even the most mundane soap opera is based typically in some specific locality, because places carry a powerful implication of social relations. In both *Beverly Hills 90210* and *Miami Vice,* the locality functions as an additional character; it is much more than a backdrop, it is a shorthand for a relatively complicated set of social and political relations.[12] The setting of Miami, for example, made it unnecessary to spell out the details of the drug cartels; it was enough to sketch the powerful Central American connections that exist in the city. So too in *L.A. Law,* there is little coincidence in the use of the title and the detailed panoramic shots of the Los Angeles skyline. The city is a symbol of materialism, yuppie values, and postmodern architecture.[13]

Advertising, the most persuasive dimension of the electronic media, is only superficially of no place. National corporations are growing more cognizant of regional tastes, and offer product variations that will connect with different styles of life. A New York advertising agency offers demographic data on eight regions in the United States, and the Campbell Soup Company recognizes twenty-two smaller regions, known to have differences in terms of food tastes.[14] Chevrolet's award-winning "Heartbeat" series of advertisements in 1987 included annotation directed to road and driving conditions in individual States. In all these instances, manufacturers increase profit via an identification of place-specific behavior, and in doing so, they reify that behavior. The reinforcement of an image via television is an extremely effective way of selling the locality back to its residents.

The Generalized Elsewhere

It is instructive to examine the responses that Meyrowitz has made to my arguments. He writes:

> Kirby's strongest arguments for the enduring significance of locality are (1) the locality remains the locus of competition over resources (housing, education and other public services), and (2) there are subtle and complex differences between life in different places in terms of weather, terrain and . . . "local knowledge." Locality, in terms of these two elements, comes close to being a clear, objective, observable fact. But the definition is also so broad, ahistorical and safe that it is capable of masking significant changes in human organization and perceptions of place.[15]

In addition, Meyrowitz submits that the profound ignorance displayed by Americans about the world does not mean that they have a localist sense; rather, they cannot read maps. He rejects the notion that organizations are coalitions of local units; instead, he favors the more common interpretation that national structures exist and are, in reality, of growing importance. He disagrees strongly with the assertion that distant events are mediated through the locality; satellite broadcasts beam fundraisers directly into the home, he cites. Fourth, he disagrees with the notion that there is anything local about local TV. And fifth, he dismisses the relegation of categories such as race and gender to the status of ideal types, arguing instead in favor of nationally constructed images of racial or sexual discrimination that are molded by television. In terms of the aims of this chapter, Meyrowitz's reasoned replies to my interpretations are very useful, for they show just how a behavioralist discipline, such as communication, sees the world glued together, while others are much more conscious of its constantly breaking apart and reforming. Let me explore this contrast in greater detail.

Geographic knowledge and map reading. I argued that Americans have a profound ignorance about the globe, which has extended to muddled and incoherent foreign policy debates.[16] One modest aspect of this is the way in which Americans are poor map users. There is a literature on the structuring of cartographic images which shows that individual cognition is dictated in large part by the collective discourse; for example, many individuals in the Pacific would use a Sino-centric projection when sketching a world map.[17] In suggesting a reason why Americans are geographically illiterate, Meyrowitz proposes that the electronic media present gestalt-like images of battles, which undermine our place consciousness. While it has become logical in recent years to equate foreign policy with warfare, this too is a social construction; more important, we have to ask, Just why does American television present war in such a manner? It all has to do with the way in which the U.S. world image is constructed; Vietnam, Panama, and Angola have no geopolitical reality for most Americans, in government or otherwise.[18] Consequently, armed conflict takes on an existential dimension in which the bloodshed becomes little more than theater. TV transmits this, but it does not create this existential sensation.

Rusty machine politics. I noted that what we treat as monoliths—the legal system, the political parties—are little more than uneasy coalitions. It is not coincidental that unions are organized via locals, which have always responded to local labor and wage conditions. As Meyrowitz notes, union membership has declined rapidly in most industrial nations, but this hardly negates my observation; rather, it offers up a germane hypothesis. Simply, unions have declined precisely because of their fragmented bases, which cannot compete with the more powerful organizational structures of global corporations. The collapse of the miners' strike in the U.K. in 1984–85 showed how different parts of the union had very different levels of commitment to the strike, which reflected the fortunes of the coal industry in the various regions, and the diverse production relations that had evolved within the various components of the industry.[19] In the United States, national corporations have become adept at playing one local against another in order to extract worker concessions.[20]

As for Meyrowitz's claims concerning the increasing nationalization of American politics, this does not stand critical scrutiny. First, we have seen a major and very public shift in the balance of power within the party coalitions from East Coast to West Coast, and from North to South. The choice of vice-presidential running mates is but one instance of the ways in which the national parties must pay much more than lip service to regional attitudes. Indeed, it is becoming quite clear that the national political coalitions are breaking down; one key indicator here is the way in which citizen initiatives, recalls, and propositions are proliferating throughout the States. This reflects a dissatisfaction with the way in which the major parties have no room for local and regional issues—such as "English only" in Arizona and Colorado, or discriminating ordinances condemning homosexuality in Oregon.[21]

In both these instances, we can see a tension between local needs and national organizational structures. In the union case, labor is indeed losing ground. Contrary to Meyrowitz's assertions concerning neighborhoods, they are becoming much more powerful in many American cities; he is hardly the first to misread this issue, though.[22]

The local and the international conscience. Meyrowitz is on stronger ground when he writes about the links between voluntarism, donation, and television. There is little to gainsay his observation that famine in Ethiopia is brought to us (albeit, again, in a gestalt-like manner) via TV and financed via toll-free telephone numbers. There is much more to say, though, concerning the way in which distant events are evaluated and interpreted. By Meyrowitz's logic, famine displaces our ability to comprehend problems— such as homelessness—that exist around us. However, the facts are not consistent with these arguments: individuals are much less prepared to give via a television fundraiser than they are to recognize the claims of the homeless within their own community, fund public television, or donate their labor to hospitals and hospices.[23] It is not plausible to suggest that images of the dead and dying arrive in our homes in a nonproblematic way— Meyrowitz skates over the fact that people do not switch on to watch corpses; they switch on to see rock stars and film stars do their stuff. The audience (presumably a limited one in terms of age) enters into a simple trade-off transaction: see this spectacle, pay a price. This really has little to do with the broader range of people who make wider choices about how they give to those in need; from my standpoint, the needs of those in Africa are filtered through a preexisting lens that includes the needs of family, neighbors, and those visible on the street.

Is local television local? Meyrowitz argues that places are commodified in generic ways. That is not a major insight: capitalism is a wave of homogenization with regard to process, even though, like Mr. Palomar, we know that the wave breaks in many different ways (as was argued above with respect to advertising). Aspen, Santa Fe, and Reno are all tourist towns, they attract visitors for identical purposes (their dollars), but they market themselves as unique entities. Part of their style is visual and visible; the timbered chalet architecture of Vail or Aspen, Colorado could not be confused with the adobes of Santa Fe or Taos, New Mexico. Part is in the activities that go on there; do not go to Reno if you want to attend a film festival.[24]

Now, no one in his or her right mind visits a town for its television, but it plays a role nonetheless. As Meyrowitz points out, advertisements do not define everyday life, but they do play a part in the definition of the parameters of style—they operate through the collective discourse. This in turn brings us back to local news, which revolves around, and adds to, that *common* sense. Meyrowitz downplays the importance of the latter; starting from the opposite direction, we might ask the innocent question, If it is unimportant, why do local stations spend so much to generate their own news programs and employ their own staff, when they could manage well enough by just relaying the network efforts?[25] The answer is clear: stations need to display local allegiances to differentiate themselves, and competitive news broadcasting is currently one currency in this strategic game.

Members of aggregates. Meyrowitz agrees that there exist geographic differences in the understanding of the stereotypes of man, woman, anglo, black, and so on. He suggests, though, that the media, in offering a view from no place, are in fact creating ideal types. This is, in my view, the most provocative of Meyrowitz's observations, with the most important implications for our understanding of the world. There is much to agree with in the assertion that television has created new norms of behavior, notably with respect to the way in which nontraditional views of women have reverberated within our society. Roseanne Arnold, Nancy Reagan, Leona Helmsley, and Madonna may, in their public personas, be media creations, but they nonetheless offer alternatives to women who would perhaps encounter only one of these ideal types in their neighborhoods. This notwithstanding, it is still not the case that homogeneity is at our feet. I do not accept that the smokers at the next table are part of a national struggle between my side and theirs. In Tucson, smoking is accepted in certain parts of restaurants. In Hollywood, it is banned from public places. As we shall see in chapter 6, the idea of controlling smoking is still novel in North Carolina. The collective discourse on the risks of smoking varies markedly from place to place.[26] The same logic applies more crucially in the case of race relations. I agree that race is now understood as an embracing factor; indeed, the urge to replace the terms "Hispanic," "Black," and "Asian" by "Mexican-American," "African-American," and "Asian-American" indicates just such a sense of relatedness. Nonetheless, there is little question that the terms of racial struggle are mediated via local political practices, local employment opportunities, local educational experiences, and the long-standing cultural forms that contribute to local knowledge. African Americans may well have their expectations defined in part by the black sports figures, talk show hosts, film directors, and comedians who invade their living rooms; but they must still translate those expectations through the reality of the personnel department, the streets, and the courts. This will be explored again in chapter 5.

This is the point at which Meyrowitz's argument drifts away. He concludes his analysis with a vision that echoes the postmodern descriptions that have become so familiar. All is change, all is choice. We can reconstruct ourselves in new locations, reconstruct ourselves as a one-person household;

and yet these choices are illusionary. Most single parents enter into serial monogamy; the form of the household is constant, only the individuals are different. People may move to small towns, but these very rapidly turn right back into big cities within a decade. However much the existential media may offer us dazzling alternatives in the living room, in the end they do nothing more than offer ideas. They can do nothing to empower individuals or collectivities in their struggles; these are generated in situ.

Meyrowitz's ideas are useful to us here because they represent a common interpretation of the power of modernity. The intellectual willingness to jettison the variations that exist within civil society from location to location is not restricted to some within the communication discipline; it is a general tendency, and an instructive one. As Berger and Luckmann observed, "The world of everyday life is structured both spatially and temporally. The spatial structure is quite peripheral to our present considerations." A glance at their writing shows, of course, that it is anything but peripheral.[27] This confusion draws upon the myths of a totalizing discourse in offering up a placeless world, a dystopia which does not exist. It is important, though, for us to understand the origins of this discourse, and the next section explores this history.

"The Reassertion of Space in Critical Social Theory"

This quotation serves as the subtitle of a provocative book by Edward Soja, who has explored the "theoretical peripheralization of space."[28] His culprit is historicism, which, he argues, has progressively displaced a comprehension of space since the rise of disciplines within the academy. Although the book is provocative, there are some problems lodged within Soja's assertion, at least as we have begun to outline the issues here. First, it is hard to be convinced that disciplines such as sociology or political science *do* claim history as their own—as suggested in the Prologue above, the character of behavioral science is best viewed as existential, neglecting both space *and* time. This does not undermine Soja's argument; rather, it would make sociology twice guilty. Soja is more correct with regard to critical thought, which he characterizes as being innately bound up with marxism. There, he is right to note a primacy of time over space, despite the countervailing voices of several geographers (especially David Harvey in the *Limits to Capital*), and those with a number of differing but sympathetic agendas, such as Foucault, Castells, and Lefebvre.[29]

The project of insinuating an understanding of the production of space back into critical thinking has a long way to go, not least because it resolves itself as a messy institutional war rather than a series of clean intellectual contests. For sociology, the rejection of space is likely to become a Verdun (if a spatial *and* historical metaphor is acceptable), a denial that will occupy more and more of that discipline's energies. Gitlin illustrates this rather well in asserting that "space is not real, only time," confirming that historicist habits are hard to break.[30] This is thrown into sharper relief by the postmodern debate, heralded by some (geographers included—Soja's project is entitled *Postmodern Geographies,* and Harvey too has written on the *Condition of Postmodernity*), and misinterpreted or ignored by others.[31] For Jameson, the postmodern is a disjuncture in critical thought:

> One privileged language in modernism, Proust or Thomas Mann for example, always uses temporal description. That notion of "deep time" . . . seems radically irrelevant to our contemporary experience, which is one of a perpetual spatial present. Our theoretical categories also become spatial: structural analyses with graphs of synchronic multiplicities of spatially related things (as opposed to, say, the dialectic and its temporal moments), and languages like Foucault's with its empty rhetoric of cutting, sorting, and modifying, a kind of spatial language in which you organize data like a great bloc to be chopped up in various ways.[32]

In short, "our relationship with the past is now a spatial one."

Historicism and Presentism; Space and Time

If there is a limitation to Soja's reinvocation of the importance of space, it is the way in which he develops a partially disciplinary lens in order to undertake that task. That is to say, in order to explain the diminution of space, he must account for the weakness of geography as a research activity. In turn, that leaves him with two options—he can either blame the victim (geography has inept practitioners), or he can elevate history (and historicism). This means of interpretation is somewhat narrow, and even old-fashioned.[33] The dangers of presentism within the history of science have been well rehearsed, and there is plenty of reason to salute already a new history of the social sciences.[34] In large measure, this work rejects the Mertonian paradigm—the internalist and presentist interpretation of the discipline—in preference for a social constructivist point of view, which recognizes that the work of the academy is like work anywhere in a capitalist society.[35] Expressed a little differently, a discipline must necessarily reflect the social formation within which it is placed, and in consequence one cannot be examined in isolation from the other.

Geography in Its Social Context

Victorian geography had an explicit role in nations committed to scientific development, overseas exploration, and colonial expansion. In France, Germany, and Great Britain, the creation of empires—both formal and informal—was grounded in the collection and organization of scholarly knowledge about the globe.[36] In contrast, the explanation of geography's limited impact in the U.S. is a restatement of the problem of American exceptionalism.[37] American leaders have frequently denied an interest in being actors with a normative global agenda, despite early declarations of a Manifest Destiny and, thereafter, the creation of an extensive formal empire in the Pacific. At the height of the country's authority after the Second World War, advisor George Kennan was able to characterize the U.S. as a "lonely, threatened power on the field of world history."[38] The attractions of informal empire (via economic expansion), coupled with periodic bouts of partial isolationism (underlined by the costs of maintaining overseas commitments), are current preoccupations; but this ambivalence rests upon a deeper ideological base. Political theory suggests that we should look to the importance of communalist ideals in American society, an idealism expressed as a strong localist tradition.[39] At the moment of independence, the republic emerged from highly dissimilar colonies, which in turn contained many isolated and disparate communities. Although all were united within "Nature's nation," no single locality could transcend the divergences between agricultural and urban interests, between North and South, and later, between East Coast and West Coast.[40] Consequently, the Continental Congress of 1774 was the first of many efforts to find a "common consciousness," to use Albion Small's words.[41] As a result, the creation of the modern, centralized state was a slow and complex affair; as one political scientist has argued, it was a process of "patching" that had to overcome local resistance and which extended far into the modern era.[42]

The relation between this social and political reality and the material dimensions of time and space has had explicit consequences for the development of American thought. As far as geography is concerned, individuals' knowledge of the spatial integration of the U.S.—and, by extension, of the globe—is minute; awareness of, or concern for, that lack of knowledge is even smaller, as Meyrowitz's comments on map reading testify.[43] Rather, there is an emphasis upon local communities and States, their traditions, discourses, and roles within the nation's political system.[44] For example, the American flag is an explicit cartogram of the States that changes to reflect the growth of the country; this transformation of a country's emblem makes it unique. In consequence, it is unsurprising that the urge to burn the flag is interpreted as an explicit threat by the state apparatus, which cannot allow challenges to the notion of ideological cohesion.[45]

From a somewhat different point of origin, Dorothy Ross has argued for the late emergence of historicism within the United States, and notes that "Americans . . . could relegate history to the past while they acted out their destiny in the realm of nature." This also has implications for our understanding of space, for, as she continues, "[Americans] could develop in space rather than in time."[46] Complex assumptions are embedded in this perspective: one is the assumption that the Frontier represented more than a symbol, and was part of a geographical consciousness.[47] A second, which emerges with force in Ross's arguments concerning political history, is the supposition of a principle of universal republican values and an early emphasis upon the sovereignty of the state. This underlines a discontinuity between a fragmented political reality (after the War of Independence and before the Civil War) and academic discourse, which was caught wrong-footed by the fragmentation exposed so starkly by the North-South conflict. It was only at the close of the nineteenth century that scholars (such as John Burgess) could look back to confront the fact that the Civil War had shredded the myth of the universal state—a reinterpretation, argues Ross, that could take place only as the country entered a gilded age in which state institutions were at last perceived to be secure.

One of the problems exposed in Ross's tempting arguments is the urge to treat the material dimensions as opposing elements—space and time, fire and water.[48] When she argues that the nation developed in space but not in time, she makes bold and appealing claims, and ones which are certainly consistent with Soja's reading of the way in which spatiality and temporality have been so frequently compartmentalized when theorized. Kant's *nacheinander* and *nebeneinander* have become dichotomous, despite their complementarity as encompassing material dimensions; as Ong observes, drawing on a remark of Dedalus in Ulysses, "I am a time man, and you are a space man."[49]

The dilemma posed by these dichotomies is that they are rooted in a particular form of intellectual experience, which has chosen to equate geography with movement, in an attempt to dispense with space as an absolute form.[50] So when Ross notes that Americans developed in space but not in time, she indicates that the transformation of the republic was occurring at the margins, not within its institutions. Of course, this was only partially the case. The changes provoking Turner to develop his Frontier thesis were anything but imaginary, but they were hardly the only transformations. The eastern seaboard was not held in a fossilized state—either socially, economically, or politically—while westward expansion occurred. As Meinig indicates, many changes were in evidence throughout the period.[51] Following Pred's logic, sketched in chapter 1, we can see that the established communities within the country continued to develop, no less than did those of the Midwest or California, such that both time and space must be invoked if we are to comprehend the social and economic palimpsests that resulted.

Cultures of Time and Space

As Giddens has shown, this is by no means the only way to illustrate the links between the material dimensions.[52] Consider for a moment Stephen Kern's discussions of the impacts of modernity upon what he characterizes as the culture of time and space.[53] He points to a sharp transformation that began approximately a century ago and instigated a state of flux that lasted through to the Peace of Versailles. Intriguingly, he interprets this as a phenomenological shift, perhaps without rational cause in some cases. His exploration of the nature of space takes him toward a comprehension of presence and absence, noise and silence, being and nothingness.[54] As he reminds us, space could be empty, as represented in literature by Conrad and art by Munch; negative, as in some architectural forms (notably Lloyd Wright); positive, notably in stage designs by Gordon Craig, and even positive negative, as in Futurist sculpture.[55] Implicit in this disjuncture was an overt break with the past, although this may be more apparent than real. Schorske observes that modernity involved a rethinking of what had passed and a challenge to history:

> Modern architecture, modern music, modern philosophy, modern science— all these define themselves not *out* of the past, indeed scarcely *against* the past, but in independence of the past. The modern mind has been growing indifferent to history because history, conceived as a continuous nourishing tradition, has become useless to it.[56]

Soja reminds us that marxism has fought this trend of indifference, but Schorske is correct to identify the eclipse of historicism elsewhere within the rush to modernity. Yet one additional factor needs emphasis, and as we shall see, it is the supreme irony of Schorske's work that he fails to recognize it himself. His book explores *fin de siècle* Vienna as a locus for development in the fields alluded to: art (Gustav Klimt), music (Gustav Mahler), architecture (Otto Wagner), and science (Freud). Implicit is the recognition that something singular took place as the Austrian empire collapsed: a large number of unique minds coalesced to produce a hothouse of intellectual development within one locality. Schorske, though, never makes the connection between the overthrow of history and the enabling condition of geography—indeed, his study never really manages to make the connections between the different spheres of intellectual development.[57] He writes that the historian is the weaver:

> The diachronic thread is the warp, the synchronic one is the woof in the fabric of cultural history.[58]

We can contrast this with Harvey's insight when he writes of making tangible connections

> between the weft of theory, and the woof of historical geography.[59]

For Harvey, the possibility of a metastatement that would constitute the weft of theory is clear: for him it is the mode of production and all that can be derived therefrom. This is not without its problems as an assertion, for it sets up theory and geography as orthogonal—that is to say, it implies that there exist processes which are not dependent upon specific spaces for their creation, manifestation, expression, re-creation, and interaction.[60] Here, I take a very different position: I agree that we can identify supraprocesses, but only in exceedingly vague terms, such as "war" and "peace." We can stay at such a coarse level of generality, but to talk of a phenomenon that pervades all time and space does little to further our understanding. As Evelyn Waugh once observed, if the constitution of the universe is malignant, then malignant ceases to have any meaning.[61]

Universals and Specifics

War, patriarchy, class struggle, and racism are universal; the creation of complex institutions—cities, nation states—is virtually ubiquitous. But the ways in which they present themselves as processes also depends in some important measure on the way in which they resolve themselves over time, and from place to place. Take the example of nuclear strategy; while it is argued that the geopolitical tacticians of an earlier era have long been irrelevant (Mackinder, Spykman, de Seversky), this ignores the legacy of two world wars—the evolution of the nuclear option was a direct descendant, and attempted resolution, of the prenuclear impasse. In consequence, the archeological metaphor developed by Foucault is necessary to probe the evolution of containment and the MAD option. The image of the chessboard, noted in the previous chapter, is apposite, for the distribution of weapons and their targets made sense only in the context of long-standing Soviet fears of encirclement and the American occupation of Germany, dating back to 1945.[62]

To summarize this account, we can see that there are many ways to comprehend the material dimensions of space and time. From Soja, we can take the inference that historicism exists at the expense of spatiality, although there must be more to the story than that.[63] While the ways in which concepts of space and time have been employed creatively can be seen to change at specific moments—the onset of modernity and postmodernity, for instance—we must be wary of disconnecting these shifts from the embracing ideologies of the state and civil society. In particular, and as we shall see again in chapter 4, there is a very close connection between the growth of the state and the diminution of spatiality within civil society. It is barely an exaggeration to argue that space—or, explicitly, spatial variation in terms of characteristics such as political attitudes—can be empowering, allowing as it does individuals and collectivities to exist in singular ways. This is the corollary of, and is to be contrasted with, the creation of spaces of control, discussed at length by Foucault; as he notes, the leper colony, the penal island, the insane asylum, and the panopticon are all ways of overseeing and marginalizing unorthodox behaviors, by restricting them to marginal locations.[64]

Common Sense

In asserting that space may be empowering, I am suggesting that the ability to generate a certain quality and style of life is both possible and, of course, beneficial for residents. This is not without its difficulties; one district's empowerment can constitute the embodiment of bigotry and intolerance for others, and there is always the problem of localities passing on their negative externalities to their neighbors.[65] Implicit in this evaluation is the reminder that we map our own values across the struggles of others only with difficulty and with great arrogance, a point that will be developed in detail in chapters 4 and 8. In probing these issues further, two questions are immediately presented. The first is the way in which the foundations for political action can be laid; the second is the possibility of success in such efforts. In consequence, this section explores the locality, as a social construction, in some greater detail.[66]

The process of social construction is complex. In order to grasp the links between individuals and collectivities, we need to understand the ways in which a *sensus communis*—which we may literally translate as a *common sense*—develops.[67] This phrase is taken from Vico, who argued that for individuals to interact one with another dictated a common discourse. Such commonality was necessarily rooted in the everyday life of the locality, and "sensory topics" shaped language to incorporate an already shared circumstance.[68] Vico provides an account of the bases of human awareness and the necessary point of departure for conjectures on the development of interaction. Of central concern in this regard is the relationship between people and their environment. Those within a locality evolve a particular set of coping mechanisms which represent an accommodation to the complexities of life-in-place. These are laid down over long periods of time, such that these effects of habit, as Darwin termed them, become sedimented.[69] Implicit in this insight is the assertion that as such habit becomes a cornerstone of social behavior, so it becomes enabling; residents know where pollution is at its worst, where flooding may occur, where crime may take place.[70]

The consequences of these quotidian processes can be marked. To take one example, the industrial experience of the Massachusetts mill towns was subtly different from the ways in which the same industrial process was organized elsewhere within the United States; the exploitation of nature, the organization of labor, worker-manager relations, ethnic friction, and political outcomes all developed in a singular manner. Some of these dissimilarities, of one locality to the next, reflected contingent peculiarities of time and place, but others reflected preexisting social, cultural, and economic relations. In each instance the singularities have in turn become part of the sedimented local knowledge which may be identified today.[71]

A particularly salient example of this process is to be seen in the current development of the United States–Mexico border region. Following the loosening of Mexican investment controls in the 1970s, there has emerged a dynamic industrial region which straddles the border and incorporates American capital and Mexican labor in the *maquiladora* plants that stretch from Tijuana to Matamoros. The rapid urbanization that has resulted from this process shows many instances of the argument explored here; new unplanned neighborhoods—the *colonias*—are appearing, employment of women in the *maquilas* is changing gender relations, and unexpected environmental problems are resulting from the pollution of water resources via human wastes and industrial chemicals. These challenges are generating new linkages between political institutions on both sides of the border, plus accommodations by the individual households that are without pumped water and other basics of life. Interaction between the two nations was not an intended outcome of the economic development strategy; indeed, the border remains an important ideological barrier within the United States. Nonetheless, the contingencies of the particular space economy are provoking political and social change which has had impacts through to the congressional level. More of this story is examined in chapter 7.

Although this process of generating a *common* sense has been examined vis-à-vis economic links, it is also identifiable in terms of the ways in which other relations are resolved. This is the case with language, with religious practice, with gender relations, and with cultural activity. Sensitive architecture reflects vernacular coping strategies, so that a hotel may demonstrate echoes of adobe or timber, re-creating (and thus commodifying) an image of the Southwest or the Northeast. Literature is rarely separated from specific localities, for place becomes a metaphor for an inchoate yet understood set of behaviors.[72]

Perhaps the most controversial aspect of this differentiation is the political question. As noted above, it is not uncommon to interpret politics in the U.S. as being beyond local concerns. This is, as was pointed out in the discussion of Meyrowitz, a singularly superficial interpretation. The American political system is implicitly organized as a compromise between the interests of different regions, as a number of prescient political scientists and historians have observed.[73] The process of pork-barreling is a glue that connects individual voters in a district with their representatives. The shift of population from centers in the Midwest and the Northeast to States such as Florida, Texas, and California continues to generate conflicts over representation (where are the legislative districts to be trimmed and reassigned?) and the distribution of resources that are based on population.[74]

As political geographers have argued, it is possible for parties to paper over these differences and to produce compromises that will allow them to function in, and represent, various regions. Attempts have been made to show how the broad-scale evolution of recognizable political practices— now reified as national electoral politics—may be little more than the forging of coalitions between various forms of sectional interest.[75] At times, these coalitions undergo major changes; the wresting of control of the Republican Party over the last two decades by the nouveaux riches of California from the brahmins of the East Coast provides one example. At other times, the coalitions may threaten to break down, and there is some evidence that another restructuring is currently imminent. There has been a consistent growth of nonparty electoral politics, dating back to the tax revolts of the late 1970s.[76] As the proliferation of ballot initiatives, recalls, and referenda indicates, this tendency has far from worked itself out.[77] Shuman notes that

> as of 1991, more than 900 localities passed resolutions supporting a "freeze" in the arms race; 197 demanded a halt to nuclear testing; 120 refused to cooperate with the Federal Emergency Management Agency's nuclear-war exercises; 126, plus 26 States, divested more than $20 billion from firms doing business in South Africa; 86 formed linkages with Nicaragua and, along with grassroots activists, provided more humanitarian assistance to the Nicaraguan people than all the military aid Congress voted for the *contras;* 80 demanded cuts in the Pentagon's budgets; 73 formed sister city relations with Soviet cities . . . and at least 10 established funded offices of international affairs—in essence municipal state departments.[78]

Each instance represents an unresolved tension between the specified concerns of groups of residents and the broader agendas of the political parties. Residents in many places feel clearly that the latter are unwilling or incapable of dealing with their issues and interests. These revolts are part of what has been identified as a "politics of place," although this has been dissected from a number of directions. From one, we can see places as areas of contestation, across which various forces—notably those related to economic change—wash; the result is that social practices and economic realities are resolved through conflicts over labor practices, plant closures, or development strategies.[79] In contrast, it has also been argued that turf politics are to be seen simply as local expressions of class contests that have become romanticized by bourgeois ideology.[80]

This chapter has argued that localities are settings within which long-standing cultural and political outlooks are sedimented; they constitute places within which a collective political discourse is shaped, and which may take as its object any number of facets of everyday life. Central to this argument is the realization that a communal sense is frequently translated into individual and collective action. This may be focused upon what Piven and Cloward termed "stop-light politics," or Cox "turf politics": that is, immediate neighborhood issues that can be resolved via land-use strategies. But there are these numerous instances in which more wide-reaching social goals may be defended, or even fought for aggressively. Resistance can be mounted within the local state against external edicts that relate to social or economic policies. In Great Britain, for example, opposition to Thatcherite politics was explicit in many localities, and this was revivified by the advent of the poll tax during Thatcher's last Conservative administration.[81] Equally combative strategies, revolving around religious freedom, state/church separation, and abortion, have also emerged in the United States. Such strategies are often highly illiberal in nature, but this should not force us to reject them a priori as examples of political action generated and organized at the local level.

As we shall see in the following chapters, these interpretations are always open to the criticism that the local state has limited autonomy to initiate its own projects, or even to resist higher authority.[82] These readings do, however, rest upon a specific decoding of legal texts, and are open to challenge on that level. It is more valuable to address the *salience* that can be exerted by the local state and its residents. Just as a small child may disrupt the household and exert her own will—despite a lack of formal or sovereign power—so too the local jurisdiction can exert some salience against the central state (see page 100).[83]

To Conclude

This chapter has laid out some reasons for bringing geography back into social analysis. In specific terms, I have shown that, contrary to some arguments, places do matter. The variations that exist there in terms of social practice are of interest in themselves; in addition, the recognition of diversity is an important step toward comprehending larger social organizations as something more than an ideal type. Throughout the chapter, I have given some primacy to political arrangements, for it is the relation between the state apparatus and its constituents that is crucial to an understanding of social development. This, then, will be the object of the next two chapters: first to lay out some principles of state maturation, and then to develop some insights on the links between the state and the local state.

THREE

THE DISPLACEMENT OF POWER

that master noun of modern political discourse, state   —*GEERTZ*[1]

Preamble

The previous chapters have laid the foundation for the discussion of the state that follows. Chapter 1 illustrated the ways in which collective action is increasingly directed against the state; chapter 2 indicated the need to examine social institutions in spatial and temporal contexts. This chapter now begins to unfold a theory of the state, but does so in a very explicit way. As this first section indicates, there is already a multiplicity of such theories on offer, and these prefatory remarks are necessary to show why this existing suite of ideas is unsatisfactory.

Many studies of the state have been driven by materialist analyses which posit a simplistic relation between capital and institutions. This tendency was most visible during the late 1960s and 1970s, when a number of structuralist interpretations were developed, but it has not disappeared entirely. As recently as 1983, we can find the question being asked, "How great a degree of autonomy does the state have in capitalist society? . . . What purpose is its autonomy intended to serve?"[2] These studies replaced an earlier emphasis upon government and the procedures of governing, which can be traced back to Weber; but they also exhibited serious limitations. Most important, they were typically ahistorical. In consequence, there was a tendency for structuralist interpretations to lead to teleology—that is to say, the assumption that the state has emerged with the purpose of doing what it currently does. Bryan Jones has observed that in such studies, we often find that the state is capable of taking on a "subjunctive mood."[3]

Since this period, there has been a flow of more sophisticated state theories, a process that reflects in part the call by Skocpol to "bring the state back in."[4] It is usual to collapse these studies into three distinct groups—pluralist, managerialist, and class perspectives—which are sometimes seen as "incompatible world views."[5] This is partly correct, although it neglects that these varied studies also have much in common. In particular, they struggle under the same burdens. Below, I identify three such problems, notably the contextual nature of theory, disciplinary elitism, and time-space exclusions.

Theories are themselves contextual. First, it is clear that there is not simply one state theory, nor even one type; there are, in fact, many of both. This multiplicity has much to do with the number of different theoretical perspectives on display, although it is certainly not the intention here to provide yet another compendium of pluralist, managerialist, and structuralist accounts. More important are the recursive connections between theory and the social contexts they have been designed to illuminate. We can illustrate this didactically in a comparison of the work of theorists such as Miliband, Castells, and Saunders, all of whose work has been cited already.[6]

Miliband's exegesis on the instrumental links between the ruling class and state institutions is quintessentially British in the manner in which it traces close connections between school, boardroom, and bedroom. Castells's work, in which he draws together the twin themes of state provision of collective consumption goods and urban development, reflects the evolution of the French state apparatus, and indeed his later work constitutes a partial critique of the French Communist Party. Saunders's work on the local state and urban politics again draws on the British case, in which large parts of the welfare state are administered via local government.[7]

We can go a bit further with this argument, and show how little these perspectives have made their entry into some grand theory of the state, by contrasting a recent American survey of the state literature, Alford and Friedland's *Powers of Theory,* with a British volume, Dunleavy and O'Leary's *Theories of the State.* In them, we find a very different emphasis placed upon the works cited above.[8] Castells is mentioned by Alford and Friedland only with respect to his book *Economic Crisis and American Society,* which is hardly a development of his broader research on the state and urban social movements.[9] Similarly, Miliband is mentioned only with regard to his errors, as exemplified in his debate with Poulantzas.[10] Saunders is not cited. Miliband fares a little better in the Dunleavy and O'Leary volume, but Castells gets short shrift (even *Economic Crisis* is not cited), as does Saunders's work.

Although this is not a systematic comparison, it does illustrate some general points. First, and to reiterate, our understanding of the state is contextually grounded in a specific set of experiences. This is not unexpected, although it remains unconscious and unexamined. Thus, the raw material used by Alford and Friedland is different from that employed by Dunleavy and O'Leary, and in consequence their respective syntheses are different. It is not surprising that the former, for instance, spend a whole chapter dealing with fragmentation within the state apparatus, using the many available American examples.[11]

Disciplines. Second, there is also a large disciplinary bias in the state literature, which additionally goes some way toward explaining the marginalization of sociologists Castells and Saunders (and, perhaps more incredible, the exclusion of Giddens) from the Dunleavy/O'Leary work, which comes out of political science. This is, though, a systematic exclusion; neither sociology nor political science pays particular attention to the work done in anthropology, all three typically ignore the products of geography, and so on. In some ways, this may be a simple result of academic specialization, but it leads to massive lacunae in consequence. More important is the implication that different groups of researchers invoke the state as a simplified, independent variable into their analyses. Each discipline has its own caricature of the state, and pays little attention to broader theorizations.

Exclusions. Third, and from the point of view of this essay most important, the absence of various slices of the literature means that the constant churning of the state synthesis machine still excludes a number of important facets, such as the evolution of precolonial and colonial states.[12] These and other exclusions do not occur without cost. In the first instance, the lack of scholarly attention to the process of state formation in countries such as Japan has allowed an unhealthy emphasis upon a small group of countries which could not, for reasons already outlined, be termed "representative" of all advanced capitalist societies.[13] Similarly, the indifference toward the literature on the creation of colonial states has hidden an interesting perspective that deals with state and society links, rather than privileging the state alone.

These issues will not be developed further at this time, but the point should be clear: a vast library of works on the state does not guarantee complete coverage of approach or subject matter. In consequence, it is necessary to return to some first principles and reexamine the basics of state formation.

Perspectives on State-Society Relations

Let us begin with the assertion that there is no such thing as *the state*—an ideal type that can cover the many political forms of organization that have existed through time and across space. The corollary of this insight is that most research is restricted to a small analytical sample—for the most part, contemporary nation states that experienced neither colonialism in the nineteenth century nor communism in the twentieth. Just as studies of political behavior have concentrated on voting at the expense of collective action around the world, so too the study of the state has neatly managed to exclude the majority of state forms.

This exclusion persists despite the fact that the isolated studies undertaken beyond the contemporary advanced capitalist societies are enormously provocative.[14] In these, we find ourselves in a political terrain far away from the familiar. For example, Geertz's study of Bali reveals institutions so utterly different that it becomes hard to use the same vocabulary to discuss them, even though they reflect a precolonial period only a century ago.[15]

Negara, the theatre-state. The theatre-state was so called because of its concern with ritual and display. This remains a consideration of contemporary state forms, as military parades in Red Square and Times Square attest. However, the purpose of such rites differs. In the present, ritual (such as that commemorating the U.S. military campaign in the Persian Gulf) demonstrates the successes of the state apparatus. In nineteenth-century Bali, the very purpose of the state was ritual:

> The court-and-capital is at once a microcosm of the supernatural order—an image of the universe on a smaller scale—and the material embodiment of political order. It is not just the nucleus, the engine, or the pivot of the state, it *is* the state. The equation of the seat of rule with the dominion of rule, which the negara concept expresses, is more than an accidental metaphor; it is a statement of a controlling political idea—namely that by the mere act of providing a model, a paragon, a faultless image of civilized existence, the court shapes the world around it into at least a rough approximation of its own excellence.[16]

Geertz summarizes this with the statement that "the ritual life of the court, and in fact the life of the court generally, is thus paradigmatic, not merely reflective, of social order."

While the study of negara is instructive in itself, it also permits Geertz to argue that politics is not necessarily reducible to mastery—"Women and Horses and Power and War"—and it allows us to draw two additional inferences.[17] The first is the reminder, albeit a simple one, that different societies and states evolve along different trajectories, and that the search for a single state theory can exist only at some level of massive generality that explains everything—and thus nothing. Second, it underscores the inference that no society reshapes itself anew with each generation—it will be re-created, but it does not alter precipitately. Aspects of the Balinese state and culture remain in the present; thus, any interpretation of the *contemporary* situation would still need to invoke Geertz's historical data.

For these reasons, there are very real attractions in undertaking "an ethnography of the state" in a contemporary society (or what Geertz calls "annalistic" study). By this, I mean the patient identification of the actors, institutions, and sedimented practices that make up the nexus of state, civil society, and economy. Such studies are rare, as already noted, but models do exist, such as Franz Neumann's *Behemoth: The Structure and Practice of National Socialism* (published in 1942, still in print in 1983).

Behemoth. Neumann's work represented an invaluable map for those in the wartime U.S. trying to comprehend Nazi Germany.[18] All commentaries on the progress of the war, and particularly the intelligence community, emphasize the power of his work.[19] In addition, his flight from Germany gave the book the added ethnographic twist of the scholar writing about a distant land; now the book has the historical significance of a record of a doomed society.

Books such as Neumann's reinforce two points. The first is that the form of *any* state apparatus is to be understood only in relation to the society within which it is locked. In *Behemoth,* he argued in fact that the German state had been destroyed by national socialism, and replaced by three or possibly four interlocking power structures. This conclusion may be counterintuitive, insofar as the terms "fascism" and "state power" have become synonymous in the postwar world. Indeed, a narrow focus on state institutions in Germany during 1933–45 might suggest a strong form of state organization. However, Neumann shows at length the way in which the judicial system was co-opted after 1933, which destroyed in turn the links between the state and the people. In their place emerged a multiplicity of "totalitarian bodies" which exercised control directly—the army, the party, the head of state, and the industrial monopolists. The operation of such a "nonstate" could be examined only via the broadest study of social interactions.

Second, *Behemoth* reinforces the view that social organization is in reality a palimpsest of many layers. Each represents particular practices, and each reflects specific historical circumstances. As Neumann argued, the phenomenon of Nazism was rooted in many facets of German experience; some, such as the *Dolchstoss* legend and the Depression, were recent, while others, such as anti-Semitism, were embedded much more deeply. In any case, historical inference was crucial. This is equally true for the United States: aspects of the premodern state are reflected within the U.S., insofar as the electoral college and other components of the state's formal organization reflect compromises made two centuries ago. In short, to understand the state in the advanced society, we once again need a long lens. In fact, a rather different historical analogy may be more appropriate; to draw once again on Foucault, an "archaeology of the state" may pay large dividends in revealing the present to us.

When Women Rebel

The excesses of structuralist argument have receded in the wake of a broad critique that emphasizes the role of human agents in the process of social formation. Giddens has been important in this trend, but valuable work has also been done in historical sociology and social history.[20] Feminist theory, too, has been crucial in terms of developing a less reductionist perspective on the state. In some cases, there has been a tendency to broaden the economism of some marxist analysis with a different functionalism that revolves around the role of the patriarchal family within a capitalist society. But in the main, a feminist analysis of the state is necessarily about difference, not reductionism. Discussions of the nature of welfare provision and of law (notably developed in terms of ethical questions related to pornography and abortion) have provided important expansions of the issues that may be discussed within the context of the state.[21]

A key dimension of the feminist canon is the emphasis placed upon the public/private dichotomy. In simplistic terms, women have been excluded from the public sphere on the grounds that their designated responsibility lies in domestic reproduction and the management of the private sphere. This demands that close attention be given to the unglamorous realm of birth, death, and the nature of everyday life.[22] However, it should not be assumed that the spheres are unconnected. Particularly powerful work has been done by Cynthia Enloe in connecting the world of the everyday to the actions of the state and also the domain of international relations. She links the violence of male-dominated society to militarism on the one hand, and personal oppression on the other. For women, neither war nor peace deflects the male violence that is rooted in many homes. In short, the implicit violence of militarism and the personal oppression of women in everyday life are simply expressions of each other. This is revealed most sharply for women who live close to military bases, who are drawn into employment as barmaids or prostitutes, both gender-specific examples of the links between the dominant culture of masculinity and the processes of militarization.[23]

The feminist analysis also offers an historical analysis which wrestles with the question of how gender relations have emerged in the way they have, and the political implications involved. Marston, for instance, argues that "the social construction of public and private life is one of the central conceptual building blocks of the modern nation-state, and the challenges to their gendered composition have proved to be vitally dynamic in the history of politics."[24] She argues that without a concept of public and private, we could not understand the way in which the American republic came into being. Most centrally, we could not understand the way in which males were automatically categorized as "citizens," while women, slaves, and Native American peoples were excluded. The same analysis holds true, she argues, for the gendered composition of the French Revolution, which was

> a direct attack upon the considerable public power wielded by the elite women of urban salon society in the Old Regime. . . . In place of the spectacular omnipublic presence of the monarch and elite women's influence over public speech and behavior, bourgeois theory proposed a public sphere composed of men having a "certain position in the property order" who could claim the right to govern on the basis of universal reason. . . . At the same time a new public sphere was fashioned which rejected privilege and tradition, a private sphere, maintained through the virtue of morality and respectability of bourgeois women, was envisioned as an essential substratum to the public.[25]

Theroigne de Mericourt. The implications of these remarks are revealed in the story of the young courtesan who returned to Paris during the unrest in October 1789, when Maillard and the *poissardes* marched on Versailles. Anne-Joseph Mericourt, astride a jet-black horse, wore a "plumed hat and a blood-red riding coat . . . carrying pistols and a saber."[26] As "Theroigne the Amazon," she became one of the many symbols of the Revolution, namely the newly liberated woman, active in the political Clubs, pressing for equality, attempting to form a regiment of revolutionary women. She also became one of the victims of the backlash against such liberated women;

she was beaten (by market women) in 1793, lost her sanity, and was confined to an asylum for the last twenty-three years of her life.

> By 1810 she had disappeared from the land of the living in all but biological
> fact. Clothes had become abhorrent to her, so she sat naked in her cell,
> angrily refusing even the simplest wool dressing gown offered to protect her
> from the winter cold. . . . Every day, she would throw cold water on the straw
> of her bed, sometimes breaking the ice in the yard to get at it, as if only
> glacial saturation could cool the heat of her dementia. Periodically, she was
> heard, still, to mutter imprecations against those who had betrayed the Revo-
> lution.[27]

De Mericourt and her sisters had sought to be included in the Republic
on the same terms as men—to be, simply, *citizens*. This was denied them.
The public sphere was not public enough to admit women, at least not on
the terms demanded by the Fraternal Society for Patriots of Both Sexes.
Women's place in the Revolution was rapidly restricted; the Declaration of
the Rights of Man and Citizen was quite literal. For the revolutionary women
of 1789, a re-creation of the state offered the opportunity for a restructuring
of social relations, via the determination of gendered human rights. As
events showed, the new state form was not a thing apart from those social
relations; the deep imprints of unequal gender relations were, consequently,
reproduced in postrevolutionary France.

The theoretical implications of this case could be developed in different
ways. One would be to infer the state's relative autonomy from social pressure; another would be to identify the webs of class and gender within the
state apparatus that resisted externally determined change. While these
interpretations would be reasonable, they would fall into the trap of trying
to lay contemporary theoretical blueprints across particular historical moments. This can be dangerous for two reasons. First, it implies that the state
has remained constant, and that our contemporary insights can be used
as leverage against it in its former guises. As the Balinese example suggests, this is worthwhile only over short historical periods. Second, it assumes that those who took political action perceived their actions through a
lens—such as class or gender—that we employ in the same manner today.

The purpose of this argument is to expose the central problem of state
analysis. On the one hand, if we use a strictly presentist method, then we
run a real risk of ignoring the unfolding of the past. On the other hand,
historical analysis may be difficult if we try to apply contemporary perspectives to distant circumstances. For this reason, the next section of the chapter moves to examine the recent work of historian Charles Tilly, who has
offered a self-contained interpretation of the process of state formation.

His work, which focuses primarily upon Europe, necessarily employs an historical method, but does not attempt to force current interpretations, except where they seem appropriate.

The Creation of the State

Tilly's book *Capital, Coercion and the European States* is important for three reasons: first, it moves us away from teleological concerns for the state apparatus; second, it shifts our attention instead to the *becoming* of the state, to borrow a phrase from Allan Pred; and third, his project emphasizes that the process of state formation is a complex and long-run one, which encompasses a large number of forms of collective action.[28] In short, he handles the three factors of time, space, and political action with which this book deals.

Tilly has synthesized the literature on European state formation for the period 990 to 1990. His masterful analysis represents a broad sweep across the European states in a period that saw the collapse of empire, a move away from fragmented sovereignty, and the emergence of the contemporary state system. We can summarize his conclusions as follows.

First, state formation is dependent on an interplay of two processes—capital accumulation and political consolidation. By political consolidation, or more simply coercion, Tilly means the way in which rulers attempted to extend their control over resources and territories. Typically, this process of extraction was achieved via warfare, and it tended to determine the structure of political organization: "within limits set by the demands and rewards of other states, extraction and struggle over the means of war created the central organizational structure of states."[29] Alongside this stood the accumulation of capital, which clearly varied in its intensity from location to location. In some regions, it was virtually absent; in others, intense activity prevailed. This had significant implications for social and political development.

Second, the relation between capital accumulation and the extension of political control is complex, but can be summarized as an inverse relationship—the greater the extent of economic activity, the smaller the impact of coercion:

> The organization of major social classes and their relations to the state varied significantly from Europe's coercion-intensive regions (areas of few cities and agricultural predominance, where direct coercion played a major part in production) to its capital-intensive regions (areas of many cities and commercial

predominance, where markets, exchange and market-oriented production prevailed). The demands major classes made on the state, and their influence over the state, varied correspondingly.[30]

Third, urban centers played an important role in this relation, acting as either economic or political foci. Economically, cities depended upon but also represented their respective regional economies, and the growth of one frequently stimulated the other (just as the stagnation of one could constrain the growth of the other). In regions of capital surplus (such as the Netherlands), city-states were common and constituted a particular form of opposition to both the religious empires and the more traditional coercive rulers. In other settings, though, urban centers represented the outposts of authority for these forms of government.*

Fourth, these processes were replicated from place to place. This reflects

> the uneven spatial distribution of capital and therefore sets off the relatively large but capital-poor states that ringed the continent from the swarm of smaller, capital-rich statelike entities that proliferated near its center. The contrast distinguishes exterior states, such as Sweden and Russia, that went through their formative years with relatively large concentrations of coercion and relatively small concentrations of capital, from interior states, such as Genoa and Holland, for which the opposite was true, and intermediate states such as England and France, in which concentrations of capital and coercion grew up side by side.[31]

These are clearly provocative, broad-scale arguments that demand more detailed examination. Let us examine these premises in turn.

Tilly observes that "extraction and struggle over the means of war created the central organizational structure of states."[32] From this, a number of conclusions follow. Wars were fought for varied reasons, but in the main to consolidate or extend territory, to obtain the resources located there, to deal with rivals, and to protect from incursions. These struggles were financed in various ways, such as direct extraction from the defeated, but those who fought became dependent upon a merchant class that financed warfare— and grew in both economic and political power as a result. Consequently, the fundamental processes of coercion and of capital accumulation can be identified throughout the course of European state formation.

---

*"Authority" is used in preference to "power," which has a number of meanings. Michael Mann, for instance, differentiates "despotic" from "infrastructural" power; both ignore Foucault's emphasis upon *resistance* (Mann, p. 5, n. 50). Authority recognizes the forces of the state, but also its legitimacy—expressed in legal codes, religious symbolism, and such— without closing off the possibility of resistance.

The relation between the two processes was never rigid, but in general terms, countries could be described as taking either a coercion-intensive or a capital-intensive path to state formation. The mercantile class could resist the coercive tendencies of the ruling class, if only because they were often sought as paymasters; but there were, nonetheless, nations where such a class was stunted. There, rulers found opposition only from within their own ranks or from other nations.

State creation went hand in hand with urbanization, although for different reasons in different locations. Where capitalism was dominant, urban places grew as part of the creation of an economic system. In coercive societies, urban activity was more representative of central authority. In consequence, Tilly differentiates cities as either part of a top-down process of coercion, or part of a bottom-up process of economic activity. In those locations where capitalism was weakly developed and there was little challenge to a ruling class, the latter could extend itself across relatively large territories. In areas where capital accumulation was more advanced—often identified as city-states—local resistance could inhibit the spatial expansion of coercive regimes: "wielders of armed force were able to cow urban ruling classes and to create extensive states in the thinly-commercialized European periphery, but tried in vain in the heartlands of capitalism."[33] In consequence, and as a broad generalization, there were observable differences between "capital states" and "coercive states" in terms of population and area.

Using as an arbitrary date the year 1500, Tilly demarcates the European experience of state formation as follows. First, there was a periphery, where the level of coercive political control was high; this belt included the Ottoman Empire, the Spanish domains, France, England, and the Nordic nations, Russia, Poland, and Hungary. Second, and surrounded by this broad belt, there existed a large number of small fiefdoms, palatinates, and city-states, where the scale of political control was highly circumscribed. We can differentiate these two groups, then, both in terms of a core and a periphery, and in terms of spatial extent. In addition, we may also distinguish them vis-à-vis their levels of capital accumulation, which was concentrated heavily in the city-states and urban centers of the European core.

From this historical baseline, Tilly moves on to identify the relations between these different types of states. With respect to interstate warfare, for example, he notes two discrete phases: first, a period that lasted through 1700, which saw the consolidation and institutionalization of power in fewer hands; and second, a period of nationalization, in which resources determined the ability to go to war, and strategic objectives determined the occasion of conflict between nations.[34]

Tilly's work is important for the way in which he attempts two things. The first is the search for a balance between political and economic domains, such that he does not confine the process of state formation to a mechanistic and functionalistic explanation of capital's needs and dictates. The second, which is potentially more relevant to this account, is the way in which he lays out a script—albeit an unfinished one—in which it is possible to place many of the dramas of collective action. This means that the latter do not remain as free-floating and unimportant aspects of struggle; rather, it becomes possible to place them directly within the project of state formation. This crucial factor will be developed in the next section.

The State and the City[35]

Because he approaches his task as an historian (or, perhaps, as an historical sociologist), Tilly allows us to see the state as something that develops and unfolds; he is far removed from the functionalistic models discussed above. In consequence, his work captures a crucial insight, namely the way in which the growth of the state apparatus involves a necessary conflict with other forms of political organization. He portrays this conflict in different ways. In the coercive states, the power of the ruler could be resisted by other factions, either within the territory or beyond. In the capital-rich states, a mercantile class could challenge a ruler's efforts to appropriate resources (if not the right to do so). While both these groups were integrated within the political system (they were not proletarian opponents, for example, such as the Diggers), their opposition was rooted in the spatial organization of the state—that is to say, they operated from a regional or an urban base. As we have seen, the clearest expression of this lay in the system of cities throughout Europe, which played a complex role in the economic and political development of the nation state.

The definition of what constitutes "urban" is never close to resolution. We can identify at least four strands of explanation, as outlined in table 1.[36] In each case, we see an attempt to identify a predominant explanation of urban growth; each is well known, so only a brief précis will be offered. In the first instance, we can deal with the geography/economics literature, which has emphasized the importance of trade to urban growth. Central place theory (CPT) is the most complete expression of this argument, and predicts a complete range of settlement sizes, plus a spatial distribution of central places. Other considerations may be incorporated (such as the importance of administrative organization), but the theory is best known for

Table 1. Alternative Characterizations of Urbanization

Urban Theory	Generative Force	Example
economy	trade and market functions	Christaller
community	citizen autonomy, trade	Weber
reproduction	collective consumption	Castells
authority	state control of territory	Giddens

its economic emphasis. Relatively little work has been done on the historical evolution of central place landscapes, and as a normative model, it is very different from the other three presentations outlined in table 1.

In partial contrast to the CPT model, with its contemporary focus, is Weber's ideal-typical city. His monumental study was directed primarily at the medieval city, which, he argued, constituted the only true urban community. In such cities, conditions of trade, fortification, some degree of political autonomy, and a semi-autonomous legal system together produced a distinctive communal style of life that both reflected and determined the ways in which cities developed and increased in overall social importance. The contrast with CPT is only partial, of course, insofar as both identify trade as a crucial factor in the development of urban life; Weber's work was, however, far more broadly based, and with a different intent, than that of Christaller.

The third strand of explanation identified in table 1 is the work of Castells, which focuses upon reproduction and the role played by cities in the provision of collective consumption (as noted in chapter 1). In these early formulations of his ideas, Castells relied heavily on a highly formalized Althusserian framework, which viewed the city as a locus of collective consumption. To summarize his argument briefly once more, a study of citizen movements extending over several centuries indicates that cities have constituted a semi-autonomous political realm, and that within this realm, social movements have attempted to improve their control of public goods. This argument develops from Weber's characterization of the medieval city, but goes a great deal further forward—both historically, in the sense of moving into the capitalist era, and in terms of an understanding of the evolution of civil society and spatial forms. These he summarizes as follows: demands focused on collective consumption, that is, goods and services directly or indirectly provided by the state; defense of cultural identity associated with and organized around a specific territory; and political mobilization in relation to the state, particularly emphasizing the role of local government.[37]

All three discussions of the city, then, emphasize the way in which the city represented crucial economic and political foci within evolving mercantile and early industrial landscapes. All recognize that urbanization constituted an *intersection* of political and economic development that was exceptionally dynamic. When Marx wrote of city air making men free, he barely exaggerated the ways in which the mercantile centers generated new economic, social, and political relations.

These principles are also recognized by Giddens, in the fourth explanation noted in table 1. He emphasizes the city in the precapitalist era as a "crucible of power."[38] His analysis echoes both Weber and Marx in underlining the relationship between cities and the countryside, and gives to such cities a powerful authoritative role, consistent with Tilly's general remarks. This, though, is limited to cities in what Giddens terms class-divided societies; subsequently, he argues, the state increases its power, the countryside loses its economic importance, and the city loses some of its preeminence as a power crucible.

Giddens's ideas are problematic ones, and instructive as a consequence.[39] The problem lies in his assertion that the city played a particular role only in class-divided societies; this was with respect to the countryside, and constituted the extension of the elite's power into rural territories. With the "maturation of capitalism," he argues, the state increased its power, the city lost ties with the countryside, and internal divisions within the city reflected class conflicts rather than the dictates of the urban *Gemeinde*. For Giddens, then, the shift from class-divided to class society marks the collapse of the city as a specific socio-spatial form.

There are central problems here, revealed once the historical contexts are examined in greater detail. Braudel, for instance, offers particulars on the evolution of cities in his monumental study of civilization, via his emphasis on "total history."[40] Did the city constitute a crucible of power? Only in certain situations. In Italy and Germany, for instance, there was no state, only cities. In France and Castile, on the other hand, the nascent state exerted controls over city functions. In some contexts, cities could exert no power over the countryside—this was particularly true of Russia—while in others the state depended firmly upon the city. For Braudel, the growth of Britain rested upon the expansion of London; in other words, the growth of the state depended upon the growth of the city, and the latter in turn was specifically an economic phenomenon.[41] In other countries, of course, this symbiosis did not exist, and there the state marked its growth with the creation of an independent entity: Versailles, St. Petersburg, Washington. The point remains, however: it is not possible to set up the city and the state as dichotomous, as a parallel to the city and the countryside. As

Braudel notes, "the great cities created the modern state, as much as they were created by it."[42]

The point at issue here rests with the assumptions being made about the nature of the city in a period of material transition. According to Giddens, once the city-countryside dialectic is diminished in importance by the onset of mass industrialization, the city loses its intrinsic significance, and the state becomes the smallest discrete unit of social significance:

> The nation state replaces the city as the "power-container" shaping the development of the capitalist societies as the old city-countryside symbiosis becomes dissolved. The precision with which the boundaries of the nation state are drawn is the modern analogue to the circumscribing of the city by its walls.[43]

But the error of this kind of interpretation is revealed by the kind of broader analysis offered by Braudel, or Raymond Williams, for that matter. As the latter points out in *The Country and the City,* we maintain strong images of both, despite the fact that the economic and social relationship between the two has shifted dramatically in the last two centuries.[44] The city has been transformed from a point of consumption to a point of production (and, to some extent, back again), but we continue to use the word "city" to describe very different urban entities. This reflects the continuing importance of urbanization within social relations.

Giddens appears to have a vision of the medieval city as stylized as the images of those contemporary artists who had not yet come to terms with perspective.[45] His view is of a city separate from that which surrounds it—unconnected, free-floating—a true city-state, to be replaced, ultimately, by a national counterpart. He fails, however, to adhere to his own thoughts on space-time language.[46] The city in class-divided societies was not an "isolated state," to borrow a phrase from Heinrich von Thünen, but part of a complex mesh of economic, social, and political links which crossed and recrossed countries and even imperial economies. In reality, the city has rarely constituted a separate entity of the sort proposed by Giddens. There were many cities, towns, and villages—a complex urban hierarchy, with economic bases and political power. *Together,* this hierarchy represented a dense web of political and economic power.[47]

These interrelationships emerged over relatively long periods of time and reflected the economic trajectory of preindustrial society. Such economic stability as existed was overseen by a political system which lacked both the bureaucratic unity of the contemporary state, and the fiscal stability and control of legitimate violence with which we are familiar. Stability necessarily rested within the "parcelization of sovereignty," as Katznelson puts it, which related not solely to cities but to all distinctive forms of economic privilege. In other words, authority lay in cities, but in rural holdings, too:

> Both the manor and the town shared another basic characteristic . . . the fusion of economy and polity. Each locus of economic activity was also a political jurisdiction.[48]

This dispersal of power remained virtually unchanged until the collapse of feudalism, which was prompted by a period of uncontrollable inflation.[49] At that time, authority was, in Perry Anderson's words, displaced upwards, thus producing state systems with concerns recognizable today: control of political structures, military coercion, and fiscal regulation.[50] As we shall see, however, this displacement was anything but total, for dispersed economic and political power was still evident on the ground.

The Drive to the Modern State

Braudel points out that the scale of mercantilism far outstripped the political stability within Europe during the sixteenth and seventeenth centuries; consequently, the mercantile sector, whose representatives enjoyed wider and wider horizons, often shored up the sphere of government and regulation. A broader scale of political reach was inevitable once the economic system began to move toward a global compass, and the rise of the state was intimately bound up with transactions of all types—within countries, within continents, beyond continents. Although we frequently think of the modern state in terms of *internal* organization and control, Michael Mann makes a very telling point. For most European states, it was not until the nineteenth century that more public funds were spent *within* the country than on warfare *outside;* in the case of Britain, for instance, this did not happen until 1881.[51] As Mann infers, this means that mono-theoretic models of the state that emphasize its capture by class interests are, at the least, too narrow.*

This insight also goes some way toward explaining what happened to local sources of authority once the state began to grow. Had this upwards

---

*What Mann does not help us to explain is why global trade moved the state toward a specific territorial form; this is explored again in chapter 4.

shift occurred for Kafkaesque purposes—that is to say, the deliberate crea-tion of a powerful organization of internal repression—then doubtless it would have come close to success in the long run. However, as we shall see below, the growth was typically for other, external, purposes; and while there was an increase in control, taxation, and coercion, it was hardly total in scope.

What, then, were the implications for local political jurisdictions once the centralized state began to grow? This is the question that should have been addressed by Giddens, but which he avoids by dispensing with the city as an object without sociological significance in class societies. Regardless of the status of the city in capitalist society (a point discussed already in chapter 1), we need to focus on this question of displacement in greater detail.

Despite the upwards movement of control, a great deal of political author-ity and economic privilege remained at the local level. Until the nineteenth century, power was still literally rooted in place, via the possession of land. Local interests pursued coherent political practices, akin to what Locke identified as a *political society*.[52] In a patriarchal society, local politics were defined by men "agreeing with other men to join and unite into a community for their comfortable, safe and peaceable living one amongst another, in a secure enjoyment of their properties and a greater security against any that are not of it."[53] As one political theorist puts it, this represented the fusion of *ius* and *dominum*—right and ownership.[54]

Personal, religious, and use values were all achieved at the local level, and were maintained via a localized political tradition. What is particularly interesting about this tradition is the way it was reproduced as an identifiable activity from place to place. When "new" societies were developed—as in North America—they immediately began to establish themselves via sys-tems of local organization. As Grant shows in detail with his study of Kent, Connecticut, the settlement of the Thirteen Colonies displayed clear ele-ments of the Lockean world.

Kent was settled in 1738 as part of the westward movement of the frontier. It was incorporated as a township in the following year, and the property owners of the town immediately requested three things from the General Assembly of Connecticut:

> Grant to us, the proprietors aforesaid, to be a town with the immunities, privi-leges and authority of a town. . . .
> We request that you would grant a tax four pence upon the acre for four years to be raised upon the divided land. . . .

And inasmuch as our situation is at great distance from persons in authority
... people transgress the Lord by trading in liquors with the neighboring
Indians, and also in other things, to the great distraction of the peace and
yet with impunity for want of proper officers.[55]

Where some form of central control preceded local polities—as in the
Colonies—we can see that such local forms were quickly sought, and were
equally quickly granted. Without local jurisdictions in place, problems of
land speculation and irreligiousness were inevitable. The outcome of this
evolution in the United States is a tradition of *communalism* that remains a
powerful strand within the skein of American political development, and
which can still be identified within contemporary political discourse.[56]

Control and Resistance

I have asserted already that authority remained based in land until relatively recently. While this is correct, it diverts our attention from the great
change that began to take place within the state apparatus as a result of
the onset of industrialization in the nineteenth century. The industrial world
soon became an urban world, of greater complexity, and also of growing
population. Agrarian political societies were overshadowed, for the most
part, by the cities described by Engels and Booth. From the outset, these
were places in which greater control was manifested. The factory and the
boarding house were experiments in spatial and temporal organization,
designed to restrict the worker to explicit tasks and prescribed forms of
recreation. These had only limited success, and were constantly replaced
by new forms of restriction, such as the frequent removal of the right to
strike.

These complex efforts notwithstanding, it was frequently the case that
the new urban proletariat took to the streets; as Katznelson observes, the
sheer number of the poor made it harder and harder to maintain control.[57]
Increasingly, the management of violence became crucial—through the
placement of troops in major cities or, as in Paris (and elsewhere), the
design of public space by Haussmann in a manner that would facilitate defense.[58]

Although working-class collective action was replicated throughout the
industrial nations, these were rarely international movements. While the rhetoric of trade unionism, for instance, displayed a global ethic, industrial
action was fragmented—organized through union locals, as noted in chapter 2. As Katznelson shows in great detail, urban politics were more fre-

quently concerned with consumption issues (akin to those described by Castells in chapter 1), and instead of being directed against the central state, political strategies were more frequently designed to capture the most immediate forms of political organization—explicitly, local jurisdictions.[59]

In part, this was expedient; marching on Paris or Washington was not undertaken lightly. But, also in part, this was a function of the real political life that existed locally. Bagehot wrote in 1867 that "we have little independent 'local authorities,' little centres of outlying authority." These were not simply outposts of the state, however: "when the . . . executive wishes to act, it cannot act effectively because these lesser bodies hesitate, deliberate, or even disobey."[60]

The discomfiture of such commentators should not be ignored. Efforts to increase the strength of the state during this period were by no means universally successful. Stephen Skowronek's book *Building a New American State* shows quite clearly that both as a set of institutions and as an intellectual construct, the nineteenth-century state in the U.S. was relatively weak, in contrast to the legal and procedural powers rooted at State and local levels. It was barely strong enough to undertake the tasks for which it was responsible. As industrialization increased in importance, new tensions revealed themselves, but there was always resistance to a stronger state. Attempts to expand and professionalize the army were opposed by the locally based National Guard network. The development of the Interstate Commerce Commission was beset continually by contradictory geographical interests. In the end, it was a series of contingent factors—the collapse of the Democratic Party between 1896 and 1910, the seriousness of labor unrest, and the need to mobilize national resources during the First World War—which allowed a central bureaucracy to push against local interests. As Skowronek concludes, the change was never a smooth one:

> Administrative expansion accompanied by a withering of party machinery and judicial restrictions on state action has defined America's peculiar approach to modernity.

An additional factor in this was the relation between capitalism and uneven development.[61] As capitalism progressed, so it became increasingly obvious that it had important geographical implications. The circulation of capital had differential impacts upon localities in ways that plagues or droughts never did. In consequence, collective action was increasingly influenced by local conditions as these changed—slowdowns or layoffs might be restricted to certain towns with particular industrial mixes, whereas nearby communities could be enjoying relative prosperity.

A second development also needs recognition. As urban populations grew, and the potential for unemployment and unrest expanded alongside, so too did the state's interest in surveillance and, ultimately, repression. Tilly has written a detailed history of the Place de Greve in Paris, which was for centuries a place of commerce and, when conditions demanded, collective action.[62] In the nineteenth century, it became an assembly point for unskilled day laborers, some of whom were picked for work in the docks or in construction. Until 1870, police spies mingled with the workers, and reports of their conversations were recorded in great detail. It seems the perfect metaphor that Baron Haussmann, prefect of the Seine, lived in a large apartment on the corner of the Place de Grève, overlooking this historic space.

Summary and Conclusions

This chapter has begun to explore the historical creation of the modern state, using both Europe and North America as its examples. This is, necessarily, a general account, but it offers up some important insights. The importance of moving away from functionalistic models will not be repeated; rather, I will simply emphasize the inferences that can be taken from such a broadly brushed picture. First, we can identify the importance of warfare to statemaking, to echo Tilly. External demands have often been much more important through history than have internal ones. Second, these demands—to raise taxes, to regulate, to coerce—have caused a shift of powers upwards, from a multiplicity of sites toward a more centralized focus. Third, this process is not complete (and probably, it is hoped, never will be). There remain important political activities at the scale of the local jurisdiction.

A commitment to local practices, and its political expression, has already been linked with the overarching concept of spatiality. This requires more detailed discussion, and this will follow in the next chapter. There, we will see that the contemporary tension between local practices and the authority of the state is important to an understanding of both entities. Taking this logic a little further, we can argue that an understanding of the contemporary state must rest upon a recognition of this tension.

FOUR

A SPATIAL THEORY
OF THE STATE

a non-state, a chaos   *—NEUMANN*[1]

Introduction: From *Leviathan* to *1984* and *Judgment Day*

As we have seen, the emergence of the modern state has been described as a displacement of authority away from multiple locations—such as cities—until coercive power resides in some central locus, itself often marked by the construction of some symbolic place, such as Brasilia, Bonn, or Berlin.[2] This process has typically involved a concentration of "the legitimate means of violence" at the disposal of the state's institutions (to use Miliband's phrase).[3]

To a significant extent, however, this reading is now outmoded. Control and uniformity are still crucial goals within any bureaucracy, but a strong physical presence is no longer required to achieve them. As geographers have argued, improvements in transport and communication technology have produced a time-space compression that brings distant regions and their populations "closer" to each other.[4] Consequently, efforts to control violence have increasingly been augmented by nonviolent methods of pre-emptive control: electronic methods of data collection, identification, and monitoring provide instantaneous global reach.

These changes have received relatively little social attention, and the concerns expressed are often misplaced. For instance, any discussion of a loss of personal freedom inherent in the introduction of identity cards is moot in a society such as the United States, where there is instant police access to driver's license information via a national computer network, a data source that is almost complete in its coverage. In absolute terms, then, state institutions are more powerful than before with respect to surveillance.

The police spies of the *ancien régime* or the Restoration, mingling with the workers in the Place de Grève, have been replaced by computers and satellites.[5] It is appropriate to remember that the rather innocuous English word "surveillance" has a more redolent meaning in French; for example, Foucault's *Surveiller et Punir* is usually translated as *Discipline and Punish*.[6]

As I argued in chapter 2, civil society is also more complex, more diverse, and more populous. In consequence, the *relative* power of the state is thus not necessarily greater than it was decades ago. The electronic media of communication are, as commodities, widely available, and their distribution has had numerous consequences. The photocopy machine has proved a powerful ideological weapon in the dissemination of books, poems, and lyrics, and in simpler tasks such as announcing rallies and meetings. Radio broadcasts can be heard across borders and by even the poorest of listeners. Video cameras started life as a lowly part of the surveillance of parking lots, but have proved to have other, significant uses: Los Angeles Commissioner of Police Gates announced his resignation in 1991 following the fortuitous videotaping of the brutal beating of Rodney King by LAPD officers (again, following electronic transfer, this time on television).[7]

The Terminator. These themes run explicitly through the recent postmodern film *Terminator 2: Judgment Day,* to date the most expensive movie ever made. I call it postmodern in that nothing is as it seems. The hero dresses as a biker, his enemy dresses as a motorcycle cop. Both come from the future; their goal is to change events in their own past. One of the main protagonists is wrongly held—for reasons of state security—in a mental hospital; several of the staff are themselves depicted as being deranged. Of the non-cyborg characters, the most heroic is both a woman and a mental patient (an unusual direction for character development, to be sure), while her son, a future hero, is depicted as a delinquent and petty thief (who, incidentally, is adept at electronic crimes such as extracting cash from automated teller machines).

There is an explicit theme running through the movie, namely the increasing power of the state; this will, within several years, result in nuclear war, the judgment day of the title. The machines that will take over the planet following this catastrophe are creations of the state, and they will be resisted by the few humans who survive. However, beneath this story runs a second, virtually identical strand, which is manifest in the theme of law and order and the endemic powers of the state. As noted already, the "evil terminator" appears disguised as three different policemen, for these are personas of unquestioned authority. When he first lands in California, he immediately uses the police computer to find his victim—who is revealed within seconds.

When Sarah Connor escapes from the mental hospital, all the forces of law and order are used to track her, and when she is cornered, the entire arsenal of the police force is brought into the open—tear gas, helicopters, vans carrying automatic weapons. It is interesting that this massive display of coercive means does not seem uncharacteristic; indeed, it is unusual to see a contemporary Hollywood movie that does not involve fleets of police cruisers being destroyed. Nor, interestingly, does the level of resistance to these forces seem unbelievable to the audience.[8]

Sarah Connor begins by passively resisting her interrogators, who are armed with numerous video cameras that record her every excess; then she escapes using a picklock; she escalates to the use of a nightstick, and is within minutes festooned with grenades and high-caliber automatic weapons. The message of the movie is clear: only the individual—not the state—can be trusted to get things right, and to achieve this, any means are justified. By its manipulation of traditional values of right and wrong, this too is a postmodern conclusion.

In short, we seem to be a long distance from the uniform electronic world portrayed in Orwell's *1984.* There, resistance was possible only passively, deep within the individual; to date, our electronic world is one of difference, in which there still exists significant opposition to that apparatus. However, this resistance provides an example of an intriguing dualism: despite the greater power of the state, there is greater difference within civil society; and the more there is difference, the more the state must attempt to control it. This is by no means a self-evident proposition, and it will, once more, be examined historically.

Spatial Organization of the State

Cynthia Enloe offers an excellent definition of the relation between the state and its citizens. She writes that

> the *state* is a vertical structure of public authority. It contrasts with the *nation,* which is essentially a horizontal network of trust and identity. The state's most visible expressions are those institutions which exert vertical authority: the civil bureaucracy, the judicial system, and the military and police. A *nation state* . . . is a state whose vertical authority structures are rooted in, and dependent upon, horizontal bonds of trust and identification among all those persons who fall under its presumed jurisdiction [original emphasis].[9]

This statement brings us neatly to one of the central tensions within the state: as with virtually any organization, it is organized vertically, or hierarchically, while the citizens overseen by the state are dispersed horizontally, or geographically.

Organization and control were most readily achieved when the dependent population was small in number and close at hand. Once authority was exerted over the horizon, more complex strategies became necessary. Almost paradoxically, the distant frontier took on greater significance than did the one close by; for logistical reasons, its loss was harder to replace. Although Vienna is now inextricably linked with the memory of the Hapsburg empire (as was noted in chapter 2), it is less often remembered that it was chosen as the capital city for precisely these geopolitical reasons.[10]

Spatial arrangements were, in consequence, the hallmark of early organization. Focusing on the example of the early Christian church, Sack has shown that a complex geographical structure developed, which has persisted as a form of territorial organization through to the present. These structures were rarely freestanding; in the first instance, the church operated within the framework of the Roman empire.[11] A second instance is that of the Holy Roman Empire, which flourished under Hapsburg control in medieval Europe, although it is frequently observed that it was neither Roman nor an empire, and was certainly not holy. Subsequent to the Thirty Years War, the Catholic church consolidated its own structure, with a "capital city"—Rome—and complex territorial arrangements. These allowed the Cardinals to maintain a rigid grip over orthodoxy and, just as important, the raising of revenues.

The interesting question about the Catholic church is not so much its territorial structures but the contrast that it makes with other religions. As Sack notes, for instance, the Jewish faith was originally associated with a national organizational structure, but this disappeared with the diaspora. The reasons for this are not hard to find. Catholicism has long been, to reiterate, a religion linked with the power of the state; Judaism, in contrast, has been a religion of otherness, and only its strict canon has allowed it to endure during persecution.

This connection between the state and territorial organization is manifested in many societies. Foucault has shown in detail how spatial, or panoptic, forms of surveillance and control—the penal colony, the asylum, the workhouse—were introduced into eighteenth- and nineteenth-century society.[12] What is sometimes overlooked is the manner in which these were representative of much broader structures of control. We can quote Foucault at length:

> Panoptism [sic] was a technological invention in the order of power comparable with the steam engine in the order of production. . . . At a certain mo-

ment in time, these methods began to become generalised. The police apparatus served as one of the principal vectors of this process of extension, but so did the Napoleonic administration. . . . From the First Attorney-General in Paris to the least Assistant Public Prosecutor in the provinces, one and the same gaze watches for disorder, anticipates the danger of crime, penalising every deviation.[13]

The police state to which Foucault refers was not comparable to that extant in a country such as the Soviet Union; rather, it refers to the attempt to create rational policies of organization. We should not forget that the etymological roots of "police" and "policy" are identical.[14] Foucault notes that Napoleon represented a watershed between the seventeenth-century assumptions of policing and the modern state apparatus that he created. A complex bureaucracy became possible as society became less *spatialized*—that is, as it shrank in physical size, as the result of new technologies.[15]

There had, of course, been forms of powerful territorial organization before this. Cromwell, for example, created the system of Major-Generals in England between 1655 and 1660—high-ranking soldiers who were responsible for the maintenance of order in explicit geographical territories. In addition, their mission was to enforce the Puritan hatred of secular pleasures, and to increase churchgoing; neither, however, proved amenable to military enforcement. Of course, the Major-Generals were a primitive experiment when compared to the organizational detail and the sheer penetration of Napoleonic France. Tilly writes:

Chinese and Roman emperors had, to be sure, constructed vaster systems of government. But they and their counterparts in other empires had essentially ended their administration at the regional level, stationing their own bureaucrats and soldiers in provincial capitals and relying on co-opted indigenous powerholders for routine government below that level. . . . The revolution and the Empire, through intense struggle, established direct connections from national government to individual communes and almost—via communal councils—to local households and kin groups. Regional and local potentates who were hostile to the current national regime could still make life difficult for its representatives. Yet they had nothing like the bases of opposition afforded their old-regime predecessors by parlements, estates, corporate trades and chartered municipalities.[16]

It is this type of experiment that demonstrates just why the successful state has a territorial form—an insight also developed by Michael Mann. As he argues, it is only via such an intense, territorial form of organization that the state can dominate, and ensure that its representatives are not simply seduced away.[17] The colonial officer who "goes native" is the archetype of this tendency. Sir Richard Burton, the eighteenth-century soldier and, later, diplomat who spoke many languages other than English, became a practicing Sufi, and frequently adopted aboriginal customs, was always suspected of moral weakness by his superiors for exactly this reason.[18]

Giddens on the Control of Time and Space

Giddens has suggested that it is with the onset of modernity that we see a restructuring of both time and space—a point already addressed in chapter 2.[19] He states three things: that both time and space have been manipulated; that space has been easier to structure than has time; and that space has been separated from place. The first of these insights is clearly correct. To take the French example once more, the imposition of state controls included both a new calendar and a new road system, the Routes Nationales that converged on Paris. Nor was this an isolated example; in Madrid's Plaza Major, a plaque shows one where to stand at the designated center of Spain.[20]

Giddens's other two assertions are more complex. It is the case that the invention of standard time was not achieved simply; indeed, the familiar time zones employed in the U.S. were introduced only with the Uniform Time Act of 1966. Efforts to standardize time further (e.g., year-round daylight savings) have been possible in wartime, but have always been rescinded later following localist political opposition.[21] In short, the definition of time is tied up with the definition of place, and it is hard to argue that the latter is the simpler process, as Giddens does. As we have seen above, the partitioning of space is an important part of the modern state. We can say metaphorically that the colonial boundaries inscribed at many peace congresses were drawn with a *ruler;* their arbitrary positioning flaunted the imposition of a new ruling class. Yet these simple geometries have proved to be extremely unstable, precisely because they were the work of what Stoppard calls "conspiracies of cartographers." Thus while Giddens asserts that space has been divorced from place—a phantasmagoric argument reminiscent of Meyrowitz—he neglects to add that social action continually attempts to reinscribe that relationship. The literal and metaphorical collapse of the Berlin Wall is a testament to reunification of more than two Germanies: it is a reunification of space and place, and one that has contemporary echoes throughout the world.

The Ideological Form

While it is important to identify the territorial imperative within the modern state, we should not forget that this is, in reality, both a solution and a weakness. As we have seen, the state employs territorial forms of organization; in contradistinction, opposition can build upon its connection to place. For this reason, the state cannot depend upon main force; it must always employ ideological patterns of control. These may take many forms, ranging from terror at one extreme through to simple exhortations at the other— such as the "harambee!" movement which has marked the regime of Daniel Moi in Kenya.[22] Successful state apparatuses have always recognized the importance of discursive control. In addition to employing the Major-Generals, Cromwell also tightly controlled the distribution of pamphlets and news throughout England. The Restoration went even further, introducing the London Gazette in 1665 to disseminate, twice weekly, the "official" version of the news.

As Foucault has shown, panopticism was much more than a system of surveillance, important as this process was. In addition, those who were involved in the systems of control were pulled into a ubiquitous scheme of designation that created new forms of order.[23] This was true of the insane and of criminals, but most interestingly with regard to paupers.

Poor Laws and the Definition of Poverty

Economic dislocation in Europe in the sixteenth century led to an increase in the numbers of the poor. Because work was available in some areas and not others, the peripatetic pauper became widespread. Local communities became adept at expelling the dispossessed and thus transferring the costs of poverty to their neighbors. In lieu of any resolution of either economic problems or social inequalities, the state offered a simple bureaucratic response that inevitably imposed uniformity upon localities. In England, the 1601 Poor Law Act determined that the parish would be the unit of pauper relief, and that each parish must claim those born there as its own. Very similar decrees were passed in the Netherlands, France, Austria, and the Thirteen Colonies.[24]

Naturally enough, this geographical solution was no solution at all. The externalities of poverty were passed back and forth, and disputes became more and more contrived. A case was heard in the Clerkenwell Sessions in

England, with the grounds of dispute being that the parish boundary passed through a pauper's bed: "the Court held the pauper to be settled where his head (being the nobler part) lay, though one of his legs at least . . . lay out of that parish."[25]

These problems reflected, in part, the primitive technics of surveillance available at that time, which made it impossible to track the origins and movements of individuals. It became common, in consequence, to redefine destitution: "poverty slides from a religious experience, sanctifying it, into a moral conception, condemning it."[26] While there were those who wrote economic treatises noting the problems of inflation, many others emphasized the idleness and indolence of the poor. Their tea drinking and fondness for tobacco were noted, and numerous schemes for control suggested. National friendly societies were proposed, and, in an early version of the pink triangle or the yellow star, those not contributing to such schemes were to have the word "DRONE" stitched in large red letters on their clothes.[27]

The resolution of this issue was the creation of the workhouse, which was designed both to control paupers' behavior and to force them to work. This was, in fact, the original manifestation of panopticism, namely a creation in which the poor could be isolated, observed, controlled, and re-created. Bentham's scheme of "pauper management" was extremely complex; it extended from a broad national, economic base to include a large number of Benthamite Houses.[28] Their internal organization was highly detailed:

> Next to every class from which any inconvenience is to be apprehended, station a class unsusceptible of that inconvenience. Examples: 1. Next to raving *lunatics* or persons of *profligate conversation,* place the deaf and dumb . . . separated as to sight. 2. Next to *prostitutes* and other loose *women,* place the aged women. 3. Within view of the abodes of the blind, place melancholy and *silent* lunatics, or the shockingly deformed. 4. Next to each married couple, place at bed-time a set of children, under the age of observation [original emphases].[29]

The panopticon represents an interesting microcosm of our discussion. It operates systematically and effortlessly, despite the creation of an artificial universe. Perhaps the most poignant example of this is the prison of Alcatraz in San Francisco Bay, an island that incarcerated both its inmates and their guards; they were effectively suspended in a space that isolated them from the society that they could all see on the horizon. Crucially, the panoptical rules cover the watcher and the watched: both are situated in this perpetual relationship, although there is always the possibility of individual action beyond the "script" of the system; the watcher may initiate punishment, and the watched may resist, as we shall see below.

It is important to repeat that the prison or workhouse is not simply a removal of certain persons from civil society; rather, it is a functioning part of what Foucault neatly describes as a *capillary* system of power that insinuates itself throughout a territory.[30] Prior to this, paupers and criminals were migratory, or lived as bandits, driven beyond the usual parameters of everyday life by the authorities. (Describing a premodernist society, Hobsbawm notes such a phenomenon as recently as 1941 in Eritrea, where a trio of brothers fled after they had killed the local governor. They took to living in a forest and prospered by robbing Italians, never locals, and thus had the tacit support of their former neighbors.)[31]

In contradistinction, it is important to confront the fact that Alcatraz and the like are not hidden; they must be in plain view in order for them to function as part of this capillary system.[32] This perspective also allows us to comment on the apotheosis of the panopticon, namely the camps where the Nazi regime placed political prisoners, homosexuals, and Jews. While many Germans claimed that they did not know exactly what was going on in the camps, this may be beside the point. In terms of the control exerted by the regime, it was enough that all who could see knew of their existence.

The bureaucratic mind created the ultimate panoptic hell in the Nazi camps. All detainees wore "color-coded" patches: red for politicals, green for criminals, violet for Jehovah's Witnesses, black for asocials, pink for homosexuals, brown for gypsies. Race defilers wore an inverted black triangle, foreigners a single capital letter indicating their origin. Those in penal colonies wore a black dot; those who attempted to escape received a red-and-white target on chest and back. While escapes were not frequent, the systems of control and extermination could collapse. In August 1943, for example, several hundred prisoners escaped from Treblinka Camp Two.[33]

In coming to the extermination camp, we also arrive at the realization that panopticism is no final solution to the bureaucratic problem of control. That lies instead in death. In part, this was recognized very early on; it was clear that neither the prisons nor the workhouses were particularly successful in their long-term goals of reordering the pathologies of their inmates. Indeed, Foucault seems to suggest that representatives of the state found the prisons useful as breeding grounds for informers and secret agents, but this seems unnecessarily functionalistic.[34] Crucial here, though, is the recognition that the closed society of the prison was also a site of resistance. It is becoming clearer, for instance, that while untold millions died in the penal colonies established by Stalin in the Soviet Far East, others survived and established a shadow society on the physical margins of the USSR.[35]

Foucault on Resistance

Although Foucault has often been interpreted on the basis of his early, structuralist writing, it is clear that his project was closely tied to the issues of power and resistance, which are, in my view, inextricably linked in his overall body of work; indeed, he stated on different occasions that "where there is power, there is resistance."[36]

Of course, Foucault did believe that power is immanent in all social situations, and the trite remark frequently attributed to him—"knowledge is power"—reflects this. However, this simplifies his position. As he emphasized, there is no necessary correspondence between power and knowledge, and his task was to grasp the many ways in which the relationship is articulated.[37] Individual expressions of power, and of resistance, are dependent upon individual motivations and strategies; and as Jessop observes, these are not reducible to an overarching logic such as class struggle.[38] This issue also emerges with regard to the origins of resistance. Foucault was left to explain the latter in terms of a basic human energy, not necessarily connected to broader, theorizable motives derived in terms of fundamental social contradictions. In consequence, as much as sociologists and social psychologists have sought to explain occurrences such as urban riots (which appear paradoxical insofar as they cause the greatest damage in the poorest neighborhoods), Foucault would likely have pointed to the problems inherent in searching for causalities when dealing with the actions of those who are described in translation as "the plebs." Resistance is, by nature, sometimes violent, unrehearsed, and brutal.

This is not to swing instead to an interpretation of resistance that has no broader limits. What Foucault termed "localized procedures of power" are transformable by "global strategies" such as the state, which is exactly why the latter has become the symbol of the twentieth century.

Kafka's Castle. We see the theme of resistance explored frequently in Kafka's work, which has become the ultimate metaphorical statement of the power of bureaucracy and the ability of the individual to resist. His writing is of interest for two additional reasons: first, because he was productive during the modernist period in which bureaucratic control shifted from the formalities of monarchy to the more complex and extensive coercive regimes, such as the Soviet Union; and second, in that he holds out some hope of individual redemption within such systems.[39]

While *The Castle* was at first often cast as a divine allegory, it is now much easier for us to see it as a parable of bureaucracy, with farcical officials engaged, like the citizens of Chelm, in an endless task of moving burdens back and forth.[40] Despite their ineffectiveness—or perhaps directly because of it—they create a system that cannot be understood, except on its own immediate terms: "Of whom should we think? Who is here apart from us?"[41] In keeping with the legacy of viewing *Das Schloss* in divine terms, it is common to question whether the edifice is benevolent or otherwise. As Sheppard observes, "the Castle appears to be all-too-human and yet endowed with divine powers of observation and intervention; to be both benevolent and malevolent."[42] The question of observation/surveillance does not need to be rehearsed once more, but it is valuable to consider, not so much the intentionality of but rather the participation of K. the protagonist. He creates an image of the Castle, in which its malevolence, efficiency, and "monolithically-purposeful" bureaucracy are uppermost—despite the essentially ineffectual nature of the latter.[43] In Foucault's language, this is readily explicable: the "micropowers" of the system have K. in their grasp. This notwithstanding, *The Castle* is very much about the possibilities of resistance, and in particular the possibilities of different kinds of struggle.[44]

In reality, different forms of collective action can emerge in very unsupportive settings. Until extremely recently, women were excluded from the formal political process. This does not mean, however, that they have been either silent or passive. Resistance can begin within the household, as we saw in chapter 1 in the case of the early shoemakers, and within the workplace. In addition, American women have shown themselves capable of taking collective action when necessary.

Women and Temperance. In 1873, women in Ohio reacted to efforts by the liquor trade to liberalize the State's licensing laws. Excluded from the franchise, they took to entering the saloons and, by prayer and song, closing them down. "Throughout the midwest that winter, the streets literally ran with rum as saloon keepers 'surrendered' to the women, signed temperance pledges, and rolled the casks of liquor into the street to be split open."[45]

The temperance movement was a natural extension of Victorian women's responsibilities for family and home, and they extended their concerns from the church and the neighborhood to the morals of the community at large. Again, the strand of communalism can be seen to connect political actions within the community over long periods of time. Of course, it is easy to read this example as a reflection of small-town America, where some moral authority resided in the institutions of the church and the family. While this is the case, it has also been possible to trace parallel kinds of protest in urban industrial settings. Next, I want to explore Hoggart's *The Uses of Literacy,* which examines the changes in working-class culture in England between the two world wars; this is to be read explicitly in terms of the issue of resistance.[46]

The Uses of Literacy. Hoggart's book is a fascinating study of class relations in England, written toward the end of the rigid distinctions that had survived both the Depression and the Second World War, but which would not outlast the relative affluence of the 1960s. Although it has a patronizing tone, it contains some persuasive insights concerning the ways in which groups maintain themselves and their practices in the face of change from outside.[47]

For Hoggart, the working class was in part defined by its attitude to authority. "The refusal to accept any publicly-offered values is related to the old pragmatic and unidealistic root. . . . Thus Pip and Joe, at the beginning of *Great Expectations*—to choose one example from hundreds—automatically hope that King George's men will not catch the prisoners escaped from the hulks." Hoggart continues:

> Anti-authoritarianism becomes not merely a nonconformity nourished by a sense of the value of personal and individual life, but a refusal to accept at all the idea of authority: "I'm not going to be used like a dog" becomes "I'm not going to be bossed around by anyone"; and there, as elsewhere, the tone is as important as the words.[48]

From Hoggart's perspective, the micropowers are pervasive. They manifest themselves in the police, of course, but also in the factory, in local government, in charitable concerns such as the British Legion; newspapers, too, commodify this sense of control. This is all defined as external and outside, and very different from what goes on with regard to "local matters"; "you will not twist a neighbour but a middle-class customer is fair game."[49]

Much of *The Uses of Literacy* is about the ways in which these forms of resistance are maintained. In part, there is a recognition of class as a bond, which emerges in many settings; Hoggart observes, for instance, that the armed forces are "held together not mainly by discipline nor by *esprit de corps,* nor by the enlightenment that Current Affairs talks bring, but by the interlocking multitude of little cells of personal relationships which men create for themselves inside the huge impersonal structure."[50]

In everyday life, it was the home—and the collection of homes that constituted the neighborhood—that provided the propinquity upon which such relationships developed:

> Home is carved out under the shadow of the giant abstraction; inside the home one need be no more aware of those outer forces than is the badger under his mountain of earth. It is as much of a relief as it ever was . . . to come back to the local known group, to come across "one of us."[51]

Hoggart's neighborhood was not solely a physical presence, although it could be recognized easily in a Lowry painting or a Lawrence short story. Rather, it was a set of relationships built up over time, each with an explicit purpose. The local shops provided various forms of credit for families facing intermittent work or just a general shortage of funds. A vast array of now-forgotten organizations provided clothes on credit, or various forms of insurance or annuity schemes. Individuals—grandparents, unmarried siblings—played particular roles on the edges of family life (such as child care) that allowed large families to function.

British sociology in the 1950s, via its community studies, came close to hagiography of these mean streets. And as factories closed and urban renewal ripped up the neighborhoods and moved the tenants out to far-flung developments of public housing, the palpable failure of these concrete creations served only to sharpen the glow that surrounded the disappearing neighborhoods. It is not my intention to follow that simple Weberianism, which saw the working class in nostalgic—and functionalist—terms as contented cogs in the social machine.

Hoggart himself placed the practices of the self-defined working class as a part of a complex process of reification and re-creation. His work was in large measure an effort to show the ways in which the print media amplified social tendencies, with respect to gender relations, the importance of family life, and one's place.[52] However, contrary to the arguments developed by Meyrowitz with respect to the flattening aspect of the electronic media, British magazines catered explicitly to readers of different classes and commented on the follies of the other.

As a number of commentators have indicated, this question of culture is complex. For some, any human practice that is not directly reducible to the relations of production becomes transferred to the dumpster of culture—the recycler of ephemera. I think that there is an element of this approach in Harvey's efforts to trace a connection between neo-Fordist techniques of flexible accumulation and the trappings of postmodernity.[53] Here, I use culture to refer to any practices that are self-sustaining for the group; in many instances, these may have political-economic overtones, and may even be achieved through strategies such as union organization or the formation of a political action committee. This is, I think, consistent with Raymond Williams's interpretations of the raw material examined by Hoggart: "the working class, because of its position, has not, since the Industrial Revolution, produced a culture in the narrower sense. The culture which it has produced, and which is important to recognize, is the collective democratic institution, whether in the trade unions, the cooperative movement or a political party."[54] Explicit in this definition is, again, the question of resistance.

Culture and Resistance

For Williams, working-class culture in the 1950s was to be witnessed in terms of institutions, such as the Workers' Educational Association, in which he himself functioned. This adult education organization created its own curricula—focused frequently on political-economic debate—in a way that was not possible had its members attended the middle-class universities. In turn, successive waves of immigration brought to Britain a number of groups who maintained their cohesion in different ways and demonstrated it more visibly. The obvious instance of this has been the carnival generated within Caribbean districts of London. On a superficial level, this suggests an innocent example of cultural artifacts—music, food, costume—that is transported out from its own neighborhoods and is displayed to the dominant social and racial groups. There is, though, much more to this celebration than a demonstration of heritage. It is an explicit example of tactical resistance that employs a spatial strategy to achieve its goals. The carnival succeeds by carrying its symbols from the neighborhoods in which it is based, out toward the dominant population. This is a long-standing urban tradition, common when ethnic groups, such as the Irish, first moved to the U.S., for instance.[55]

Lipstick Traces. Practices of culture/resistance can be maintained anywhere, as Marcus indicates in his study of art and music.[56] He traces a straight line from the Communards of 1870, the Dadaist movement in the 1920s, through to Adorno and the Frankfurt School in the 1940s, the Situationists (SI) who manifested themselves in the 1950s, on to Paris during the events of 1968, and through to the likes of the Sex Pistols in the 1970s. All are connected via a condemnation of mass culture and a critical need to offer a radical alternative.

Marcus explores the ways in which the dominant ideologies of society can be confronted from the periphery or the underground. He uses the lyrics of the Sex Pistols' "Belsen Was a Gas" to show how it is otherwise impossible to confront tropes that have passed into the realm of the untouchable, the unspeakable. Only violent, nihilistic performers can reappropriate such images of horror and re-present them to us, and then in a complex, dualistic way—the horror of the original act is compounded by its juxtaposition with an unrepentant artist.

In most senses, artists are on the periphery, their statements only rarely becoming appropriated, commodified, and presented to the world via the mechanics of mass culture. From the Situationist perspective, it is more logical to avoid the performance altogether, and to move straight to looting or terrorist acts that drive directly against the state. In the infinite regress of the absurd, the surrealism of Breton's character shooting wildly into the crowd becomes the terrorism of the Red Brigades or the Ulster Defence Force. And as was noted above in our discussion of K., such dramas attack only the architecture of the state; they do little to dismantle the more pervasive capillary system.

It is significant that Marcus subtitles his book *A Secret History of the Twentieth Century;* while he can trace the extremity of the opposition that is displayed within the SI or the Dadaists, it remains the case that not one in a million has ever heard of Debord or Huelsenbeck. This is resistance of the most desperate sort, taking place in forgotten warehouses and clubs, after hours, after the rest of the world has fled; it is the parallel universe of Warhol's *Factory* or *Paris Is Burning,* where gender, sexuality, race, and class lose some of their traditional meanings.[57]

From Mattachine to Political Machine

The example of gay culture is an extremely important one for the discussion of resistance and the concomitant changes in civil society emerging here.[58] To do any kind of justice to the issue would require a separate study; Foucault himself was at work on the fifth installment of his study of sexuality when he died of AIDS complications in 1984. This caveat aside, I want to develop a number of themes: the aspirations of gays as a political collective; the early development of such a political consciousness in the Mattachine society; the innovations of the Stonewall movement and its contemporaries; the examples of political organization that have taken place in San Francisco and West Hollywood; and the criticisms that have been directed at the gay movement, notably in terms of its gentrification.

Sexuality and the State

Foucault has shown that the *concept* of homosexuality was absent in early societies, and has depended upon the reconstruction of public and private life within the last two centuries for its emergence as a social practice—indeed, the term "homosexuality" seems not to have been used until 1864.[59] He observes this process to have been part of a widespread reorientation that was instrumental in the creation of the modern state: "at the juncture of the 'body' and the 'population,' sex became a crucial target of a power organized around the management of life rather than the menace of death."[60] There was a pronounced change in the way that individuals were cast; whereas sexual actors had once been defined in terms of their acts, they instead became defined as *types:*

> As defined by the ancient civil or canonical codes, sodomy was a category of forbidden acts; their perpetrator was nothing more than the juridical subject of them. The nineteenth century homosexual became a personage, a past, a case history, and a childhood.[61]

Through changes in medical practice—notably the emergence of psychiatry—and the greater emphasis upon control of private life, the definition of homosexuality as deviance or difference became possible:

> Whence the setting apart of the unnatural as a specific dimension in the field of sexuality. This kind of activity assumed an autonomy with regard to the other condemned forms such as adultery or rape (and the latter were condemned less and less): to marry a close relative or practice sodomy, to seduce a nun or engage in sadism, to deceive one's wife or violate cadavers, became things that were essentially different.[62]

In consequence of these changes, male homosexual activity became, in the nineteenth century, more typically a clandestine venture. (The marginalization of women and the interdiction of their sexuality caused there to be less policing of lesbianism.)[63] Scandals such as the 1907 Eulenburg affair in Prussia implied that the armed forces of Europe might be incapacitated by perversion and unable to fight—a fear that generated a massive attack on vice.[64] E. M. Forster depicts a similar situation in Edwardian Britain in his novel *Maurice,* which was not published until after the author's death because of the controversial nature of its content. Little changed there until the 1960s, as the diaries of Joe Orton testify.[65]

Like many repressed groups, male homosexuals developed rather than tried to diminish their invisibility. Through code words and discreet behavior, they endured as individuals at the expense of a collective existence. In the U.S., this began to alter after the Second World War, when there emerged a number of unusual political alliances. Harry Hay, a Communist Party member, established the Mattachine Society in Los Angeles in 1950; it took its name from medieval male brotherhoods. With its rudimentary sense of a political agenda, this was in itself virtually a revolutionary development.[66]

With his experience in the Party, Hay was able to organize his colleagues. Using data from the recently published work of Alfred Kinsey and the example of the civil rights movement, he was able to develop the notion of homosexuals as a large oppressed minority within American society—an important point of departure for organizing. Collecting funds from wealthy but invisible supporters, the Mattachines fought an entrapment case in 1952, and soon had over 2,000 members. However, the backlash against Communism and all activities defined as "un-American" effectively destroyed the movement later in the 1950s, and pushed gay activities back out of sight.

Stonewall and After

A crucial development in gay resistance occurred in 1969, when a routine raid on a gay bar in Greenwich Village ended in several nights of violence. The climate of political opposition had shifted—in step with inner-city violence led by blacks and draft resistance by college students and members of a self-styled counterculture. But crucial in this development was the quiet shift in urban development that had taken place in the 1950s and '60s. The dash to the suburbs had drastically altered the social composition of America's central cities, with the result that medium- and high-income neighborhoods had become zones of transition, with rooming houses and communes replacing single-family dwellings. Areas such as Greenwich Village, Haight Ashbury, and North Beach in San Francisco, Bunker Hill in Los Angeles, Colfax in Denver, Dupont Circle in Washington, and their counterparts in dozens of other cities became centers of social change. Homosexual men, used to being invisible within straight society, could now base themselves within these milieux without undue attention, i.e., without police harassment.

"Coming out" thus became possible for many because of the support of neighbors, but as an act of resistance, it rested upon much more than propinquity. As Adler and Brenner have observed, "gay men require a physical space in order to conduct a liberation struggle," and they did this by putting their disposable income to work—buying and then renting out homes, purchasing businesses, taking over public spaces such as bars and clubs, and thus creating bases from which to challenge the dominant discourse.[67] Spatial concentration was a precondition but also a point of organization for such groups. (Importantly, while lesbians are typically treated as invisible in these discussions, Adler and Brenner argue that some of the same issues of concentration have been true of lesbian women, although they have been inhibited by the sexism and limited economic opportunities that impede women everywhere.)

Once gays became established—and this is very well documented for San Francisco—they took their place within the bartering system of city politics. They had votes to give, and they expected something in return. In San Francisco, support for Mayor Moscone in 1975 was followed not long after by a switch to district elections for city supervisors, which permitted the election of Harvey Milk from District 5—the Castro, the Haight, and Noe Valley.[68]

It is not the intention of this chapter to document in great detail the successes of the gay movement in San Francisco. Suffice it to say that the concentration of both gays and lesbians has permitted the creation of a base, from which key components of a homosexual consciousness have been developed. As Miller indicates, this has extended into the spheres of religion and law enforcement, and these key ideological institutions have been reshaped by their personnel and the quotidian settings within which they operate.[69] Not all has been simple: in the early days, the assassination of Harvey Milk brought gays back out onto the streets of San Francisco; more recently, they have reappeared there to mourn the passing of friends and lovers who have died of AIDS, using symbols such as the Names Quilt to express their dissatisfaction with government spending priorities. More radical groups, such as ACT-UP and Queer Nation, have presented a more militant face to these demands.

Political Correctness and the Politics of Identity

In his study of San Francisco, Jackson points out that by projecting the usual Kinsey statistics, there are probably in excess of three million gay Americans below the poverty line and nearly half a million homeless with the same sexual orientation. He notes that "these are sobering statistics that need to be taken seriously by the gay community if it is committed to repairing the range of social inequalities that characterize contemporary society, not just those that are defined in terms of sexuality."[70] In more specific terms, he points out that concentrations of gay male professionals have led to widespread gentrification and the displacement of low-income tenants, notably from the Mission. This is an insight that is worth examining for several reasons, but particularly because it is very indicative of a certain form of political criticism, rooted in the traditions of a marxism, itself grounded in certain forms of privilege.[71] In basic terms, Jackson is demanding that gays align or even subordinate their own political issues to those such as homelessness, a demand that is explicitly rejected by self-styled "queer theorists."[72]

In terms of the broader argument being developed here, we can examine alliances within the politics of difference at a number of levels. First, in order to place this discussion in perspective, it should be noted that San Francisco does in fact have unusually liberal ordinances dealing with homelessness (to take one example). Indeed, *Forbes* magazine has criticized the city for its "anti-business" posture.[73] We might well assume that gays have contributed to this stance. Second, although homelessness has not gone away, neither has homophobia. It makes little sense to argue that gays should broaden their political platform when their own base is a very shaky one. The New Right attack on abortion provision is only one strand of a reversal of attitudes that has been going on since the late 1970s; gays, for instance, now face greater discrimination within their churches than they did two decades ago.[74] Third, and most crucial, AIDS has ravaged the definitions of both the self and the collective. Even a decade ago, Foucault noted that "homosexuals do not constitute a social class," and that their political objectives were necessarily limited to explicit questions of sexuality and personal freedom.[75] The importance of these restricted goals has been underlined in the intervening decade, which has illustrated just how recalcitrant the left has been in terms of finding common cause with homosexuals; Clause 28 in the United Kingdom and AIDS funding in the United States have been issues marked by indifference from liberal politicians and organized labor.[76] Even in cities such as San Francisco, gay groups have found themselves fighting to maintain the political and human rights that they have wrested for themselves.[77]

Thus on virtually any level, it is both naive and presumptuous to argue that a collective defined in terms of sexual orientation should act monolithically to accept the "map of meaning" defined by those with a different political agenda, such as a concern for neighborhood displacement.[78] Such a concern could emerge *strategically* in certain situations; the political incorporation of West Hollywood, for instance, was the result of an alliance between gays, rent control activists, and Russian emigrés.[79] But it should be emphasized that these are not interchangeable components of a homogenous underclass; and just as it is no longer enough to base our politics on the economistic divisions that constitute capitalist society, so it is inadequate to reduce the politics of difference to a group of interchangeable axes. Race, gender, and sexuality are canonical, even though racism, sexism, and homophobia are mutually reinforcing.

To summarize, a group with a collective discourse and a geographical identity will develop its own priorities, and these may—or likely may not—be close to those of an external observer. Gays, to use Jackson's own logic, are a cross-section of the broader population; and consequently there exists there tension between men and women, between races and ethnic groups, between young and old, and between affluent and poor. Moreover, while these tensions will be accommodated within the collective discourse of the group, the latter will also differ from location to location. While gays can claim that "we are everywhere," being gay in West Virginia is not the same as being gay in California. As Miller indicates, different quotidian realities dictate different alliances and strategies. To expect all members of a minority defined in one sphere to automatically hold identical opinions on other spheres is, tragically, to miss the point about the fragmented nature of urban society and also the differing potential of new social movements.

Conclusions

My concern in this chapter has been to demonstrate the following: First, while the state apparatus may be increasing in technological strength, these artifacts are double-edged swords, to use a metaphor from an earlier era. Second, resistance to the display of power is rarely absent, and deeply buried individuals and groups may emerge to exert their resistance. Third, spatial concentration is a powerful basis upon which to build patterns of resistance, and to consolidate any social and political gains that are made. The key issue is the recognition that resistance can develop within the neighborhood and the locality without being crushed by the state. More important, these developments represent a continual procedural challenge to the legitimacy of the state; they constitute difference and otherness within a bureaucratic system that yearns for order and standardization.

It is important to recognize that the examples that I have developed here are not directed explicitly against the authority of the state. The styles of life that are discussed form in themselves the pattern of resistance; a change in class position is not the goal of the groups, and such alliances are by no means inevitable. Rather, these are much more subtle—and thus much more dangerous—challenges to the state. As Lefebvre observes, "This is why conflicts between local powers and central powers, wherever they may occur in the world, are of the greatest possible interest. Such conflicts—occasionally—allow something *other* to break the barriers of the forbidden."[80]

FIVE

LOCAL STATES AS SOCIAL CONSTRUCTIONS

a field little disturbed by the transcendent insights of great thinkers —*MAGNUSSON*[1]

Introduction: Homage to Catalonia

Having pointed to the patterning of resistance in chapter 4, I turn now to the development of a consistent principle of the state and its constituent parts, that is to say, the development of an account of the state that has a literal place for local affairs. I begin with an example that is far from routine, insofar as I want to emphasize yet again that we are not dealing here with prosaic events. The case I use is that of Catalonia, one of several places within Europe where a premodern autonomy has endured.[2]

In beginning the history of the conflicts between Catalan people, their institutions, and the Spanish state, we might opt for a generic political-geographic lens, such as ethnic regionalism. The latter has been invoked in studies of Canada, the Lebanon, and a number of European cases where the relation between people and territory has attracted interest.[3] The problem with such a framework is the way that it excludes some insights (e.g., the forms of political practice) and pushes us toward an organic interpretation of the territorial state.

Ethnic regionalism would be unhelpful in the Catalonian case, where powerful ideological interests have long been present. Alternative interpretations are offered by communication theory and cultural analysis. Gifreu, for instance, interprets Catalan political struggles as follows. He begins with the recognition of a Catalan culture, identified in terms of, first, a territorial consciousness and, second, a language; these he restates as a principle of political sovereignty and a principle of communication. The existence of

Catalonia as a distinct unit that displays these principles is under attack, he argues, by the incursions of the state apparatus (which threatens political sovereignty), and the neocolonialism of the United States, which threatens the linguistic distinctiveness of the region. The control of the electronic media by American transnational corporations is simply another example of the way in which a hegemonic nation within the core of the world system may impose its economic order upon other nations within the core or semi-periphery.

In short, Gifreu identifies two "cultural and social" phenomena which have had important impacts upon Catalonia:

> 1. the extent and depth of the Francoist oppression during nearly 40 years (1939–75), which enforced the imposition of the Spanish language and culture (and through it favored the imposition of an increasingly prevalent American mass culture), and 2. the immigrant waves coming to Catalonia, mostly from the south of the Iberian peninsula, and so carrying Spanish language and culture with them.[4]

Gifreu's analysis is limited in its emphasis upon culture and language, i.e., his principles of sovereignty and communication (but see also Diaz Lopez).[5] Within his own logic, a good deal of the threat to Catalonia's autonomy should have abated post-1978, with the dismantling of the fascist state. Indeed, the existence of a region possessing cultural autonomy represents only a limited threat to the state apparatus, as other European cases indicate. Linguistic singularity (to take the most salient example of such cultural independence) is frequently the reification of marginality, for that language can be easily excluded from the daily interactions of the state and the economy—this would be true for Gaelic and Breton, for instance.

Instead, Catalonia has to be understood not solely as a *cultural* entity, but in addition as a *political* space. Language and culture may be seen as determinants of the form of a political space, but its trajectory is to be understood in terms of the conflict between the state apparatus and its sovereign components. The very persistence of Catalonia is a reminder of the fragmented sovereignty of the Iberian peninsula, and is as such a representation of the tensions within the Spanish state. In short, we understand Catalonia, its past and its future, not in terms of cultural phenomena (although the latter are clearly not insignificant) but in terms of the essential struggles associated with the process of state formation. A perspective that gives privilege to cultural forms, and their maintenance and reconstruction, misses the more fundamental struggle at work within countries such as Spain, Italy, and the United Kingdom, where subnational political spaces present themselves as explicit challenges to the continued process of state formation. Culture and its communication are media through which a political space is maintained, but the latter has existence in terms of the most traditional expressions of sovereignty—that is to say, in terms of capital accumulation and local authority. It is on these terms that struggles are waged between collectivities within political spaces and the national state.

Orwell and the Civil War. One of the reasons for highlighting the Catalonian case is to underscore that the politics of territory need not be diversions from greater struggle (and this is, ultimately, the criticism leveled by Jackson against San Francisco's gay residents, noted in the previous chapter). Catalonia has not existed solely as a relic of premodern Spain; rather, it has possessed a distinctive ideological cast that does not derive solely from its concern for autonomy.

Orwell's account of the Civil War is a detailed source of this history, and he shows clearly that Catalonia has had a very complex political past. As he notes at one point, when discussing the street fighting in Barcelona,

> the people of Barcelona are so used to street fighting and so familiar with the local geography that they know by a kind of instinct which political party will hold which streets and which buildings. . . . To the right of the Ramblas, the working class quarters were solidly Anarchist; to the left, a confused fight was going on among the tortuous side streets, but on that side the PSUC [the socialists] and the Civil Guards were more or less in control.[6]

Even more now than it was fifty years ago, Barcelona *is* Catalonia; and I want to use it as a point of attack against our basic question: How do we construct a theory of the state that contains a space for such a social and spatial entity?

Spatial Fetishes

The British literature in sociology and geography has expended a great deal of effort on "localities research" in the past decade. This work stems from an initial study undertaken by Massey in the late 1970s, which began to explore the ways in which reconfigurations within British industry were being manifest within the space economy. To the surprise of no one—except, it seems, some geographers and sociologists—contractions in some sectors and expansions in others generated explicit spatial patterns of affluence and decay. The subsequent locality studies have been attempts to comprehend these changes.

Inner Cities

Such analyses have a relatively long history within British social studies. The community analyses of the 1950s have already been mentioned. In the 1970s, a number of investigations were undertaken under the auspices of the Community Development Projects, which explored how communities could develop strategies of political organization and resistance. In the same decade, several inner-city studies were undertaken at great expense, which also showed, with varying degrees of sophistication, what was going on in the cores of several large British metropolitan areas.[7] The state-sponsored study undertaken in Liverpool emphasized the theme of structural manufacturing change and metropolitan collapse; that done in Birmingham invoked race and urban infrastructure, while that done in London took a broad view of housing problems, police actions, employment potential, and bureaucratic organization. At this time, too, government acted to close down the Community Development Projects, which had begun to report their findings from studies around the country; virtually all the documents turned out to be radical critiques of British class structure and the operation of industrial capitalism.

Academic opinion was divided. Some argued that the inner city was a publicly created space dependent upon housing subsidy and welfare checks, and that in consequence the poor quality of life there was an equally public responsibility. Better schools, better homes, higher welfare payments, and increased aggregate demand should, logically, bring back the stores, provide jobs in construction, increase the chances of children completing their education, and provide the bases for personal development. Others argued that an interest in the inner city was nothing more than a spatial fetish that obscured the weakness of the British working class in a period of economic restructuring within the world economy; nothing other than a change in the relative balance between finance capital and manufacturing capital would even begin to resolve this outcome. With hindsight, it is now possible to argue that both of these positions were correct. The inner areas were but one spatial manifestation of the class structure and the country's ethnic balance. They would disappear—as cores of unemployment and deprivation—only via change within that structure. And of course, that was not happening; neither the white working class nor their West Indian and Asian neighbors were able to provoke such changes, and until that occurred, only spatial fixes or palliatives were possible. The real irony—which would not be so obvious until the second Thatcher victory in 1983—was that the whole question of change within the inner areas was utterly moot from the moment that the Labour Party went into governmental exile in 1979.

It was not apparent immediately that the country was being thrown forcibly down a new policy path; and so the academic debate continued, with major SSRC initiatives reporting in 1981.[8] These reports failed to capture the causal factors of the problem, with the most important of these neglected issues being the broad question of the role of the state within the policy process. For some observers, inner-city analysis had indeed begun to metamorphose into one of intergovernmental relations, for example, and it became plain with some speed that central government intervention in the urban areas was only a part of a larger process of struggle between the state and units of local government.[9] The terrain had, in other words, shifted; it was no longer a question of channeling funds, but much more a question of controlling public expenditure. The inner-city question and the broader issue of central-local relations have been a part of a structural conflict taking place in the state apparatus for a much longer period.[10]

Local Government

Parallel to these works has been a refocus upon local political practices. Using the umbrella term of the local state, a number of commentators have worked to employ Althusserian tropes in a study of local government—striving, in essence, to bury local political entities within the state apparatus (more will be said of these developments below).[11] Central to both these strands of argument was a concern to demarcate the theoretical importance of spatial variation within the social formation; that is, to delimit the importance of spatiality within the sphere of reproduction and consumption (these connections between reproduction and the locality were explored in chapter 1). While it was possible to argue with great sophistication that the accumulation process could be understood only within a spatial domain, it seemed equally *im*possible to argue the same for reproduction.[12]

Most frequently, this issue has emerged in terms of a supposed "fetishization of space." A sample quotation will suffice to convey the flavor of this argument. Duncan and Savage, a geographer and a sociologist, write that

> this social importance of localities is one part of postmodern society and localities research is thus one index of "postmodernity." [We] reject this position as basically just a new form of spatial fetishism. [We] argue instead that spatial variations should be incorporated into the analysis of social processes as appropriate to any particular research problem—and this means that there will be no pregiven sociospatial objects like . . . localities—for the scale, logic and importance of the inevitable spatiality will vary from case to case.[13]

The assumptions here are pretty clear, and not so different from those raised by Jackson in chapter 4. First, the world is there for the purpose of analysis—human practice cannot exist outside the grid of analysis and does not generate its own social constructions; and second, to reify space is to necessarily downplay "social processes," for the two are clearly antinomies.

The need to explore these assertions in detail has already been made; as we saw at the outset, there are no "social processes," at least not in the sense of processes that transcend time and space. As was noted in chapter 2, some very anodyne statements could, I suppose, be made about patriarchy or capitalism, but these are so generalized as to be meaningless without recourse to situating these activities in time and space.[14]

Localities and Local States

In this section, I want to review these two blocks of argument—the first dealing with the concept of the local state and the second with the locality—in greater detail and with an eye to comparison.

Local State

This term was first used consistently in a 1977 study of local government in London by Cynthia Cockburn. Going beyond the analysis of local government as a set of legal and political instruments, she moved toward the political forms which operate at the nonnational level. The local state is made up of local government per se, plus a whole panoply of other organizations: bodies dealing with water, education, recreation, and employment. She placed these units within an Althusserian framework which took account of their existence but provided them with scant independence. She summarized her position as follows:

> Local authorities, including local health, water and transport authorities as well as local education, housing and planning authorities, are aspects of the national state and share its work. When I refer to Lambeth borough council as "local state" it is to say neither that it is something distinct from "national state" nor that it alone represents the state locally. It is to indicate that it is part of a whole.[15]

The terminology of the local state was broadened by sociologist Peter Saunders, although his purpose was very different from Cockburn's. His study of urban politics—also in London—moved toward the internal actions and policies of a jurisdiction, with an emphasis upon the functional specificity of such a local unit—that is to say, the way in which the local state is responsible for the reproduction of social practices, while the central state is responsible for the rate of accumulation. This was underscored with reference to O'Connor's work on the nature of state intervention, which Saunders reapplied to the local scale.[16]

The evolution of this literature was driven by an interest in local political practices as an alternative to the emergence of the New Right throughout Europe.[17] This notwithstanding, it too has been branded fetishistic—Duncan and Goodwin, for instance, go so far as to ask how Cockburn and Saunders managed to get "the concept into such a mess."[18] They take Saunders to task on three grounds: first, for the creation of a dichotomy between production and consumption, resulting in the equation of the functions of the local state with collective consumption, to the exclusion of any other forms of activity or struggle; second, for the presentation of the local state as an ideal type, with the consequent exclusion of any hint of historical evolution with regard to the forms of government or the political struggles that have molded its evolution; and third, over the question of whether these political struggles are to be seen as class struggles rather than more ephemeral political activities.

Saunders's response is also instructive. In accepting the need for an historical perspective on the evolution of state forms, he quotes approvingly from Castells on the value of "a theorized history of states." He is more forceful with respect to the issue of class struggle, arguing that there exist a series of conflicts which relate specifically to consumption questions— housing, transportation, land use, and so on—and that these cannot be interpreted as class struggles: "The political groupings which arise around housing issues, education cuts, welfare agencies, and so on, are not class-based but are constituted on the basis of consumption sectors (council tenants, parents, the elderly), which bear a necessary non-correspondence (analytically though not, of course, empirically), to class categories."[19] This takes us back to the arguments introduced in chapter 1—arguments that are without any final resolution. Duncan and Goodwin note that Saunders's work has been crucial in identifying the roles of the local state, but inoperable because of its ahistoricism:

> Capitalist states have developed historically, as one part of the social relations between subordinate and dominant classes. They did not suddenly appear as an autonomous entity standing above society in order to regulate the squabbles of competing capitals, nor were states just called into being by dominant classes as a convenient tool in their subordination of other classes.[20]

This position echoes the argument that has been developed here.

Localities

Work on the local state has been overshadowed dramatically by the development of a related but very different set of literature. As Massey notes, the economic restructuring that has manifested itself across the globe appeared to have important social and political consequences. As she argues, "causal connections were being made between changes in employment and occupational structure and wider social, economic and political changes. We were facing the end of the working class, the end of class politics, the new ideology of individualism, a politics of consumption, the dominance of what were referred to as 'new social movements.'"[21]

To comprehend these developments—to understand the causal connections that linked global processes and outcomes—involved detailed study, and the British experience has been documented in several places.[22] In light of that evolution, it would be apposite to repeat the question asked ten years ago, namely, How did this work get into such a mess? Following the discussions of both Massey and Harvey, we can see a number of problems. First, there has emerged an analytical distinction between abstract work (on, say, the global economy) and concrete work (on "real people" in "real places"). Second, and logically, locality work has become branded as empirical (read "empiricist") and thus of little importance. Third, the whole issue of postmodernity has reared its head. This is perhaps the most crucial issue for our project.[23]

The postmodern condition has been addressed, as we saw in chapter 2, by a number of analysts, including Soja, Harvey, Jameson, and Lyotard. Consistent with a call to address "otherness" is the examination of those real people in real places, rather than abstractions such as the median voter, the immigrant, or the blue-collar worker. With a concern for multiplicity, fragmentation, and chaos, it is logical for postmodernism to embrace local research and the complexities of place. Harvey, however, sees this complexity as illusory: space is not becoming (as was argued by Pred; see page 12) but is static and nostalgic.[24] This is a profoundly British interpretation, of course, seeing place as a bounded area, a region of control—that local *authority* at work once more. To get away from this, Massey swings in the other direction, defining the locality in terms of *interaction:* setting for interaction, spaces of interaction, juxtaposition of social phenomena, are all phrases that she develops. In short order, we return to the position asserted by Jackson and by Duncan; that is, the locality is a research trope, not a social construction: "The particular social relations and social processes used to define a locality will reflect the research issue . . . which in turn means that any locality so defined will *not* be the relevant spatial area for the investigation of all and every social process deemed in some way to have a local level of variation or operation."[25] The implications of this position are that there is no such thing as "the locality"—only a constantly changing set of geographical taxonomies, which, like epistemes or durées, might be altered to suit a whim. Thus when Massey argues that "localities are not simply spatial areas you can easily draw a line around," she is being disingenuous; it may not be easy, but her first task in working with a locality *is* to begin imposing some exogenous criteria upon its extent.[26]

While this evolution is understandable, it does not make it any less unsatisfactory. The locality cannot be a sampling grid, to be placed over an appropriate or useful area; it is, to repeat, a *social construction.* If it exists at all, then it is as the creation of social, political, and economic (inter)actions rather than a backdrop for such behavior. This is in contrast to the local state, which must be recognized as a juridical entity. It is the product of formal deliberations, agreements, and disagreements, and while it is always subject to change dictated by residents or by those in other jurisdictions, it is not subject to the whims of academic definition. To be explicit, the local state is a creation whose existence is defined by its political history, manifested, in part, by its boundaries. By helping us escape this procedural quicksand, this alone would be enough to make us work within the local state framework and abandon the locality on the scrapheap of forgotten debates, alongside corn circles and cold fusion.

Moving to State/Local State Theory

After this long and disappointing detour, the reader has a right to be placed back on course. It will be remembered that in chapter 3, we explored the displacement of power within the state apparatus from local to national bases; in the next chapter we saw the ways in which resistance may be maintained within the local setting. We must now move ahead to unite these two insights within state/local state theory. As should be clear, one cannot recast state theory without the local; equally, one cannot create a theory of the local state without situating it within the broader political institution and the economic system. In exploring this further, I will initially develop four basic issues that together define the local state:

- the way in which economic development within the local state underpins the social relations that exist in a place;

- the instrumental links that tie together a group of political and economic managers, and the struggles that can emerge in opposition;
- the way in which jurisdictional boundaries act to contain and amplify social relations;
- the external relations that connect the local state with the central state and the global economy.

1. Local Economic Development

First, I want to reemphasize that while this argument deals primarily with political theory, it is not isolated from the economic base. As we saw in chapters 3 and 4, material issues have been predominant in shaping both the form of the local polity (see page 53) and the emergence of the modern state.

Here, I build on the insights already generated on the space economy, notably the case of the Lowell textile mills which was explored on pages 3–4. In line with the historical accounts being highlighted here, it is important that we continue that case further. A number of external events subsequently altered the economic circumstances within Lowell; domestic competition led to falling rates of profit, which in turn generated management responses, including speed-ups and pay cuts. A cycle of labor replacement was initiated, with successive immigrant groups replacing their predecessors, who were forcibly removed from the mills and company homes.

This cycle defined the industry in terms of the manipulation of labor rather than product development or technological change. Consequently, whenever widespread recessions occurred, textile production within New England was always hit hard. Conversely, there were occasional upturns— notably wars—which staved off the final collapse a little longer; the two world wars and the Korean conflict, for example, all re-created the demand for blankets, uniforms, and other goods.[27] Equally, the cycles of immigration continued, and in the middle of this century, both Puerto Rican and Southeast Asian families moved to Lowell, Lawrence, and the other mill towns.

What we see from this example is the way in which a local space economy was locked into a particular trajectory of economic development. This is consistent with the analyses undertaken by Massey in her studies with McDowell of different localities in Britain. They show, for example, how gender relations at the beginning of the century were very different in various areas—the coalfields versus the textile towns, for example. These then constituted a template within which subsequent relations emerged: deferential women in coalfield settings were readily used as cheap part-time labor when long-term male unemployment in the mining industry emerged in the 1960s; conversely, women with a history of unionization in the mills were not attractive to mobile assembly industries.[28]

The same general cycles emerged in New England. From the early part of the twentieth century onward, economic and political leaders led efforts to attract new capital to their jurisdictions, but this was not an undertaking to reconfigure local plants or labor skills. Ultimately, by the 1960s, the former had disappeared, leaving behind a labor force whose collective talents were no longer in demand. This sequence was broken only by the arrival of new industries, notably electronic assembly firms such as Wang, which were able to use cheap land and equally cheap labor for their production purposes.

Of great help in decoding this and parallel examples is the work of Logan and Molotch.[29] In their studies of places as *growth machines,* they have incorporated key materialist concepts into the study of urban economic development. As they note, places are neither produced in nature nor consumed and discarded as are other goods, and are in consequence subject to complex social and political manipulations. There is a large cast of players within the growth coalition, and their search is to maximize exchange value. They confront residents, whose struggle to maximize use value within the community places the household against the larger institutions that seek profits within the growth machine. The management of these replicated contests is a constant activity within the jurisdiction, not least as the disutility of growth increases in many localities and intense political responses have emerged.

It has been argued that these contests do not define local politics: "much of local politics is not about localised social structures per se."[30] Let us be clear about this point: what goes on within the local state is not occurring in a vacuum.[31] There are certainly many organizations that are busy lobbying for legislation at both the State and the national level, for instance. But this does not at all indicate that there are no *local* politics to speak of. Legislation passed—even at the highest levels—must still be implemented *in place.* Bills dealing with civil rights or workers' rights (such as OSHA) depend upon implementation in the plants, in the schools, and on the streets—and this will depend upon the collective discourses manifested within places (this question is explored in greater detail in chapter 7).

This point is clearly demonstrated with respect to the 1973 Clean Air Act (CAA) and subsequent legislation in 1990. Currently, one-third of the U.S. population lives in cities where the standards of the CAA are not met because of photochemical smog. High ozone levels present dangers of pulmonary collapse and seriously threaten the quality of life in major cities such as Los Angeles, Philadelphia, Chicago, and Denver.[32] This problem will become particularly acute if global warming accelerates, as photochemical smog becomes more intense as temperatures rise—in other words, the generic problem will have some explicit, and geographically concentrated, impacts.

These problems continue in specific places because federal law has not been implemented. EPA studies suggest that in order to bring Los Angeles into compliance with the CAA, tough regulations would have to be introduced, dealing explicitly with the ways in which Los Angelinos live.[33] But basic legislation remains unacted upon because environmental issues are reconstituted as problems of jobs and personal freedom, which make it hard for residents to develop an independent risk calculus that permits them to identify the serious problems associated with present practices. In consequence, growth and development questions have to be struggled over in situ, and they must be resolved—collectively—using local tropes and a *common* sense (see page 33).

These tropes are always open to manipulation within the growth machine. We are cut off from the natural environment in our cities, and residents lose track of the links that connect nature and the development process. Take the examples of urban development in Houston and Tucson. In both, there is a natural constraint upon the extent of growth: in Houston, it is the provision of water and removal of sewage; in Tucson, it is the provision of water and the control of flooding. In both, there is a limited popular awareness of these risks, because development interests have recast them as economic and procedural questions that can be negotiated for the benefit of the community at large. In Houston, there is a serious infrastructural shortage of water, and from 1970 to 1984 there was an extensive trade in water and sewer permits. A locality with an understanding of its natural base would have placed this resource question on the political agenda; instead, it became a fiscal issue, resolved by a proliferation of inefficient water districts. In Tucson, there is both an overuse of water (leading to aquifer depletion) and a continual destruction of natural floodplains via residential and commercial construction. The arrival of water from the Colorado River seems to solve the supply question, but this ignores the massive potential for flood destruction within the city. However, the bumper stickers in the city that ask rhetorically "Does your job depend on growth?" make discussion of floodplains and other dimensions of the environment politically impossible.

In short, the struggles that emerge within the local state are cast within the histories and the experiences of its residents; despite their universality, neither the struggles nor the outcomes are uniform.

2. Local Political Discourses

If development issues are rarely what they seem, this reflects the way in which politics within the local state are subject to a simple instrumentalism of the form developed by Miliband—that is to say, the control exerted by a closely interrelated group whose members hold positions within real estate, industry, and elected office. Such groups have been identified in many studies of local political interactions, such as the "Suite 8F" group in Houston who did much to direct the economic development of the city during the New Deal, or L.A.'s "Committee of 25."[34] Connected interests, plus a collective experience in terms of school or college, religious attendance, and recreation, can generate a closely knit organization capable of directing the political discourse. In Gramsci's terms, such groups display leadership, which may be backed by coercion when necessary; police forces, for instance, often act within local settings to break up strikes and demonstrations, or to attack neighborhoods thought to be centers of drug distribution or gang activity, and in doing so they exert force against specific groups— workers, residents, gays, ethnic minorities, or any combination thereof.[35]

Within a limited geographic space, the micropowers can be particularly important in the maintenance of such a system. Personal networks connect large numbers of institutions, in a way that can make coercive power a last resort. In Tucson and Pima County (which together have a population of approximately 650,000), for example, there are extensive personal interconnections, as is shown in note 36. These links are never proof of uniform decision-making, but they are very much consistent with an instrumentalist model.[36]

Conversely, the scale of the local state also makes it possible for alternatives—networks of resistance—to develop. As was noted, union locals played significant roles in shaping collective action during the most intense periods of industrialization; in some situations, class positions remain important, and wages still form the basis of opposition to economic change.[37] Elsewhere, tenants' groups—as described by Castells—and neighborhood associations have pressed for their concerns.

Neighborhood action in Tucson. I have noted above that Tucson has displayed classic growth-machine tendencies. Yet as Marston has also demonstrated, opposition has been influential, culminating in the election of a mayor who was supported by neighborhood groups in 1988. She identifies three reasons why these groups have been successful, and I reproduce her arguments at length:

- *fragmentation of growth interests.* Within the metropolitan area there have been up to fifteen separate agencies, both public and private, whose mission is economic development.
- *extensive spatial development of the city.* With a classic sunbelt spatial structure, the built-up area sprawls for over 150 square miles. There is no one group of business people or land entrepreneurs who speak with a single voice for the business community across the entire domain. The Downtown Business Association, which represents only one of the city's spatially concentrated business communities, is at times at odds with the objectives of the Southern Arizona Homebuilders' Association, whose focus of attention is frequently occupied in fringe locations of the metropolitan area. Furthermore, both of the major daily newspapers are owned by national syndicates, and the power of the press in supporting the local business community has been diluted as homegrown weeklies and monthlies have frequently championed residents' concerns over economic development.
- *neighborhood and environmental groups.* Opposition has been significant owing to members' level of education and relative affluence. The driving force behind these citizen organizations is a cohort of college-educated men and women who are sufficiently well informed about the machinations of local politics to have created interest groups with a great deal of political savoir faire. A strong preservationist and conservationist philosophy underlies the civic commitment of the citizen organizations in the city who want to balance growth with the maintenance of a unique desert and urban environment in order to avoid the "losangelization" of Tucson. In a city where a significant proportion of economic development capital flows from tourism, this is certainly no panglossian position. Add to this the important field training provided by the federal programs of the 1970s, and it is not surprising that citizen organizations in the city have been quite effective in taking advantage of fragmentation in the business community and in demanding a forum for their concerns in the local political arena.[38]

Summary. The local state is defined by political struggles over issues of immediate and common concern. Molotch and Logan are correct to argue that exchange value interests are very important in such matters, but these are often balanced by interests revolving around use values and the quality of life; chapter 6, a study of gun control in the community, indicates that the quality of life can be defined extremely broadly. In short, they observe that

> current urban arrangements . . . represent the physical and social conse-
> quences of cumulative strivings by capitalists bent on profit, rentiers seeking

property returns, and neighborhood groups striving for use values from place. Each group, within its limits, has left no stone unturned in the attempt to mobilize and manipulate every political, cultural and economic institution on its behalf.[39]

3. Internalizing Issues

Although Logan and Molotch focus explicitly on the urbanization process, their analysis should be seen to hinge on the jurisdictional question: the extent to which there is an arena within which the commodification of place can be determined. It is this juxtaposition of political, economic, and social actions *within a jurisdictional grid* that makes it possible—and necessary— to emphasize the social construction of the local state, rather than the complex processes and competing forms that we recognize as "urban" (or those which have been placed in the "locality"). Our analysis of the formal structure of local administration will take us into questions of sovereignty, but that task will be reserved until chapter 8. Here, we will just examine the composition of the jurisdictional grid.

The United States has a very fluid system of governmental units; this reflects our earlier discussions concerning a nation developing in space but not time (page 29). Conversely, older nation states, such as Japan, have more rigid units. The consequences are straightforward. Jurisdictions that change only rarely in extent may become dislocated, in the sense that population movements—perhaps from city to suburb—are not reflected in new administrative boundaries. One of the simplest manifestations of this can be a wide difference in terms of the voting populations found in jurisdictions, with suburban units finding themselves wildly underrepresented in terms of delegates.

These demographic shifts can be rectified, of course, and even relatively small and stable societies can exhibit rapid spatial change. Britain saw extensive local government reorganizations in 1972 and in 1986; the first reflected population shifts, while the second was explicitly about relations within the state apparatus.[40] In the United States, the proliferation of incorporated areas and special districts has continued virtually unabated since suburbanization became marked in the 1940s, and we can often identify a good deal of isomorphism between social groups (defined in terms of income, age, and race) and the jurisdictions in which they reside.

Inevitably, these differences become reified in fiscal terms, although typically in an inverse manner: that is, local jurisdictions with high-income populations are often able to keep their tax rates low, as their residents do not demand *public* services such as housing or trash removal. In addition, there exist many formal ways in which to exclude populations that might need such support: large-lot zoning can exclude low-income families, and urban renewal can remove them from existing neighborhoods.

It is the fiscal question that has come to characterize the basic difference between older urban jurisdictions and newer places—suburbs or new townships. With a balanced portfolio of businesses, modest budgets on public services, and low-cost infrastructures, the new local state is in much better shape than the metro area that contains an elderly infrastructure and a population with low aggregate incomes and high needs. As some local states have sought to deal with their problems in a manner demanded by residents, so then they have sought funding from higher levels of government, have increased levels of taxation and floated bonds. Indeed, the fiscal metaphor of the 1980s in the United States has been the junk bond, the high-risk effort to raise cash by strapped municipalities; the profit from the trade of these bonds has done little other than finance the buy-outs of innumerable corporations, whose demise has further weakened the economic base of the self-same cities. These cycles of economic disparity have contributed to complex fiscal problems within the state apparatus, and these are, in consequence, passed up and down the bureaucratic apparatus.

4. Externalizing Issues

Many commentators have come to define the local state in terms of its fiscal relations with other layers of government. A dominant argument in these analyses is the dependence exhibited by the local unit, many of which receive a significant proportion of their revenue from external sources.[41]

We should be clear what the movement of funds between levels of the apparatus represents. On the one hand, it is part of the glue that binds local states to the center, and despite its commonplace nature, we should not overlook the fact that residents do pay taxes to the central state and are very conscious of the funds that they and their districts receive in return. On the other hand, fiscal transfers are a crucial part of the state's bureaucratic mission to ensure that there is some uniformity of expenditures on broad programs designed to educate, provide health care, and maintain infrastructure. Without this, there is a return to the medieval problem of the indigent being passed from place to place—and, in fact, this does occur with the homeless in the U.S., precisely because federal programs are lacking.[42]

Interpretations of the past decade have pointed repeatedly to the way in which the state has tried to rein in the expenditures of local units in an effort to control public borrowing and avoid fiscal crisis. These are important questions; they are hardly the only issues that count, though. Studies that reduce the relationship between the state and the local states to one of fiscal transfers—and, more important, reduce the significance of the relationship to questions of fiscal crisis—are again missing the longer historical record. Once more, the historical evolution of the relationship is foremost; the fiscal question is one indicator of that evolution.

As we have already seen, the need for transfers is compounded by the asymmetry of the economic development process. The business coalitions that take for themselves leadership roles within the local state are hardly the arbiters of their own economic destiny. Many decisions that have implications in one place are taken in another—a simple insight that can be seen as a benefit or a disbenefit. Those who argue for the essential weakness of the local state see only the disbenefits, insofar as those in the jurisdiction are not in command of their own future. The same could be said of the nation state, which operates on the same terms within the global economy. We might just as easily turn this argument around in order to reflect upon the benefits; for instance, many jurisdictions are adept at passing on their costs to their neighbors, and this is by no means a one-way street. Suburban jurisdictions may benefit from an imbalance in terms of low-income populations, but then some central cities benefit from the sales-tax dollars of visitors and commuters.[43]

State/Local States

The issues covered above are basic factors within the determination of the social, economic, and political relations of the local state. We can summarize them as follows:

1. There is no predictable way in which relations within the local state are resolved. It is not the case that capital interests always win; to put this another way, it is not the case that neighborhood or citizen activists always lose. There are particular contingencies that will determine just how local politics will resolve themselves from place to place, and these are always subject to change from one period to the next.

2. There is no predictable way in which relations between local states will resolve themselves. Neighboring units may have very similar concerns or may routinely pass their problems back and forth. There may be diffusions of

problems from one jurisdiction to another, in realms such as infrastructural development or the construction of negative externalities.[44] Neighboring jurisdictions may take very different stands on social issues, with the result that legislative solutions may be sought in the courts or in higher legislatures (see the case of reinterpreting the definition of the family in San Francisco and Concord, noted in the next chapter).

3. *The complexity of relations within and between local units dictates that there is a very predictable relation between the state and local states.* The complexity of these relationships—within and between units—necessitates that the state apparatus must try to maintain order out of chaos by setting narrow standards of control wherever possible.

This basic bureaucratic drive operates at various levels. A recent newspaper column, for instance, observes that without uniform rules, travelers cannot know what is permitted from place to place:

> The District of Columbia has decreed that . . . toilet paper must have 20 percent recycled content and paper towels must have 40 percent. . . . New York and Rhode Island have passed different definitions of "reusable" and "recyclable." . . . This movement has the potential to produce so many conflicting homegrown rules and regulations that the average person travelling across state lines . . . could in the future find himself locked up in Tiny Town for violating some obscure community standard he couldn't possibly have known about.[45]

This may sound a little thin, but we will see in the next chapter that it was exactly the argument developed by State lawmakers in Florida with respect to gun control ordinances. Moreover, the imposition of uniform standards is also normal in more sensitive settings, such as those where national defense interests are invoked.

Local state and local states. These examples take us to the core of a crucial issue, namely the autonomy of the local state. While this is developed in some detail again in chapter 6, it is important that we deal with a common characterization of the local state as an entity that exists only by the whim of the central state, and within which accommodations to exogenous economic and social factors are reached.

Most important is the differentiation between the local state as an ideal type and the broad configuration of local states that exist within any national unit. While it is possible to characterize the ideal type as "dependent," a victim of broad economic restructuring, it is not possible to go far with such an argument when *all* local states are drawn into the equation. The way in which the continual process of economic restructuring is manifested in any one local unit cannot be predicted; nor can the attendant social and political developments.

When we explore the relations between local states and the national apparatus, we find, in consequence, a complex web of interactions that are expressed in systemic form: the operation of the electoral process, contests within the courts, and fiscal transfers. Each will be addressed in turn.

Elections. With the exception of Israel, where all issues come predefined as national in scope, industrial democracies employ a system of sending local representatives to national assemblies. In certain periods, representatives have organized themselves into geographical blocks, and at other times they have sought to represent specific class or racial interests; in some situations, these may coincide. Political parties have become analogues of the state–local state relation in the ways that they try to hold together different local traditions, needs, and expectations within a narrower ideological framework.

In many industrial nations, basic tensions between classes have been represented in socialist and conservative parties, with fascists and communists taking outlier positions in many countries. At present, there seems to be a general trend toward the blurring of ideological linkages in Europe and the United States, as parties with clear "left" or "right" positions find themselves not to be in control of representatives with strong regional or localist sympathies. In Britain, for example, studies show that voters no longer automatically reflect their class position, even when opposition to Thatcherite policies has been stressed by the Labour Party.[46] Analysts also identify "three Italies," in which different political parties hold sway.[47] In the U.S., the inability of the Democratic Party to maintain its traditional coalitions reflects, in part, the collapse of relations between African-American and Jewish voters in cities such as New York; riots and deaths in Crown Heights in 1991 were just one example of this.[48] Again in the U.S., it is also common to point to referenda and the increase in the number of citizen initiatives as evidence of a more general failure of the formal party system.[49]

The meaning of these shifts in electoral organization will be touched upon again in chapter 8, but it is important to note here that the national electoral system is always a compromise—between, on the one hand, the needs and aspirations of voters in the many electoral districts and the regional political cultures in which they operate, and, on the other, the bid to create a unified sense of a national interest which facilitates the process of government.[50]

Transfers. We have already touched upon the fiscal transfers that move between levels of the state apparatus. While these reflect a broad spectrum of goals—bureaucratic, organizational, economic—they also reflect explicit competition between local states for largesse. Many commentators have discussed the expenditures and social actions of the state using functional criteria, and such studies suggest clues about the responsibilities of the state.[51] They say little, though, about the distribution of funds, and for that we fall back on a number of studies that have sought regularities in the distribution of programs, funds, and their outcomes. One such strand of research has sought to identify the holy grail of "territorial justice"—that is to say, the transfer of the state's funds to regions and localities in proportion to levels of need. Naturally enough, this is much more common in settings where there is a political ethos that can be related to some notion of a welfare state.[52] In the United States, there have been many more attempts to identify divergences from such a principle of equity—this work could be summarized as a search for the pork barrel.[53]

In large measure, and typically because they focus on narrow government policies rather than the state, these approaches overlook the similarities that unite both cases. Examples of territorial justice and of pork-barreling *both* exist because of the state's responsibility to its constituent units. Let us be clear about this. Many instances of pork-barreling arise because they are demanded by sectoral interests—agricultural producers and processors, defense contractors, specific unions—but the distribution of funds also reflects, in many cases, a spatial imperative. Perhaps the clearest example of this in the U.S. is defense spending. This has turned into a veritable form of military Keynesianism, with broad connections to urban and regional policy.[54] While strategic thinking has driven the organization of the military at specific moments (such as the movement of bases and armament plants during World War II), other considerations are now common. What we might call "positive externalities," such as contracts, are frequently distributed with some crude notion of territorial justice in mind—the B-1 aircraft, for instance, employs parts built in all forty-eight contiguous States. Negative externalities, such as weapons dumps, are placed in locations where opposition will be minimal.[55] Base closures are determined for party political purposes.[56] All in all, and to reiterate, fiscal transfers are a glue that holds the state and local states together.

Courts. Despite this adhesive, relations between states and local states can become unstable in various ways, and at that juncture, issues may spill over into the courts. Individuals and groups can challenge the legality of local ordinances, and local states may use the courts to dispute the actions of neighbors. Common examples of such legislative challenges would include spillover effects, such as efforts to construct public housing in unincorporated areas, and even "border" disputes.[57]

Frequently, cases move up the legislative ladder. The example of gun control, discussed in chapter 6, displays such a development; legislation was introduced in the Florida State Legislature in 1987 to overturn local ordinances. Such issues can then move—given time—up to the level of the Supreme Court; this has occurred, for instance, with a broad challenge by developers to local land-use control within the State of California.[58] Indeed, the current Supreme Court is actively intervening in federalism issues. Cases such as *Garcia v. San Antonio Metropolitan Transit Authority* and *South Carolina v. Baker* give signals that the Tenth Amendment, commonly understood to apply to the separate and independent existence of the States, is under reassessment.[59] In its ruling on the *Baker* case, the Supreme Court observed that "States must find their protection from congressional regulation through the national political process, not through judicially defined spheres of unregulable [S]tate activity."[60]

These developments emphasize that there is persistent conflict between the different components of the federal system over just how the balance of power is to be interpreted, and indeed, there is evidence that this balance is shifting in different ways. The furor over the loss of States' and municipalities' tax-exempt status, as revealed in *Baker,* reflects a harsh economic reality, and perhaps an indication of direct taxation on these jurisdictions for the future.

As has been noted, however, all legislation, even at the highest level, must be implemented in situ. The events surrounding the civil rights movement, and particularly the integration of public schools, are instructive in this regard. When *Brown v. Board of Education* was approved by the Supreme Court in 1954, white schools in the South received five times the support received by black schools. Federal legislation did not change this situation; if anything, it made matters worse, insofar as many local school boards took action to resist this interference. An extreme example is Prince Edward County in Virginia, which closed all its public schools rather than integrate them. Symbolically, the State of Georgia added the Confederate emblem to its flag in 1956, in order to indicate its defiance toward desegregation. Change in education began only amidst broader social transformations a decade later, and the intention of full integration has never come about, because of the flight of white families to newer and more exclusive communities in the suburbs.[61]

There is now a burgeoning literature on the contexts of law.[62] This aims to place, in a literal sense, legal interpretations within the settings from which they arise. In addition, interesting studies have shown how reforms and controls are interpreted differently in different situations. For example, several States have continued to move forward on the definition of individual liberties, going far beyond the minimum of protection afforded by the Constitution.[63] What is especially interesting about this work is the way that it allows us to trace the relative abilities of different jurisdictions to create law for their own purposes. Implicit in this inference is the assumption that local states have some autonomy.

Autonomy and the "Tenuous Existence" of the Local State

It is common to view the local state as the very last link of the governmental chain, a unit without autonomy. The latter has been defined as the capacity of local states "to act in terms of their interests without fear of having their every decision scrutinized, reviewed and reversed by higher tiers of the state."[64] In fact, since "bourgeois theories of local government condemn the local polity to a tenuous existence,"[65] many observers see no such autonomy:

> Local government is part of the apparatus of the state. It has no independent existence and the functions it is called upon to perform represent—in both quantity and quality—perceptions of the role of local government held by those who control the central state apparatus.[66]

It is not hard to see the fallacious reasoning within this perspective. While it is the case that the state has the ultimate means of control at its disposal—and violence has been used on occasion against residents of local units—these balance sheets of powers have to be placed back into a meaningful theoretical context.[67] Most important is the recognition that central control is only one side of an equation—on the other is the determination of local states to pursue their own independent actions on matters such as public spending, education, social relations, and the rights of the individual. As Magnusson argues, however, a changing view of local government itself has been part of the upwards displacement of power, with economistic legal interpretations adding to the diminution of the local state's standing.[68]

A clear example of this shifting discourse surrounded the dismemberment of the Greater London Council (GLC) in 1986. As Duncan and Goodwin as well as Wolch have shown in detail, this was a struggle between a central government, committed firmly to New Right values, and a large, supralocal state unit that was equally firmly pledged to the promotion of New Left ideas.[69] This had not, of course, been the intention of those who redesigned local boundaries in England; spatial reorganizations within the National Health Service, for instance, had imposed boundaries upon London that were totally at odds with the social geography of the city, a move consistent with a principle of disrupting the territorial bases of local opposition to bureaucratic restructuring.[70] Nonetheless, the GLC became a "red base," and the promulgation of socialist values within the very capital of the United Kingdom became a reality in the early years of the Thatcher administration. In consequence, the GLC was dismembered in 1986, along with a series of changes in the fiscal relation between the state and the local states.[71]

The British case is instructive in this context, for it shows quite clearly that the process of power displacement is still in effect, and it shows, too, that this is continually resisted. While an instance such as the 1985 miners' strike in England was a highly visible example of opposition to the Thatcher government, much of the concerted reaction to New Right policies was based in the local states. The restructuring of the fiscal relation between Westminster and the local states may seem to have brought this struggle to an end; indeed, Duncan and Goodwin argue exactly that.[72] However, this again overlooks the long-run dynamic of the state apparatus. The conflicts within the system may be suppressed in various ways, but this hardly indicates that the struggles are concluded. Again, the strict reading of the balance sheet of powers and responsibilities indicates that local states are helpless, but this ignores the long-term salience of local traditions and local opposition.

Salience

A particularly useful methodology with which to think of these relations has been presented by Michael Ward in his study of power within the international system of nation states.[73] Standard readings of dominance within the world order emphasize that there is a limited number of important players, whose ability to act autonomously depends upon the accumulation of economic wealth and military hardware. This interpretation explains well enough why France has greater autonomy than Niger.

Ward then goes one step further in this process of reasoning by examining a vast data set dealing with political events throughout the world between 1950 and 1980. The events recorded extend from actions that are cooperative—such as signing peace treaties—through to actions that are conflictual, with war being the ultimate example there. Using a series of complex simultaneous equations, Ward explores two sets of relations within the data: by analogy, stones entering a pool of water, and second, the ripples that result. Ward examines the splash made by each political event and the extent of the ripples that it causes.[74]

When the question of power is reevaluated from this perspective—Ward uses the phrase "salience" to distinguish it from the accumulation of wealth or hardware—we find a very different collection of key players. While the U.S. and the USSR still appeared to be important, the other most salient nations are North and South Korea, Israel, and Egypt. This does not take much elaboration; the Korean conflict has had repercussions since the 1950s, while the Middle East struggles have overshadowed events in the western hemisphere since 1967.

In short, these relatively small nations have displayed an influence that is quite unrelated to their size and wealth. Their salience, according to Ward, rests on their position in time and space; their ability to have an impact upon events is a function of the context within which they operate.[75] To use another simple analogy, a small child has no formal power over her parents, but she frequently can get her way—and is more likely to be able to do this in certain places (such as the supermarket) or at certain times (the dead of night).

Local states must be addressed in this same contextual manner. A single unit can declare its own educational policy or its preference for polygamy with impunity, although this depends very much upon the setting. Clark, for example, gives the example of the Amish in Pennsylvania, who have resisted public schooling. We might also consider the isolated Mormon communities in Arizona that continue to condone polygamy. In both instances, groups in secluded rural areas are pursuing sincere religious views, and their "deviance" is silent and thus permissible. Other cases become pivotal because the stakes are higher. In two decisions rendered in 1986, for instance, the U.S. Supreme Court overturned a Los Angeles County ordinance and a provision of the 1972 California Coastal Zoning Management Act (*First English Evangelical Lutheran Church of Glendale v. County of Los Angeles, California* and *Nollan Et. Ux v. California Coastal Commission*). Both had been appealed by development interests because of the broad land-use controls that they contain.[76] It is consistent with this argument to suggest that both State and local legislation was overturned because it upheld residents' rights at the expense of strong attacks on the rights of developers. In a parallel development, Shuman shows how federal agencies have attacked local jurisdictions in the courts over their presumption to address foreign policy (e.g., divestment in South Africa), an arena in which federal governments have traditionally claimed a monopoly of interest.[77]

This is reminiscent of Catch-22. Yossarian was frequently asked what would happen if everyone did as he did, to which he would reply that if everyone were to behave that way, then he would be a fool not to join in. Of course, if everyone does join in, then it ceases to be a local issue. Once that happens, a struggle between state and local states is likely. However, there may be safety in numbers. Local communities throughout the South and Midwest, for example, have opposed permissive federal abortion legislation since *Roe v. Wade,* and have succeeded in placing that issue back on the national agenda. Indeed, it is not at all coincidental that anti-abortion activists have fought out their differences in particular locations, such as Wichita, Kansas. In part, the anti-abortion campaigns of the 1980s echo the tactics of the women of the Temperance Movement a century before (see chapter 4). The strategy of creating loose networks such as Operation Rescue has been successful in cumulating influence within localities rather than solely manipulating the lobbying process at the national level.[78]

Summary. Let us now pull these different strands together. This chapter has repeatedly emphasized that there is political activity at the scale of the locality—and, more important, that this cumulates to be at the core of struggle taking place within civil society as a whole. Individuals and groups attempting to close down abortion clinics, say, are trying to change conditions within their communities, while they recognize that their actions contribute to a broader discourse via the media of communication. Consequently, these replicated struggles can have repercussions—in neighboring communities, in State legislatures, and thus throughout the state apparatus.

For this reason, we can accept that the local state occupies an indistinct but important place in the relations between the state, economy, and civil society as we outlined them in chapter 1. It can be seen that the local state is part of civil society and is also, as a jurisdictional unit, part of the state. (It also has existence, of course, as an economic setting, but we need not belabor that point for the moment.) In consequence, we can see that Giddens is correct when he interprets Hegel to the effect that civil society and the state "come into existence in conjunction with one another."[79] Crucially, they do so in the form of the local state.

Between Civil Society and the State

In making these claims about state and civil society, we can return explicitly to Hegel, who argued that local governments, as corporations, were not part of the state; rather, they were expressions of civil society.[80] In subsequent years, however, they have been drawn—historically, if not philosophically—into the apparatus of the state, as power has been displaced upwards. Hence my interpretation of the local state as being both within and beyond the state.

While this may seem an arcane argument with regard to something as quotidian as the local state, we should bear in mind the contradictions between the state and civil society that were identified, in their different ways, by Marx and Hegel. Both saw the distinction between persons as *individuals* and as *citizens,* with regard to civil society and the state respectively. While they disagreed fundamentally as to the historic role of capitalism in this relation, both identify the contradiction which can be seen to lie at the core of human existence—is the individual just that, or part of the collective?[81] However, this ignores the position of the local state in civil society *and* within the state. In consequence, it is possible to show that for residents to take political action within the local state is to bring together simultaneously their roles as citizens and as unencumbered individuals, roles within and yet beyond the state.[82] As I will argue again in chapter 8, the recognition of this position provides an exciting way of considering our place with regard to the state in the future.

In Conclusion

As I argued in chapter 1, and as I have shown above, the terrain of civil society is no longer restricted to class struggle; rather, it is an unruly assortment of examples of collective action. Some of these movements have broadly sympathetic aims, and there is an equally broad coalition of resistance; both confront each other in the claims and counterclaims of what is and what is not "politically correct"—the ways that we educate our children, the ways that we think about people of colors other than our own, our views on others' sexuality, and so on.

As movements without an explicit base (as was found in the workplace a century ago), these could be seen as ephemera. It is, in particular, very difficult to develop political parties that are not based on class divisions, religious affiliations, or regional allegiances. The locality is, however, a setting where these transformations can occur, and if enough changes, then, as we have seen, the threat to the state can be perceived as large. In the next two chapters, these arguments are given life by way of two empirical examples, one dealing with gun control, the other with the MexAmerican border.

SIX

ORDNANCE
AND ORDINANCE

*Are pistols and such things Institutions on
which you pride yourselves? Are bloody
duels, brutal combats, savage assaults,
shootings down and stabbing in the streets
your Institutions?   —DICKENS*[1]

Introduction

In this chapter, we will examine in greater specificity some of the general
ideas already established. In particular, I want to explore the potential of
local actions, not solely in terms of struggles over the immediate quality of
life, but also in terms of changes that can take place across other regions.
The first example to be developed—that of gun control—explores the tensions that arise between the institutional urge to create, and maintain, uniformity on the one hand, and the entropy of local conditions and practices on
the other.

Gun control is one of the most consistent issues to be found within the
blender of American politics—one of Dickens's characters was asking an
American questions about law, order, and gun use 150 years ago. A full
account of the battle lines that have been erected over the succeeding
decades would take excessive documentation, but we can at least lay out
some of the contemporary facts here.[2]

The American Arsenal

It has been estimated that Americans possess some 150 million firearms,
and approximately half the country's households own at least one weapon.

About 12,000 persons are killed each year by handguns, and approximately 15,000 commit suicide in the same way; a further 2,000 people die accidentally from gunshot wounds. In summary, nearly 100 people die daily as a result of shootings in the United States.[3]

This mayhem has not proceeded without legal constraint. Federal law restricts the sale of automatic weapons and identifies persons (such as felons) who may not possess firearms.[4] In addition, there are another 20,000 gun laws in the U.S. at the State or local level.[5] These vary, of course, in line with local needs and practices, but may extend to total bans on the possession of handguns within a jurisdiction, as we shall see below.

Mass shootings, which are the most sensational manifestations of proscribed gun use, have provoked efforts to restrict the sale of firearms further in order to avoid future incidents, but little has changed.[6] In 1991, Congress debated restrictions being placed on extra-large ammunition clips, such as the one used in the worst civilian massacre (42 persons were killed or wounded), which occurred in the ironically named Killeen, Texas. Despite the fact that this debate happened within hours of the massacre, the vote was not even a close one.[7]

The national organization Handgun Control Inc. (HCI) has urged that the waiting period for the purchase of a weapon be extended. In doing so, it has established itself as a lobby to oppose the National Rifle Association (NRA) on specifics such as the sale of armor-piercing ammunition and the interstate transfer of weapons. There is now a complex collective discourse on gun ownership and use. In keeping with its credo, the NRA and its members have lobbied strenuously against a number of gun-control measures, including the banning of armor-piercing "cop-killer" bullets and the sale of plastic handguns that cannot be detected by airport radar devices. The rigidity of the NRA's stance has even pitted it against the law enforcement community: a survey of 226 police chiefs in 1987 showed that 195 believed that the NRA had "gone to extremes" with its legislative program, and 192 answered negatively to the statement "The NRA is a friend of law enforcement."[8]

Guns and the Constitution

The NRA has long sought to keep the issues of gun control at the level of constitutional debate and has been very successful at this: according to polls of individuals on the street, more than 50 percent of those interviewed still believe that they possess a constitutional right to possess arms.[9] The NRA argues explicitly for what it calls the "Constitutional right of firearms ownership" through its monthly magazine *American Rifleman,* its lobbying activities—reported to cost $12 million annually—and even its Washington, D.C. headquarters, which has the phrase "The right of the people to keep and bear arms shall not be infringed" displayed across the building.[10]

Although many Americans are familiar with the latter phrase, it is as such quoted out of context. The full text of the Second Amendment is:

> A well regulated Militia, being necessary to the security of a free State, the right of the people to keep and bear Arms, shall not be infringed.

The emphasis given to the third clause by the NRA, which in consequence represents a broader interpretation of the Amendment that extends the right to bear arms to all citizens, has received no support from the United States Supreme Court. The latter has not addressed this issue directly in recent years, seeing no reason to supersede its earlier rulings, which consequently remain as precedent. In 1939, for example, the Court upheld a federal law prohibiting shipment of a sawed-off shotgun across a State line, despite appeals that the law violated Second Amendment rights. The ruling made reference to the fact that such a weapon had no relationship to the efficiency of State militia.[11] In a parallel interpretation, the Sixth Circuit Court of Appeals has stated that "it would unduly extend this opinion to attempt to deal with every argument made by defendant and amicus curiae, Second Amendment Foundation, all of which are based on the erroneous supposition that the Second Amendment is concerned with the rights of individuals rather than those of the States."[12] As Lawrence Cress shows in some detail, it is difficult to find historical evidence that shows any intent by those who created the Constitution other than the maintenance of communal rights against the powers of an "assuming government."[13]

The Legacy of Morton Grove

As the NRA has intended, recourse to the Second Amendment has placed the firearms issue on a high shelf, such that opposition to gun ownership becomes a virtual attack on the Constitution itself. However, while this rarefied argument has proceeded without resolution, a great deal has also occurred on the ground, so to speak. Most of the effective gun-control legislation that does exist is at the level of the locality. Fully three-quarters of the U.S. population lives in jurisdictions where guns must be registered, and many jurisdictions have more exacting gun laws.

The apotheosis is the case of Morton Grove, in Cook County, Illinois. In

1981, the trustees of the community of 24,000 passed an ordinance that prohibited the private possession of handguns within the locality, and allowed until February 1982 for residents to surrender or sell their armaments.[14] This was challenged in both the U.S. District Court for the Northern District of Illinois and the 7th Circuit of Appeals in 1982. In both instances, it was ruled that the ordinance was a "proper exercise of police power," and in no way violated the U.S. Constitution, given that "the right to bear arms is inextricably connected to the preservation of a militia." It was ruled that "Illinois municipalities therefore have a constitutional right to ban ownership or sale of items determined to be dangerous."[15] Clearly, this ruling neatly sidesteps the Second Amendment arguments employed historically by the NRA and its affiliates, and extends the terrain of conflict away from constitutional debate and toward the possibility of local legislation that outlaws handguns and thus reduces the risk of firearm-related injury.

Residents in many other localities have developed their own versions of the Morton Grove ordinance. Broward County, Florida (which contains the city of Fort Lauderdale) had tight restrictions on gun ownership until 1987, when there was, as we shall see, a change in State law. In order to apply for a concealed-weapons permit, residents had to submit to a background check with respect to criminal history, undergo a mental examination, be endorsed by the chief of police, be interviewed successfully by a hearings officer, and demonstrate a valid reason to possess a firearm. In addition, successful applicants had to pay $500.[16] As a result of these very strict controls, it is not surprising that only twenty-two of the county's 1.2 million residents had applied for, and received, a permit at the end of 1987; the thousands of other inhabitants who possessed a weapon were in consequence liable to fines or the confiscation of their weapons.

Disarming the Local State

In the local state, of course, these legislative efforts have not occurred without dissent. As we saw, some residents of Morton Grove appealed ordinance 81–11 through the courts, without success. In Florida, the tension between those in favor of and those against control was displaced upwards into a conflict between local units and the State. On May 12, 1987, the Florida State Senate passed two bills (SB253 and SB254) which nullified over 400 local ordinances and removed the control of gun permits from local jurisdictions. Ostensibly, this preemption of powers was legitimated in two ways. First, the rising rates of violent crime in Florida necessitated some political response; this was achieved by symbolically dismantling gun controls and thus allowing private citizens to rearm themselves and protect their property. Second, the disarray of local ordinances was described as generating confusion and disrespect for the law: State Representative Johnson, a sponsor of the bills, observed that "there ought to be a statewide policy so law-abiding citizens will know the law as they travel, and not violate the law if they have guns as their cars cross county lines"—not a minor consideration in a State where over half the motorists appear to carry guns regularly.[17] Similarly, Fort Lauderdale's Mayor Cox wrote to Florida's Governor Martinez, noting that his city had consistently opposed the tough Broward County control ordinance, and that his official position was that "this issue is too important to be fragmented among 67 counties to the detriment and confusion of both our residents and visitors."[18]

Florida is the twelfth State to pass preemptive legislation against localities' ordinances, and is an interesting case for several reasons. First, it is much larger than others in this group (it is the fourth most populous State in the country), and may point to future developments elsewhere. Second, a high degree of opposition to the State legislation has been mounted by the law enforcement community, which sees no benefit in statewide standardization if it also involves looser gun control. The chief of the Tallahassee Police Department observed that "these groups [the NRA and affiliates], which many of us once considered friends of law enforcement, have created a situation that will be far-reaching for the law enforcement officers in terms of liability, personal stress and—inevitably—unnecessary loss of life."[19]

The third, and perhaps most interesting, dimension of this history was the political maneuver that preceded the 1987 legislation. The passing of HBs 251 and 253 and SBs 253 and 254 was not a spontaneous political development. It was, in large part, the result of lobbying activities by the NRA Institute for Legislative Action and the Unified Sportsmen of Florida, a move which represents a tactical break from more traditional, constitutional claims. An NRA spokesman observed that "the debate has shifted from national to State levels where hard-fought campaigns, similar to Florida's are being waged."[20] He continued that "firearm owners should be ever vigilant on their home turf since Handgun Control Inc. . . . a 'national gun control group' . . . recently announced the opening of regional offices in California and Minnesota to extend its reach into local firearms and hunting issues."[21] He concluded with the exhortation for NRA members to "take time now to discuss firearms issues with law enforcement to create a cohesion in your area that could mirror the Florida experience."[22]

This explanation is as interesting as it is disingenuous. First, the law enforcement community is presented as a natural ally of gun users, despite evidence to the contrary. Second, note how Handgun Control is branded as a *national* organization which has no understanding of *local* matters—that is to say, the rights of the community to arm itself as it pleases. Third, note too how this preemptive strategy is cast as a move to *protect* the locality, a tactic that raises powerful images of Locke and de Tocqueville.[23] I describe it as disingenuous insofar as the *National* Rifle Association is in this instance casting itself as something other than a nationwide organization—a claim that has not found support elsewhere. In Maryland, a 1988 State law dealing with the control of so-called Saturday night specials was opposed by the NRA, which pumped over $5 million into a campaign throughout the State to overturn the legislation. A referendum to rescind the law failed, amidst claims that the NRA had created a "David and Goliath struggle." This indicates that Maryland residents possessed a clear sense of local interests, which were seen to be antithetical to the NRA's broader national agenda.[24]

Summary. We can see that the contours of conflict over gun control have been widened, first by residents and subsequently by the NRA. The way in which the law is being used to try to resolve firearms issues has shifted in a concomitant manner. The Florida example reveals that local ordinances can be preempted by State legislation. However, and as we shall see again below, State bills do not put an end to communities' efforts to control their own quality of life.

The case also reveals an interesting paradox: it is easier for a political lobby to exert pressure on a State legislature, which can pass preemptive legislation, than to fight individual jurisdictions over their rights to control the quality of life within each locality. As we will see below, this interpretation reflects once more the salience and the resilience of the local state.

Conflicts over Local Ordinances

The Florida case points us then to two things: first, the efforts that can be taken by jurisdictions to maintain control of the quality of life within the locality; and second, the existence of significant conflicts moving within the legal system—both between local states and the state, and between the local state and other institutions, such as the NRA or corporate interests.

The attacks on the local state are undertaken in a very regularized manner, using wherever possible the language of bureaucratic standardization and preemption. Consider, for instance, the transport of military hardware and nuclear waste.[25] Such cargoes are extremely dangerous and have the potential to cause devastation following truck accidents or derailment. In consequence, local politicians have made strenuous efforts to impose strict controls on shipments that come through their jurisdictions, or even to ban them altogether. The departments of both Energy and Transport (DOE, DOT) have moved to preempt State and local legislation, with the result that numerous ordinances are at stake. These include some that dictate truck and railcar inspections; the imposition of fees on radioactive shipments; and mandating that hazardous cargoes bypass cities.

Controls designed to assuage community concerns have been overruled as barriers to interstate commerce. As noted above, efforts in Ohio to direct trucks with hazardous cargoes to an interstate beltway around Columbus generated opposition from the DOT, even though these were consistent with federal regulations. The DOT efforts to overturn such controls stress the necessity of federal preemption in the national interest, and invoke the 1974 Hazardous Materials Transportation Act (HMTA):

> Congress indicated a desire for uniform national standards in the field of hazardous materials transportation and gave the department the authority to promulgate such standards. While the HMTA did not totally preclude State or local actions in this area, it is [the DOT] opinion that Congress intended, to the extent possible, to make such state or local action unnecessary.[26]

As this is summarized by Wallace,

> DOT perceives certain areas in which the need for national uniformity is so crucial and the scope of Federal regulation is so pervasive that it is difficult to envision any situation where a State or local regulation would not be inconsistent.[27]

Note how this issue of standardization repeats itself. In its evocation of statist language, the rationale employed by the NRA precisely echoes the quest for uniformity emphasized by the U.S. Department of Transport:

> The preemption bills . . . will prohibit cities, counties and municipalities from adopting "gun control" laws. Further, the bills will restore the rights of law-abiding citizens in Broward, Dade, Palm Beach and Pinellas counties, among others, where severe restrictions are now in effect making Florida a patchwork of gun laws.[28]

The Local State and Corporate Interests

So far, we have discussed lobbies, such as the NRA and HCI, and federal agencies. As can be expected, however, corporations are also key players within local affairs in their own right. The following example indicates that quality of life issues can rapidly spill over into struggles where residents confront important corporate interests within the locality.

On November 10, 1989, 30,000 voters went to the polls in Greensboro, North Carolina. By a small majority of 157 votes, they approved a local ordinance that would allow restaurants and stores to ban smoking if they chose. While this may not seem particularly innovative, the story must, again, be placed in context. North Carolina produces approximately half of the nation's tobacco, and 14,000 farmers in the State depend upon the crop. Any attempt to legitimate the anti-smoking movement thus has immediate economic implications for farmers and for taxpayers, who can see the long-term contraction of one of the State's most profitable industries.[29]

The anti-smoking forces, led by a resident who was "tired of having smoke blown in her face in checkout lines," were resisted by both corporate and labor interests. Lorillard Inc., producer of Kool cigarettes, employs 2,300 workers in Greensboro. Union leader Earl Jaggers evoked the tobacco industry as a local interest, in contrast to the national issue of smoking bans. He argued that the representatives of legislation were themselves transient: "These people are going to move on to other cities."[30] This same theme is echoed in the title of the citizen group—"Greensboro Citizens for Fairness"—that lobbied against the ordinance. This was bankrolled by Lorillard and R. J. Reynolds, one of the larger tobacco interests in the State.

As we saw in chapter 5, it has been common for corporate interests to overshadow the local political discourse in a manner that makes the development of alternative strategies very difficult. For this reason, the Greensboro case is innovative. It shows that residents can separate quality of life issues from economic interests, however much corporations attempt to tie them together. Moreover, it suggests that if residents in a "tobacco state" can develop such legislation, then many things are possible.

Military Spending

Parallel examples can also be found in the intense discussions taking place within many localities over the degree of military influence there. Despite the cash transfers that flow from military contractors and bases, residents are often tired of the pollution that is generated during the production of military hardware, the constant overflights by noisy planes and helicopters, the movement of armed troops through the streets, and the intrusive militarism that pervades their communities. As noted on page 43, feminist scholars have drawn a short, straight line between the implicit violence of military culture and the reality of violence in the home.[31] Conversely, other residents are concerned about contractions in the federal budget, which spell unemployment, the loss of base privileges, and the erosion of the tax base. In consequence, there can be heated political discussion about the possibilities and liabilities of base closings, with some residents fighting to keep a military presence and others pointing to studies which suggest that closure can be, in time, an economic *boost* to a locality. Resolution of these debates over a military presence ranges from coast to coast, with, for instance, the rejection of U.S. Navy homeporting plans in both San Francisco and New York.

Affirmative Strategies

These examples may seem to imply that residents can take only reactive positions—against corporations or the military, for example. There is also evidence, however, that the local state is a setting within which experiments in social legislation can be begun. It is telling that Andrea Dworkin and Catherine MacKinnon developed their strategies against the sale and display of pornography within local settings. First introduced in Minneapolis in 1983, the ordinance was passed by the city council twice and vetoed by Mayor Fraser on both occasions. It was also introduced in Indianapolis, where it was passed by the city council and signed by Mayor Hudnut in 1984. The Indianapolis ordinance was challenged twice, and in February 1986, the Supreme Court conclusively upheld a second appeals court decision.[32]

Dworkin and MacKinnon had been asked to intervene in Minneapolis by residents of neighborhoods where sex stores had been concentrated as a result of land-use regulations. By shifting the pornography debate to the question of subordination—not obscenity—they opened up a new avenue of public debate and attack. Communities have used the local state as an experimental polity in a number of instances; examples include ordinances that restrict picketing around abortion clinics and the provision of premises for the homeless, the mentally ill, and persons with AIDS. Changes in zoning codes also permit the placing of these facilities in residential neighborhoods rather than the twilight zones of the inner city.

A good deal has been written about the Minneapolis ordinance, and it is clear that such legislation in a local setting permits—or even necessitates—an intense public response.[33] Such prolonged involvement is unlikely in a national debate, such as the Thomas-Hill Senate hearings. The importance of such debate rests, of course, on the tantalizing possibility of *action*. For the anti-pornography activist, there is no possibility of closing down the studios or the movie distributors. There is, however, the opportunity to close down the theaters and the video arcades. There is also the chance for prostitutes and other sex workers to complain about this interference with their lives, which seems a legitimate opportunity for all involved.[34]

Struggles *between* Local Jurisdictions

In some places, the style of life is liberal or even radical in intent, and communal strategies, such as support for AIDS hospices, reflect that. In other places, the collective discourse is determinedly conservative, which manifests itself in terms of the picketing of abortion clinics until they close, the passing of English-only ordinances, and in one notorious case in Georgia, an ordinance that mandated all households to own a firearm.

One of the outcomes of the socio-spatial restructuring that has reshaped the American landscape in the last century is the propinquity of very different communities.[35] Using the analogy of nation states, such neighbors may become extremely hostile, as was noted in the previous chapter. Two examples may suffice.

Definitions of the family. In California, 1991 saw another explosion of anger over sexuality. Just as the Minneapolis example took issues of pornography away from obscenity and toward issues of domination and violence, so on this occasion the debate centered less on homosexuality and more on definitions of family. Bill AB101, passing through the California legislature, permitted same-sex partners to be defined as a family for the purpose of benefits—not a minor issue where health-care coverage is concerned. This bill was vetoed by Governor Pete Wilson, after protests by a coalition of conservative Republicans and the organization Traditional Values. Going one step further, in Concord, a community separated from San Francisco by the Bay and the radical chic of Berkeley, Proposition M was placed on the ballot explicitly in order to remove homosexuals from the category of persons receiving protection from discrimination.[36]

Mohawks at the Mercier Bridge. My second example is a good deal closer to war between nation states than a tussle between local states. Throughout Canada, Native Americans became increasingly vocal about their lack of self-government and the indeterminacy of many land claims at the end of the 1980s.[37] In national politics, this resulted in the collapse of the Meech

Lake Accord in 1990, and locally in a strategy of erecting roadblocks that sealed off many reservations.

This tactic was developed first in Quebec, by Mohawk Indians who blocked entrances to the Kahnawake reservation in July 1990. (See fig. 1.) This was precipitated by proposals to turn an aboriginal burial ground into a golf course on the nearby Kanesatake reservation. Roadblocks closed the Mercier Bridge, which also connects the affluent suburb of Chateauguay to schools and offices in downtown Montreal. For four days and nights, while Mohawks looked on, suburban residents attempted to storm the bridge; chanting "savages, savages," they threw rocks and Molotov cocktails and burned Native Americans in effigy.[38]

This is a complex and nasty example, far from the niceties of the town hall and the legislature. It indicates that deep tensions—over race, in this instance—can become reified and amplified by political geography. For their part, suburban residents do not like the proximity of Indian reservations, with their bingo halls and discount cigarette stores.[39] Native Americans resent the controls exerted over them by the state and the actions of their neighbors, who often try to develop lands that are of considerable religious and cultural significance.

Conclusions and Implications

This chapter demonstrates that the local state possesses salience—to employ Ward's term—which reflects its historical position as an arena of collective political discourse. This salience is the key to any understanding of the long-run shifts within the state apparatus, insofar as there exists no simple balance sheet of powers between state and local state. In some instances, the state will exert its abilities, through either fiscal or juridical means, to control the entropy of local decision-making. In some nations, this appears to be a linear process, although that would be a hasty conclusion; the weakening of the state in countries such as Germany and Italy following the Second World War would be a clear example of the way in which the state can lose ground or be redirected. In other instances, the internal conflicts are much more cyclical, and the case of the U.S. would be central to that inference. As we have seen, the local state (and to some degree the States as well) is much quicker to deal with contingent conditions than is federal government. Localities can introduce ordinances— dealing with technologies, diseases, growth issues—with a rapidity that cannot be matched by the state apparatus, which is left frequently to react

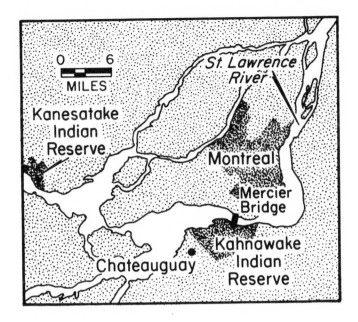

belatedly to these innovations (the U.S. Supreme Court ruled in 1987 on the 1972 Coastal Management Act in California, for example).

In addition, the local state can exert a behavioral power that can press, cumulatively, for support from higher courts and national politicians. As we have seen, there are dangers here for the local state when home-rule provisions do not exist, for it may be vulnerable to a concerted attack from partisan interests with regional or national resources. Once again, we must note that such battles are constantly moving from turf to turf, and the issues themselves are shifting constantly. For this reason, the importance of understanding the locality—of bringing the local state back in—is reiterated here.

What do these and many similar cases have to tell us about state theory as it is evolving in the U.S.? In the first instance, they point to the vibrancy of the local state's efforts to mandate the quality of life within the local jurisdiction. Local ordinances represent a display of salience that may threaten actors such as development interests or lobbyists such as the NRA, and which forces the latter into fighting such legislation through State or even higher courts. Again, the outcome of such efforts—which have been, perhaps predictably, in favor of strong interests and to the detriment of the local state in the examples used—is less important than the broader political tensions that they illustrate. That is to say, the fact that the local state is able to mount resistance to higher authority is indicative of the existence of a continued communal political tradition. Equally, the targeting of the local state by national interests is an insight into the ways in which the latter attempt to create leverage within the state apparatus, a tactic which can be discussed only by a broadening of current state theory. In addition, we must consider the implications of these kinds of examples for the local state itself, for present defeats do not rule out future successes. Past cases—in the fields of the ERA, abortion limitation, and nuclear warfare—all show how an issue can move up the legal and political hierarchy and influence regional and national decision-making, if local political practice is well organized.

SEVEN

NEW PLACES, NEW POLITICS

adjusted to the local needs
—W. H. AUDEN[1]

Introduction[2]

In chapters 5 and 6, we have seen the ways in which residents can make a difference in their everyday lives by taking political action. In the last two chapters, I want to look forward to a change within the relations between state, economy, and civil society, and in particular I want to explore the adjustments that are both possible and likely between the state and local state. I will evaluate these changes in greater depth in the last chapter, but here, by way of establishing the terrain, I want to point to two forces that are pulling the nation state apart. The first of these is the continued transformation of the global economy. Although not all agree (a point that will be raised again in the next chapter), it appears to have moved into yet another phase of its evolution.[3] We have witnessed the collapse of state socialism and the final penetration of capitalism into the former state-socialist countries. This has two important implications: first, there is a massive new circuit of capital investment available to corporate interests in the west; and second, the bipolar world of the superpowers has disappeared. It will be replaced by other conflicts, to be sure, but the political fundamentals of the international order—as they have existed since 1945—have been thrown to the winds.

The implications of these changes are many. First, the move toward global reach continues to undermine the meaning of the nation state. As Mingione observes,

On the one side, there is the internationalization of economic and sociocultural operations, the consolidation of large multinational conglomerates, the globalization of the financial sector and the formation of supra-national bodies such as the UN, the EEC, the FAO, the World Bank and so on, which restrict the ability of nation-states to control and regulate social life in an independent and different way.[4]

To be sure, there is a superficial increase in the rhetoric of nationalism, manifested in instances of bitter words passing between America and Japan, or America and France; but this reflects the frustrations of politicians losing the battle to maintain an "imagined community," to use Benedict Anderson's phrase, in societies that are penetrated by external sources of capital and related cultural icons. For example, it is now impossible to disentangle the complexities of automobile manufacture—is a Toyota or Honda produced in Kentucky or Tennessee an American car, a Japanese car, or something else again? What is an Isuzu built in Japan with an imported Chevrolet engine? It is in these incremental ways that familiar concepts of "domestic" and "foreign" become blurred.[5]

Second, the political and social meaning of the nation state, as we have understood it since 1945, is also subject to change. To all intents, the superpowers have spent themselves to a standstill on their arsenals and can no longer hold together their alliances and their acolytes. As the threats of nuclear war diminish significantly, so the nationalist imperative also retreats. In consequence, we have seen in rapid order the reinterpretation and collapse of the imagined community in a number of places. Nation states that have existed for decades are suddenly springing apart, as ethnic and regional tensions—long subdued by both force and ideology—reappear. As we watch, the world map and its analogues, such as the United Nations, are transforming; new entities are appearing and old formations are withering. As Mingione continues,

> The mounting complexity of local socialization mixes, which is reflected in the relative failure of the grand national and universalistic welfare programmes, is putting back on the agenda the importance of decentralization, self-government and local solutions. In the countries of the European Community, this highly contradictory process of the dismemberment of nation-states and the move towards supra-national and local aggregation is already apparent.[6]

In short, then, we can argue that events are increasingly assuming significance on two spatial scales, the global and the local. While industrial production does, of course, occur in specific locations, this is part of an interlocking system of production and distribution that is supranational—to use Lefebvre's term, it takes place in "world space." As was argued in chapter 1, it is thus realistic to state that the scale of production is global.[7] Conversely, the local—the scene of everyday life—is increasing in importance as the nation state loses its grip upon our imaginations.[8] In this chapter, I want to explore a very dynamic case study that highlights some of these developments, namely the forging of a new collection of social relations in a "new" place—the Mexican-American border zone. As we shall see, within the setting of an immanent transnational economic base, new forms of political organization are appearing. These have little to do with the nation states to which we are accustomed, although this is not to say, as we will see, that the state is giving up without a fight. This notwithstanding, new places are forming, and their political and social relations are of great interest; if, as Michael Watts observes, the border is the appropriate metaphor for the postmodern subject, it is also the appropriate laboratory for political study.[9]

The Mexican-American Borderlands

This chapter takes as its object an area of intense economic, social, and political transition—the border zone that connects Mexico and the United States, which stretches from Tijuana in the west through to Matamoros in the east, a distance of over 2,000 miles (fig. 2). This zone is in intensive political-economic transition, as traditional activities in Mexico, based until recently on subsistence agriculture and a state-controlled economy, have begun to confront a new expression of core capitalism, the *maquiladora* system.

The 1,800 or so *maquilas* (the noun is taken from the medieval Spanish word describing the miller's levy for grinding others' corn) are American offshore assembly plants that enjoy the benefits of cheap labor and the proximity of a politically stable neighbor; moreover, the transfer of unfinished and finished goods has been allowed to proceed with a minimum of taxation and control. The *maquilas* thus represent a unique symbiosis that bestows advantages, albeit differential ones, upon both countries. American corporations increase their profits as a result of the low costs of Mexican labor, which proceeded to fall in real terms throughout the 1980s, as the peso continued to devalue. The Mexican economy has been stimulated, via an increase in labor participation—approximately 400,000 jobs were created during that same decade—and approximately a billion dollars annually in foreign currency. To the satisfaction of nationalist politicians, this has been achieved without the full-scale penetration of foreign companies. The relax-

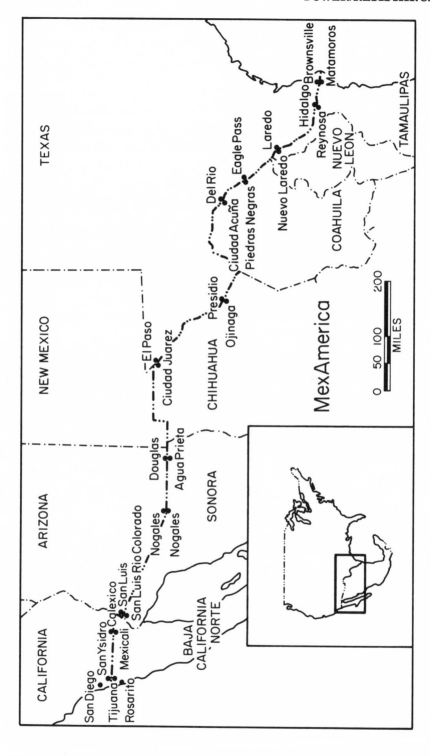

ation of border inspection was planned, but as we shall see, there has also been minimal regulation of environmental standards.

In short, there is something that can be identified as a border economy in transition. This is not achieved without massive changes, though, which will have further repercussions. The explicit interlocking of the Mexican and American economies in this region is leading to provocative cultural collisions and social transformations. McDonald's not only offers gringo food, but will also change pesos for dollars.[10] Television, too, is a field of contest, in an interesting example of competition within the electronic media. American programs are becoming popular in Sonora, Chihuahua, and Baja California as satellite dishes become available, and as more and more workers sense the importance of learning English as a precursor to migrant labor. Conversely, Spanish-language stations, broadcasting within the U.S., are also building their audiences. Presenting a mixture of American economic sensibilities, pungent soaps, and ribald Mexican humor, they provide an irresistible alternative to their stodgier Anglo counterparts, and are defining a new and distinct border style of the geographical *mestizo*.[11] Unsurprisingly, their content has been the subject of criticism from conservative elements of the traditional Mexican-American community.[12]

This economic and cultural reconstruction of the border extends into many facets of life. The induction of large numbers of women workers into the formal and informal economies on both sides of the border seems likely to have major implications for family structure and subsequent social relations in a relatively conservative and patriarchal region. Nor is it coincidental that PRI (the state socialist party) has lost its monopoly of political power within Mexico, and is weakening most visibly along the border, where the free-trade party PAN boasted a gubernatorial incumbent in 1990.

The Maquila *System*

Inevitably, these developments are generating tensions. Among business observers, the *maquila* system is treated nonproblematically—indeed, it has been claimed that there exists a "consensus as to the tremendous benefits to be derived from it." Of course, such a perspective glosses over the real disadvantages of the *maquiladoras* for Mexico.[13] These include, for instance, the lack of backward linkages (insofar as only 2 percent of inputs other than labor are derived from Mexico) and the absence of genuine technology transfer:

> Much of the technology in use in the maquiladoras is actually a relocation rather than a transfer. Sklair . . . argues that since maquiladoras merely as-

semble high-tech components, Mexican technicians only learn isolated parts of the technology. For technologies to truly be considered as transferred, there needs to be evidence of absorption, adaption and development of new technologies. There is very little evidence of this type of spin off from the maquiladoras.[14]

It is also important to emphasize that the border zone does not constitute a regional economy in the sense that the Third Italy has been so described.[15] There is little product specialization, and consequently there are few benefits to be identified from agglomeration economies. The plants are located along the border primarily for reasons of low labor costs, and there is little in common between them except for their reliance on semiskilled workers performing repetitive tasks with a relatively high degree of precision but at low cost. Because many of the *maquilas* are branch assembly plants, there is little likelihood that a broad range of business services (advertising, packaging) or higher-order establishments (leading to independent product development) will emerge.[16]

There are also more generalized problems, such as safety in the workplace. Mexican labor is becoming more vocal about the differentials that it observes between its earnings, job safety, and health benefits and those of Americans working farther north, doing comparable jobs, and often for the same corporations. Unionization has already occurred in some *maquila* plants, and this decade began with strikes in Matamoros. Pollution is also widespread, and is manifested in terms of poor air quality, generated by the burning of garbage and the smelting of copper; the contamination of water resources by coliform bacteria, due to inadequate sewage treatment; and the dumping of toxic and other wastes in unmonitored sites on both sides of the border.[17]

Urban Development

The economic expansion has generated urban growth in all border towns, although frequently this has occurred in marginal intraurban locations that lack basic facilities such as water and sewage hook-ups or electricity. Residents of the *colonias populares* squatter settlements that exist on both sides of the border are termed *paracaidista*—those who have dropped or parachuted into the area. To date, their politicization has been limited, as their energies have been absorbed by their efforts to move into the unfamiliar territory of wage labor and urban life in a binational setting. Nonetheless, using Manuel Castells's insights as a guide, we can argue that it is inevitable that collective consumption struggles will erupt over quality-of-life issues—

the need for potable water, the regularization of landholding, and the provision of education.[18]

Summary. It is the intention in this chapter to offer up this border experience as more than a distinctive case of what may occur when a core economy comes into close contact with the semi-periphery.[19] Here, I will argue that the MexAmerican example contains some important pointers to the ways in which local social and political constructions emerge, often despite the best efforts of national institutions to inhibit their development. In this instance, we shall see that there exist extensive networks that straddle the border, in contradistinction to the ideological and practical apparatuses that define the international frontier.[20]

Nation States and Borders: Metaphors and Realities

A border zone is intriguing for two reasons. First, it is the physical representation of the integrity of the nation state—it is the furthest extent of the nation state's sovereignty. As Giddens points out, this representation may be cartographic at best, as is the case with the control of the oceans; nonetheless, it is an important representation of the state.[21] Second, and in contrast, the border zone is a setting in which the peripheral and distant locality should display the most independence from state fiat (as we shall see below with regard to the Environmental Protection Agency). This is an interpretation that has depended historically upon the problems of interacting with distant locations, but even in contemporary situations there exists a discontinuity between those "at the head office" and those "in the field."[22]

The border is thus, almost by definition, of crucial dialectical importance in the annals of state formation. This notwithstanding, the study of international boundaries seems to offer "a rather parochial body of knowledge."[23] A reprise of the political geographical literature, for instance, is a depressing collection of empiricist accounts, based upon a long tradition of attempts to find physical similarities between very different realities.[24] Lost in these overwrought comparisons is the recognition that the border is a complex social construction, and of only secondary importance is its existence as an assemblage of physical features.

The survival of the nation state is, as we have seen, closely bound up with its territorial existence; and that very existence can be reified by its boundary conditions. Since the constructions of the emperors of Rome and

China, we have seen the importance of defending the peripheries of the state, and the need to mark these frontiers with, so to speak, a concrete representation. In part, this is now specious; as both the Maginot Line and Hitler's Atlantic Wall proved, modern warfare can usually destroy any attempts to keep out enemies and neighbors. Nonetheless, the edifices recur, with the Berlin Wall being perhaps the most poignant, frozen symbol of the world order post-1945.

The need to maintain such extreme symbols (in both senses) rests upon the ideological imperatives that drive the nation state. The imagined community must, on occasion, be turned from a metaphor into a reality. The boundary that separated the two Germanies was less a military construction than an ideological and panoptic one, a literal negation of the ideologies of capitalism and state socialism that faced each other. The rigid brutality of concrete and barbed wire is, of course, never enough to exclude all external influences. As we have noted, electronic messages will cross unscathed, as will most manifestations of commerce. Even during the depths of the Cold War, it was possible to identify "business as usual," first in terms of commodity exchange, such as the Vodka-Cola trade, and later in terms of banking and investment. Indeed, the collapse of the Warsaw Pact has revealed the surreal truth that the debts incurred by the anti-capitalists, secure within the Iron Curtain, were commensurate with those generated by the right-wing dictatorships of Latin America.

In the case of MexAmerica, the border has a complex reality; to use de Certeau's phrase, it plays a "mediating role."[25] Despite the fact that core and semi-periphery are separated by a wire fence, people and things both move back and forth with some ease through official checkpoints.[26] In addition, those without documents may stroll through a break in the wire or, as happens in Juarez, can be carried across the Rio Grande by porters. Capital too moves from north to south, and back again.[27] Although Mexican governments were committed for many years to a principle of import restrictions and a process of import substitution that protected domestic industry, this too has changed, and since 1964, the Border Industrialization Program has begun to pull American, and other, sources of international capital into the country.

Of central importance in this analysis is that these developments are not restricted solely to one or the other side of the border. Unionization within the *maquila* system (as has taken place in Matamoros) is action taken by Mexican labor against American corporations. Political debate over improved public services in the *colonias populares* is directed toward government in Sonora and other frontier areas, but also implicates the economic system that revolves around the *maquiladoras*. As Martinez argues, a complex ecology of border residents is emerging, which includes migrant workers, bicultural residents, and those who are truly binational—the *frontizeros.*[28]

Here, I too want to emphasize the *duality* of an international border such as that between Mexico and the United States, and its mediating role. As we have seen, the *material* reality is that the boundary between the two countries is virtually nonexistent; rather, it is in *symbolic* terms that we can detect the need to maintain the power and the detachment of the nation state. There is a small literature that has identified similar symbolic actions in other border settings—Newman, for instance, has noted the Prussian efforts to control the Posen region, and those of the Dominican government along its border with Haiti. He also discusses the way in which vehicle license plates in the Occupied Territories of Israel constitute another mark of otherness; they are colored to distinguish between Palestinians (blue) and Israelis (yellow), so that guards and other officials always have a clear idea of who is approaching them.[29]

In MexAmerica, the ideological presence of the border is also revealed semiologically. Take, for example, Interstate 19, the freeway that connects Tucson with the border town of Nogales, Arizona. It is the only highway in the U.S. marked in metric units, and the use of kilometers is a recognition of the transnational traffic on the road. Not all the road signs are in metric units, though: despite the inconsistency, the control signs—such as the 65 mph speed limit—are expressed using miles. In addition, much is made of this being a peripheral area, once more notably in terms of control. Border Patrol personnel are in evidence all along Interstate 10, and distinctive vehicles are frequently pulled over for examination—expensive cars driven by Hispanics and unmarked trucks are common targets. In addition, I-19 displays emergency phones positioned every two miles (rather, every 3.2 kilometers), with prominent signs reassuring Anglo travelers that the road is patrolled twenty-four hours a day—a feature not available to interstate travelers elsewhere in the West.

The symbolic dimensions of the border are manifested, then, in terms of the presence of police forces of various types, and in recent years the so-called Drug War has become a way for the state apparatus to coordinate and legitimate these activities.[30]

The War on Drugs

As the Cold War has wound down, others have been initiated, notably the effort to control the movement of drugs into the United States.[31] In addition to local law enforcement units and traditional federal departments, such as the Drug Enforcement Administration, the U.S. Customs Service, the U.S. Border Patrol, and the FBI, new institutional arrangements have been created to maintain the sanctity of the border. Several Joint Task Forces have been constructed, which coordinate the activities of federal, State, and local units, and which also amalgamate active service units drawn from the Navy, the Army, the Marine Corps, and the USAF. Joint Task Force Six, based in El Paso, Texas, emphasizes on its crest that its mission is "service to the nation." Its literature underscores "the threat" that it faces as follows:

- 70–80 percent of illegal drugs entering the U.S. cross the Southwest border;
- there is a vast area of unprotected border with Mexico;
- there are 150–200 Mexico-based groups involved in smuggling, armed with sophisticated weapons and other equipment.[32]

The extent of the drug trade should not be dismissed; for example, nearly half a billion dollars' worth of cocaine was seized in Arizona alone during 1991. The biggest operation yet intercepted, discovered in 1990, smuggled drugs through an elaborate concrete tunnel connecting Douglas, Arizona and Aqua Prieta, Sonora. Yet although the illegality of drug transport is not at issue, it is the rupture of the national border that is being emphasized in this interdiction. This is presented both in literal terms (the "unprotected border") and in relation to otherness—the actions of "Mexico-based groups."[33]

Economic activity—running drugs or undocumented workers—has now spawned a reactive institutional apparatus, designed to protect the *ideology* of the nation state that is upheld by the integrity of the border. Even in one State, the list of agencies involved is almost endless: sheriffs' departments for various counties, the Arizona Department of Public Safety, the Tucson Metropolitan Area Narcotics Trafficking Interdiction Squad, the U.S. Border Patrol, units of the National Guard. The armed forces also bring to bear an array of materiel that includes the most recent technologies available within the services, such as long-range audio detection and night surveillance equipment. The most elaborate hardware is the static balloon, six of which are tethered across Arizona, New Mexico, and Texas. Each costs $20 million to purchase (three have already been replaced) and $500 per hour to operate.[34]

It is important to restate here that this activity and these potent devices constitute the symbols of the state's efforts to secure what is viewed as a lawless frontier. Much is made of the artifacts that are seized—the billions of dollars' worth of drugs, the weapons, millions in cash, the thousands of confiscated vehicles—insofar as these represent readily understood and tangible evidence of defensive action. Conversely, very little attention is paid in official publicity to those arrested (who are often unspectacular messengers, carrying drugs in burlap sacks on the backs of mules), or to the wider question of drug control. Indeed, Border Patrol agents readily admit that they do not know the full dimensions of the drug traffic and also acknowledge that they "miss a lot."[35]

In short, as the integrated economic base of the border economy expands, so it seems that the symbolic divide has necessarily increased. There is a detectable process taking place, whereby the state apparatus is increasing its presence along the border; in MexAmerica itself, this is frequently identified as the "militarization" of the borderlands. There is a constant call for greater visibility, and greater vigilance. As the director of the U.S. Border Patrol argued, when pressing his case for more military assistance for his organization, "there's a strong feeling that the Border Patrol ought to be on the border, as the first line of defense to stop the illegal-alien problem."[36] In this way, the sanctity of the nation state can be seen to be maintained, although contradictory signals may be sent in the process. Even as the North America Free Trade Agreement (NAFTA) was beginning to be embraced, the deployment of National Guard units along the border in 1988, plus the invasion of Panama in December 1989 for drug-related reasons, generated a fear in Mexico that United States forces were about to cross *la frontera.*[37]

As cross-border trade and interaction of all types increases, we can see that the state's institutional efforts to maintain the integrity of its territory must also increase. From the discussions already initiated in this volume, such developments are entirely predictable. Also of interest, however, are the actions of individuals and groups along the borderlands. For them, the nationalist imperative is overwhelmed by the shifting dynamics of their everyday experience, one that confirms their status as *frontizeros,* or geographical *mestizos.* As we shall see, the militarization of the border does little to deflect the social construction of new localities, places that straddle the formal international boundary.[38]

Intergovernmental Links and Recombinative Networks

Although there are predictable tensions between the state and local units, it is not easy to anticipate how these will be played out in the chaotic reconstructions taking place within border zones. While the imperative of control is manifested in organizations with a national reach, these institutions understand little about distant borderlands; for example, Arizona is overseen by a regional office of the Environmental Protection Agency (EPA), located in San Francisco, a thousand miles away. In consequence, there are in MexAmerica rather weak ties between the local state and its national counterpart. This is certainly true in Mexico, where the northernmost provinces have been regarded as backward and unsophisticated; as a result, *la frontera* has, through neglect, undergone much greater foreign influence and political change than other regions within the country. This is less true in the United States, although it remains the case that border communities are peripheral in every sense of the word, as we shall see below in the example of the EPA. Far from the economic and political cores of even their respective States, they are rarely important economic foci in their own right.[39]

In such contexts, formal interactions between nation states (often negotiated in Washington or Mexico City) are only one way in which political transactions are completed. State governments interact across a national boundary over issues of shared concern—such as the environment—in venues such as the annual Border Governors' Conference.[40] Local officials, too, can pursue their own agendas, in line with the more widespread evolution of "municipal foreign policy." For example, some city officials have ordered police officers not to cooperate with INS officials in their search for undocumented workers and refugees seeking sanctuary in the U.S.[41]

In addition, there are many unofficial grids that connect both individuals and their institutions. Such networks typically, though not exclusively, involve government personnel who interact outside the restrictions of formal bureaucratic channels. Because they are formless, they can be described as recombinative networks, but it should be emphasized that their impacts can be large. Observers in border settings have noted a number of such procedures, and these shed light on the becoming of the border zone. The following examples are taken from the case of the twin cities of Nogales, which together constitute the single metropolitan entity of Ambos Nogales. Recent economic development there has generated a population of approximately 250,000, of which 20,000 are in Nogales, Arizona, and the remainder are concentrated in Sonora.

The Creation of Ambos Nogales

Ngugi wa Thiong'o writes that "the missionary carried the bible, the soldier carried the gun; the administrator and the settler carried the coin.

Christianity, commerce, civilisation: the Bible, the coin, the gun; Holy Trinity."[42] Although Ngugi's remarks were made with regard to the white colonization of Kenya, his observations on the processes involved hold up well in many situations, the development of Nogales included. We can trace the role of each of these forces—the Bible, the gun, and the coin—in turn to show the ways in which this region was developed from both north and south, thus laying the foundations for contemporary interactions.

Missionary ingress. Franciscan missionaries from Mexico City first passed through the Nogales area in 1539, a trip which stimulated Coronado's expedition the following year, in search of the mythical Seven Cities of Cibola. To the Spanish, the region was known as Pimeria Alta, a name derived from the Pima Indians. In 1687, Jesuit Eusebio Kino established the chain of missions that linked Sonora, Sonoita, and Arizona, a development which heralded the Anglo settlement of the Southwest. The Tumacacori mission was built in 1691, and permanent Anglo settlement in the Santa Cruz valley began in 1737. Permanence, though, was a relative concept. Pima Indians destroyed Tubac and other missions in a revolt in 1751, which was suppressed following the establishment of a Spanish garrison the next year. The mission was destroyed again, by Apaches, in 1794, and was eventually sold in 1820 and abandoned in 1848.

Military control. The tenuous foothold in the Santa Cruz was the base for the extension of Imperial Spanish authority into North America. The first expedition to northern California left Tubac in 1775, arriving in the Bay Area the following spring. However, this was the highwater mark of Iberian influence; by 1822, Mexico had achieved its independence from Spain, and controlled much of the region. This was the case until the Gadsden Purchase replaced Mexican by United States garrisons in 1854.

Economic development. An American corporation, the Sonora Exploring and Mining Company, moved into Tubac in 1856 and began to employ miners from Sonora. This development was interrupted by the Civil War, which removed army garrisons and allowed a renewed Apache presence, but a restored Anglo military renewed mining by 1867. Lead, silver, zinc, and copper were extracted throughout the region, and large-scale ranching was also prevalent.

The emergence of Nogales itself can be traced to a Mexican land grant in 1843. Its growth depended upon the construction of the New Mexico and Arizona Railroad, beginning in 1881; a connection was made with the Sonora Railroad in 1882. Once these linked the region with the world economy, there was steady economic expansion and population growth, which has in turn accelerated dramatically since the development of the *maquilas* in the 1960s.

Political Relations within Ambos Nogales

Massive alterations are taking place along the border, but they do not seem likely to lead to institutionalized political conflict between either the two communities or the two countries involved. The changes are leading to various forms of rapprochement, on both formal and informal levels. The imperative of maintaining levels of economic development (legitimated by proactive organizations such as the Border Trade Alliance, the Arizona-Mexico Commission, the Organization for Free Trade and Development, and the Mexico-Texas Bridge Owners Association) is carrying along new forms of social and political development—such as NAFTA—in its wake.[43]

Using the example of other rapidly growing cities in the sunbelt, we can predict that the real tension along the border will ultimately emerge between economic interests, committed to the pace of growth, and those that try to achieve distributional changes in terms of the quality of water, air, and other resources that contribute to the level of living.[44] Research has revealed the consistent ways in which separate institutional entities on each side of the border have relatively close links in matters of resource distribution. Such networks are an explicit recognition that some cooperative principles already connect both countries:

- El Proyecto Arizona-Sonora, a transnational educational program dealing with persons with AIDS on both sides of the border. There are few services for residents of Mexico, and this voluntary group provides support for those seeking medical care in the U.S.; approximately 60 percent of those requesting help from the Project are Mexican nationals.
- Hands across the Border Foundation, an educational program funded by the Kellogg Foundation, designed to facilitate student exchanges throughout MexAmerica.
- Medical agreements between hospitals. Mexican residents cross into Nogales, Arizona to obtain free medical care at the Carondolet Holy Cross Hospital, as the facilities in Sonora are so inferior. Hospital staff have initiated a program of supply to improve the level of care at the Sanatorio Municipal Gonzalo Guerrero Almado, in order to provide alternative opportunities for indigent patients.
- Aid between city governments. Historically, firefighters from both Nogales, Arizona and Nogales, Sonora have had an agreement of mutual assistance, and water is frequently pumped from the U.S. to Mexico when water pressure is low or when there is a periodic shortage.[45]

Environmental Issues in Ambos Nogales

The demands placed upon environmental resources are of social and political importance throughout the borderlands. Population growth, plus a massive expansion in industrial capacity, has led to difficulties in terms of sewage treatment and the monitoring of many forms of toxic waste, generated by the hundreds of *maquilas*. As noted above, there is substantial air pollution—some of it generated by the long lines of vehicles that crowd the border crossing stations—plus a growing demand for water in a semi-arid zone.

The competition for water defines the economic position of the different consumers. Residents and corporate users in Nogales, Arizona exhibit relatively high levels of water use. Corporate customers in Nogales, Sonora, particularly the *maquilas,* enjoy private wells which are isolated from the periodic shortages that face domestic users, notably in the summer months. At the lowest end of the hierarchy are those neighborhoods that remain unconnected to mains supply, and which have no sewage disposal—approximately 40 percent of the total households in Nogales, Sonora. These neighborhoods rely on the intermittent delivery of water supplies, and are frequently dependent on water storage in fifty-five-gallon drums that have often held toxics and other chemicals.[46]

The broad question of water treatment has led in recent years to a new binational agreement and an expansion of the capacity of the Nogales International Wastewater Treatment Plant.[47] The treated water is lost to Mexico, however, as the water is discharged into the Santa Cruz, flowing north through Arizona. Also of concern are longer-term questions of water contamination, emanating from the seepage of industrial byproducts and wastes into the aquifer that is used by Ambos Nogales. Of crucial importance in this development is the recognition that both communities are inextricably tied together, and that problems can be solved only in tandem. In particular, it is important to balance the geographical location of pollution—Mexico—and the source of pollution—the *maquilas,* frequently under American ownership; in short, there is an interdependency that makes it futile to apportion blame or to claim resources as sovereign.

Pollution threatens the level of investment and accumulation in the region; for example, the verification of newspaper reports such as the following could quickly damage the large Mexican produce industry: "Sewage contaminants may be coursing through U.S. food supplies as border packing houses ship produce and seafood chilled with ice that may be laden with parasites and viruses."[48] In consequence, we might expect that the state apparatus would have taken action to contain the problem, but this has never been the case. In Mexico, the Secretaria de Desarrollo Urbano y Ecologia (SEDUE) has had tough environmental standards, but has lacked the personnel to enforce them (the agency was renamed in 1992). Its counterpart, the EPA, showed little interest in border pollution until the latter was used by critics of free trade as an argument against NAFTA. Then a document, the *Integrated Environmental Plan for the Mexico/U.S. Border Area,* was hurriedly generated by EPA staff in the San Francisco office and consultants from Lowell, Massachusetts.[49] Although this is presented as a collaborative plan, it has been charged that SEDUE officials had little hand in writing the document. Certainly, local officials and policy experts were not consulted in the generation of the report. The plan offers little other than some general statements on the desirability of environmental clean-up in the larger border cities in MexAmerica. There is no hint in the document of the financial assistance that would be necessary for successful enforcement of even the existing legislation.[50]

The vacuity of the *Integrated Environmental Plan,* notably in terms of its lack of a coherent budget, is in contrast to the many millions of dollars that are pumped into border militarization, and even the provision of infrastructure to facilitate economic development.[51] Once again, we see the discrepancy between the state's strong commitment to the maintenance of the border as an expression of difference and its very limited commitment to collaboration on fundamental quality-of-life issues.

Summary and Implications

In this brief exploration of the MexAmerican borderlands, I have emphasized the significant divergence between the institutions of the state and those of the local state. As indicated here, individuals and institutions on both sides of *la frontera* have many shared interests, even if their encompassing economic and political systems have divagated for many years. In consequence, the ties that bind the *frontizeros* together are in many instances much stronger than those that connect them to their fellow nationals. In other words, the networks of everyday life are more powerful than the tendrils that go to make up the "imagined community."

These recombinative networks occur in the face of very real countervailing pressures. There is a strand of nativist political discourse—of which David Duke is a vocal representative—that identifies a present threat from immigration, and which calls for both an end to movement across the Mex-American border and a forced deportation of "nonwhites."[52] Although the institutions of the state do not use the same inflammatory rhetoric, there is the same appeal to an ever-present threat—reified, for instance, in terms of a tidal wave of drugs descending upon an unsuspecting population. In fact, the state's representatives detect many issues along the border that threaten national sovereignty, and in such cases, their response is typically to generate a symbolic profile of defense.

The question of environmental pollution can quickly become part of this nationalist rhetoric, and border politicians in Washington are not immune from this imperative. There is a consistent theme of apportioning blame upon Mexico, which is portrayed as dragging its feet with regard to environmental issues. Senator Lloyd Bentsen (D-Texas) has stated that he wants to see "some laws that are reasonably comparable to our own on environmental protection, with the understanding that Mexico has a lot farther to go on this." As noted above, this is unrealistic—Mexican legislative standards with regard to the environment are comparable to those in the U.S. in several areas.[53] Dennis DeConcini (D-Arizona) is correct to suggest that implementation is the problem, but he too casts this in national terms, with a culprit and a victim: "Mexico lacks the resources to respond to emergencies that sometimes affect *us*" (emphasis mine), a statement which ignores the reality that Mexican citizens are also affected by such emergencies, which are themselves in large measure the result of American corporate activity.[54] In contrast to this bombast, local officials have gone about their business in a different mode, recognizing that while problems exist, they are communal ones. In 1990, for example, detection of the polio virus in the Santa Cruz in Arizona led to chlorination efforts by Mexican authorities in Sonora. This was despite the opposition of health officials in the State of Arizona, who echo the attitudes of national institutions in demanding American control of American problems.

Such conflicts are a part of the wider tension that exists between the state and its local counterparts. Yet even where there has been an imposition of powerful centralized control, there are always patterns of resistance, institutionalized within communities. In the future, there will be major challenges for local governments in such settings. There will be a tension between the search for some central guidance and central legislation to deal with such issues, on the one hand, and the urge to investigate solutions within and between neighboring communities, on the other. When localities take the lead in such contexts, the results are dramatic. With community initiative, higher-order governments can be induced to lower their defensive postures and to initiate formal agreements. This is not to suggest that all will be resolved simply. The borderlands are sites of unequal exchange. Industrialization will be the cause of continuing social problems, revolving around overly rapid urban growth and housing shortages; in addition, the low rates of pay and minimal benefits offered by the companies dictate that there will be no immediate increase in prosperity or standard of living. However, this is to lose sight of the basic logic of the argument developed here, namely that it is the conditions of inequality and dependence that make cooperation between the residents and the institutions of localities so crucial.

EIGHT

EMPOWERMENT WITHIN THE LOCAL STATE

*It is only in a shared belief in the insistence
that there are practical alternatives that the
balance of forces and chances begins to
alter. —WILLIAMS*[1]

Reprise

This chapter begins with a restatement of the central themes that have been developed within the book so far. From this recapitulation, I will then move on to lay out some additional comments on these and additional tropes.

1. Initially, the most basic thesis within my argument has been that the state must be addressed and understood historically. As a set of institutions and as an idea, it is a *state of becoming.*

2. In order to understand this evolution, the state must be placed in the broadest contexts of social development. Within most societies, political and economic power has been displaced upwards, away from its original bases, which were localized. This process of displacement has occurred as the scope of human interaction has increased; this is particularly true of the expansion of mercantile and, subsequently, industrial reach. The displacement has manifested itself in institutional terms as the construction of bureaucracies, attempting to impose central authority across a territory.

3. This shift notwithstanding, social and economic interactions have endured at the local level. Individuals and institutions have an everyday existence that is contained within particular locations. In consequence, it is important to note that the displacement can never be either total or complete.

4. There is, consequently, a basic tension within the state apparatus that

revolves around the terms of this displacement; the state is not a single monolith but consists of many disparate parts, created through time and expressed
across space. This spatiality can be interpreted as a *state of chaos* that defines a contradictory relationship between the state and its components.

5. Historically, conflicting relations within the state have been confined
by force; however, the increased complexity of civil society—an increase
in spatiality—has militated against that. In its stead, surveillance has been
increasingly employed, but the technologies used have proved themselves
to be open to exploitation, not only by governments but also by citizens.[2]
In consequence, there is greater scope for resistance to the state than has
been possible for some considerable time, a resistance that also has its
origins and its existence within the horizons of everyday life.

6. Localized collective action can be theorized as taking place within
local states. We can view the latter as legal and political arenas within which
basic issues of personal and collective choice can be manifested. Following
Hegel, we can argue that the local state, as a corporation, is part of civil
society; it is, though, in terms of its political and bureaucratic responsibilities, also a part of the state. Local states thus possess a distinct analytical
form, reflecting their location between the state and civil society.

On the Withering Away of the State[3]

In developing this argument, I have suggested that there may be good
reason to emphasize changes that are currently taking place with regard
to the intersections of the state and the local state. I am not the first to note
that a period of globalization implies crucial changes for the stability of the
nation state, be it a global extension of economic relations, communications,
or political ideologies. Giddens, for example, suggests that the nation state
is too small to deal with some questions but too big to deal with others.[4]
While we should always follow Foucault's caution when trying to view our
times as special or as disjunctures, we can certainly note a number of
factors that are contributing to important changes:

* continued transnational transfers of capital, leading to a virtual hypermobility of investment and disinvestment;[5]
* a consequent emphasis upon supranational economic ties between
  capitalist nation states—notably in Europe but also, via free trade, in
  the Americas;
* the weakening of ideological chains which have maintained the integrity
  of the nation state in diverse situations—as in Yugoslavia, Canada,
  and India.

In short, we are seeing the dissolution of the state system from both directions. Localized pressures, such as ethnic regionalism, can indicate that many nation states are too large and have tried to create an imagined community where none can exist; equally, material changes underscore that many nation states are too small to survive.

Some international-relations analysts might take this as evidence that there is an optimal size for the nation state which will permit it to function within the global order of the future without losing control of its internal factions, be they geographical or otherwise.[6] Here I will simply note that these tensions are real ones, and they are without a simple resolution. The survival of the territorial state is an eternal compromise, and it remains to be seen how this will be resolved on a case-by-case basis. As the example developed in the preceding chapter indicates, a challenge to the nation state commonly results in an effort to increase the centrality of control. The example of the MexAmerican border shows that a defense of the borderland assumes a heightened importance and extreme symbolic significance in the face of economic integration.[7] However, this defensive posture is likely to prove unsuccessful. As Paul Kennedy has argued, the state that attempts to defend its image aggressively has probably already entered into a period of decline.[8] Moreover, in a period of dislocation, it is common for voters to think less and less about military successes, and more about the costs of military spending and the environmental degradation that attends the construction and maintenance of war hardware. Without effective external perils that threaten global war and planetary destruction, the imagined community cannot be maintained so readily. In such a period of change, then, it is logical for individuals to place greater emphasis upon their immediate realities and the more familiar settings of everyday life—the economic circumstances within the locality, the conditions within cities and neighborhoods, the changes taking place in schools and city government. In consequence, we see a situation in which the residents of the local state are more likely than before to develop a discourse wherein issues of personal and collective mores can be addressed.

In part, this brings us back to the title of this argument. As we have seen, the state is the apparatus that attempts to resolve difference. This occurs with regard to the basic axes of society: class, of course, race and ethnicity, religion and language, gender and sexuality, age and ability. But these axes are in some ways formless, as the social struggles and the coalitions they engender are constantly developing and redeveloping over time. As these struggles become manifested and have their reality *in place,* they are transformed into the complexities of the everyday: employment change and immigration, residential dislocation and gentrification, the costs of housing and homelessness, drug distribution and the spread of HIV, crime and gun control—these become the more familiar expressions of difference and struggle. Consequently, the *chaotic state* reflects too the multiplicity of styles of life that we find in society. A relation such as capitalism becomes reinscribed in complex articulations, like those that we see in the *mestizo* borderlands. The same is true of the many axes noted above—people can attempt to resolve their contradictions via local polities that may have very little in common, one with another. It is important that we recognize that these diverse resolutions are not to be accounted for simply in terms of the mode of production or the evolution of the late capitalist state (terms which are both too complex and too simple to capture the terms of social change). Rather, they represent the many contingencies and contradictions that emerge as the patterns of modernity fall apart.

The Defense of Modernity

These kinds of discussion are common in the postmodern arena. Increasingly, the latter has become a site of criticism, the result in part of a perceived lack of seriousness—Donna Haraway goes so far as to term it "the funhouse." In particular terms, postmodern argument has been criticized for its "nostalgia," its whimsy, and its unwillingness to challenge capitalism and the Enlightenment project. This is an important issue, and the critique will be considered in some detail. Two examples will be used, from the work of Nancy Hartsock and David Harvey.

Hartsock suggests to us that the discovery of otherness and subalternity is valuable on one level but essentially regressive.[9] In very general terms, the argument goes as follows:

- we reject the master narrative of the Enlightenment;
- there remains only intellectual chaos;
- there can be no structured alternative to modernity, only a continual rejection of its premises.

For Hartsock, this means only oppositional politics; there can be no engagement in an alternative praxis. While this is an interesting argument (reminiscent of the limits to atheism, forever tied to religion in an effort to reject it), it does rest on some specific assumptions, not least that these alternatives are not alternatives at all. She argues, for instance, that there exists no possibility for resistance within the exhortations of Foucault; but as we have seen above, this is really not the case at all. We might well say, in fact, that Foucault's intellectual life, and his death, were about resistance in one form or another.[10]

Harvey is, characteristically, more complex in his argument, and more obdurate. His study of the condition of postmodernity is intensely critical of multiple realities, and we should in no sense be surprised by this; the power of his entire body of work has rested on the search for an encompassing rule of social development. His rejection of postmodernism, though, goes much beyond a rejection of difference. It is, as we saw in chapter 5, explicitly an attack on what he sees as nostalgia and a failure of political will to "challenge capitalism."[11] He argues that while opposition movements can control specific spaces, "they are subject to the power of capital over the co-ordination of universal fragmented space and the march of capitalism's global historical time."[12]

Iris Murdoch once wrote that "it is always a significant question to ask about any philosopher, what is he afraid of?"[13] In Harvey's case, as in Hegel's, the answer is *contingency.*[14] Once the principal struggle against capitalism is relinquished, then the accepted axes of meaning within society shrivel up, and one struggle becomes as legitimate as any other. There are no master narratives, only contingent struggles. This fact is a challenge because it means that we have no route maps for these new social movements, and no way of telling what the outcomes of different collective strategies will be. In such situations, there is a real temptation to go back to familiar terrain, to try to relive former victories. Bachrach and Botwinick, for instance, call for greater efforts to achieve workplace democracy, although their manifesto reveals this to be a myopic yearning for some bygone age.[15] In complaining about the recent extension of rights at work, they distinguish between "workers" on the one hand, and "women, minorities, handicapped and homosexuals" on the other, as if the struggles of the latter are as unimportant now as they were deemed to be fifty years ago. Clearly, these are not the individuals who are really in need of empowerment, who must be, by default, healthy straight males![16] A similar nostalgia afflicts Gottdiener, in his proclamation of the death of local politics.[17] In terms of the historical measures of political action, masterminded [*sic*] via the political machine, he may be correct; but in his willful ignorance of other forms of collective action, he reveals himself to be a luddite of impressive proportions.

From a different standpoint, another—and more creative—level of response would be to ask what constitutes a realistic political agenda after modernism. Harvey demands that we confront capitalism, a goal that has preoccupied social critics for a century. Yet as Allan Pred observes, "homogenizing influences that may be produced by corporate capitalism, the [s]tate, and the mass media do not easily translate into the homogenization of resistance and conflict."[18] In other words, strategies that have worked in one arena are not automatically successful in another. Control of the accumulation of capital would not necessarily constitute an attack on the micropowers that make up the state apparatus, and vice versa. Equally important is the question of determining strategies subsequent to any broader social shift: how could alternatives—such as socialism—be achieved within the territorial state as we comprehend it today? As Walker notes, the twentieth century underlines that there is nothing more grotesque than the enshrinement of a principle such as socialism *within the state.*

It is in an effort to move forward from this strategic impasse that I have concentrated on the local state as an important setting for action. The centrality of the local state lies exactly in the possibility of making a difference— residents can resolve some of their own needs, but can also attempt to participate in a broader discourse. As we have seen, local states were able to try, throughout the 1970s and 1980s, to generate ties with other communities throughout the world, via what has come to be known as "municipal foreign policy." In some jurisdictions, of course, this was impossible, as a majority of residents rejected such strategies as "un-American" in ballot initiatives and other propositions. However, even when rejection occurred, it contributed to a broader discourse about peace and informal networks, while reflecting residents' own priorities. Such events, replicated in hundreds of jurisdictions, have pushed hard against states' monopoly in the international arena and the assumption that foreign policy is above the individual's level of expertise. It has been necessary for those who maintain the status quo to repeat the received wisdom, which is that "the United States, to be effective in foreign policy, must speak with but one voice. It cannot have a cacophony of different [S]tates and municipalities seeking to speak about foreign policy issues."[19] Again, such defensive posturing indicates the salience of the local state's challenge. More broadly, it has also focused attention back on our understanding of key concepts, such as citizenship.

Rethinking Citizenship

At the core of my interpretation is a series of exciting developments. On one level, there is a reassessment of supranational linkages: being European or American is increasingly meaningful, and no longer simply in terms of defensive economic or military alliances. There is also global debate, emerging over issues such as the Law of the Sea on the one hand, and climate change and biodiversity on the other.[20] This is at once sentimental and neocolonial, with the industrial nations demanding that the LDCs should not repeat the environmental mistakes that the former have made.[21] Nonetheless, a forum such as the Earth Summit offers some naive opportunities for action, as the weight of international opinion has proved effective in putting moral pressure on countries such as the United States to conform on certain environmental standards.

As this trend toward globalization appears to accelerate, the sovereignty of the nation state is also open to question.[22] The lurch into an era of post-socialist capitalism is ushering in another frantic round of reinvestment, as productive capacity is established in Eastern Europe and South America. While leaders flirt with the rhetoric of isolationism, this only underscores their powerlessness in the face of transnational corporate activity. In such situations, the *meaning* of one's nationality is increasingly eroded. As Walker indicates,

> Neither the spatial boundaries of the territorial state nor the geographical points of the compass (North, South) provide much help in understanding how patterns of stratification, inclusion and exclusion are being transformed on a global basis. The conventional opposition between class and nation has become yet another false dichotomy.[23]

As the territorial state's existence is opened to scrutiny—or even to indifference—there occurs a reinterpretation of citizenship, which again reflects a move in contradictory but essentially positive directions. Citizenship has been defined historically in terms of the individual's rights and responsibilities within the state. The definition of these has remained contested, and can be traced back to Locke, on the one hand, who stated that rights are subsumed within natural law, and to Hobbes, who argued that the responsibilities of the individual include the recognition of the power of the state.[24] From these alternatives, the principle of sovereignty has been rescued in various ways. Rousseau's *Social Contract,* Hegel's concepts of state and civil society, and Kant's ideas of constitutional government were all ways to ground the construction of sovereignty within the territorial state. Any recognition of globalization must also recognize that the state can no longer claim to guarantee the individual's rights. For example, it can now barely intercede against the actions of the market, for the latter has become a moving target. As such, it is increasingly difficult to guarantee property rights, which are themselves dependent upon the stability of national currencies and trade balances; it can no longer form simple alliances with labor, via the trade unions, to maintain wage rates for male workers and thus try to ensure political stability.[25]

In consequence, we see the state rolling back in terms of the ways in which citizenship is defined; the grandest evocations of *pax americana* or the British Empire are being replaced by limited horizons and equally limited expectations. This redefinition is situated, not in the abstract terrain of nationality but in terms of the gritty parameters of everyday life. In the United Kingdom, for instance, a new *Citizens' Charter* focuses on the very starkest of phenomena, such as patient waiting lists in public hospitals. The *Charter* emphasizes the workings of public service institutions, not as large monoliths but as more accessible institutions staffed by individuals with a human face—and a name tag.[26] In reality, this is an attempt to distance the state from the performance of its welfare institutions. As we saw in chapter 1, the increase in domestic projects has enlarged the centrality of the state in everyday life; as fiscal crisis now dictates that the infrastructure of welfare support be diminished, so the state's institutions are dissociated from the performance of its components, such as hospitals. In the British context, it is argued that this is to be achieved by encouraging individuals to take charge of themselves and to become "active citizens." While this contains echoes of empowerment, it also indicates that the state's institutions are placing clear limitations upon their ability to support citizens. For the individual, the responsibilities of this new relation appear to far outweigh the rights and benefits that they may expect from the state apparatus.[27]

In the United States, the posture of the state has differed; welfare support for those in poverty has traditionally been minimal, for instance. In consequence, the reconstruction of individual rights within community norms is taking place with clearer objectives, as is revealed by a recent study by the Kettering Foundation, *Citizens and Politics*.[28] The document notes that "Americans participate only in specific areas (found mostly on a local level) when they believe that a fundamental political compact exists to suggest that, 'when I participate there will be at least the possibility to bring about and witness change.'"[29] As we have noted above, these possibilities are seen in the daily sphere—the right to shelter; the right to worship in certain ways; to profess a sexual orientation; to carry or not carry weapons; the right not to witness pornography (which may contradict the right to display sexual orientation), and so on. In some ways, this may seem like the end of the grand secular experiment of the Enlightenment that freed people from an earlier control, namely the church. It may seem regressive, insofar as the state can no longer guarantee human rights, and is reduced to making promises about the length of time one will have to wait for a hip-replacement operation. Groups that have struggled to achieve the prospect of emancipation through the state—via strategies such as the Equal Rights Amendment—are likely to see this development as antithetical to their historically determined design.

The Janus-Like Image of the State

The legacy of welfare statism in the industrial nations is a powerful one. Several generations have now known only the support of the "cradle-to-the-grave" institutions of the type sketched by Michael Teitz (see page 7). Coupled with this network of support has been reform legislation that has dismantled the worst excesses of nineteenth-century racism, sexism, homophobia, and individual exploitation. Together, these two strands have defined for many the notion that the state is the final arbiter of justice in a way that cannot be achieved via the partial and exclusionary tendencies of the local community.[30]

This assumption rests, however, on a schizophrenic notion of the state. It ignores all that we know about the power of the state and all of the commonplace ways in which we characterize the latter as "big brother." Throughout the globe, we can characterize the endemic condition of statism as the "world of pain," as Eckstein terms it.[31] Consequently, for us to appeal in the same breath to the state as an arbiter of enlightened legislation demands that the state possess a Janus-like quality—it assumes that the state can be periodically captured by liberal and nontotalitarian interests. The presumption that it can be harnessed for good purposes, such as the maintenance of abortion rights, is thus based upon inconsistent premises. At the very least, we would need to specify exactly the conditions under which the state is likely to act in one way and not another. And crucially, while there are, as noted immediately above, examples of such legislation, it must always be remembered that they are dependent upon the local state for their implementation, which brings the argument full circle.

More complex versions of this Janus-like view of the state are proposed by a number of contemporary critics. For example, Bachrach and Botwinick pin their theory of workplace democracy upon some broad-scale changes within society that would reconfigure the role of large corporations and place them firmly in the public sphere. They are rather coy, however, when it comes to detailing just how the public sphere will bring this about, although it is clear that the state would have to be invoked.[32] Similarly, in her study of the politics of difference, Marion Young argues that local communities are unjust, insofar as they rest upon exclusionary practices, manifested in terms of land-use zoning and the like (this issue was explored in chapter 5). She proposes, instead, a spatial restructuring that would re-create the dynamism of the city, a political-geographical solution that would transcend smaller communities. Superficially, this has attractive elements, although it seems to have some historical contradictions built in (not least of these is the fact that consumers fled cities for exclusionary motives). Consequently, we have to reflect that it is unlikely that individuals would willingly reconfigure their jurisdictions—and so we are left again with the *deus ex machina,* the state that swoops down to restructure our local states in order to create greater autonomy and justice. This is truly the most extreme example of the state that is both gigantic yet gentle.

In consequence, when we ask, *Can* minority rights be guaranteed within the state? the answer is: Only to a degree. Any such project to guarantee rights of citizenship must be, by definition, highly homogenized. In contrast, the local state can represent a space within which more complex characterizations of the individual and the collective can be manifested. These cannot be ratified by the state in the first instance, but they can certainly be placed on the agenda of collective debate and sought in situ. Moreover, in the longer term, the collective discourse may also shift its ground.

There are many layers of inequality and difference within capitalist society that would not automatically disappear within an alternate mode of production. Gender relations and other bonds of control at the level of the micropowers remain undisturbed by broad social shifts.[33] Distributional questions, too, are inevitable within a society of complex spatiality; nor are these resolved without political action. Issues of human conscience are also left unresolved. It is precisely these struggles that Harvey would have us downplay as nostalgic, yet at the end of the day, we have to ask ourselves what the more traditional contests have accomplished, and how much they alone can achieve in the future. Struggles defined around capitalism and its political expressions have reflected exactly the same myths of linear narrative and progress that have marked modernity in other guises and have left many other axes of inequality untouched. Such conflicts cannot be relinquished, but additional struggles are overdue. These new social movements may remain unproven; but as Foucault observed, "those . . . having found a new way of looking, another way of doing, will never . . . lament that the world is full of error."[34] The legacy of our antecedents is clear—and a fairly dismal one. In its concerns for a space for new political forms of expression, this book ends with a plea for optimism and for experiment, one we are unlikely to regret.

NOTES

Prologue

1. I. Calvino, *Mr. Palomar* (New York: Harcourt, Brace Jovanovich, 1986).
2. Ibid., p. 5.
3. J. Berger, *Ways of Seeing* (Harmondsworth: Penguin, 1972).
4. A process which is usually compounded by the fact that many contemporary marxists began their academic careers as more "traditional" social scientists.
5. Anyone who doubts the accuracy of these claims should examine the work of Erik Olin Wright, John Roehmer, and Jon Elster, whose attempts to fuse class theory and various forms of statistical analysis, game theory, and calculus are, in a narrow technical sense at least, highly sophisticated.
6. C. Geertz, *Local Knowledge* (New York: Basic Books, 1983), p. 4.
7. For a discussion of the potential of ethnography in a postmodern intellectual climate, see N. K. Denzin, "Review Symposium of Field Methods," *Journal of Contemporary Ethnography* 17 (1988). This piece contains the challenge for us to become "seriously existential."
8. M. Foucault, *Power/Knowledge: Selected Interviews and Other Writings, 1972–77*, ed. C. Gordon (Brighton: Harvester Press, 1980).
9. See M. Foucault, "Clarifications on the Question of Power," in *Foucault Live* (New York: Semiotexte, 1989), pp. 179–92. Foucault is at pains to point out that we cannot see power as a thing that confronts nonpower; rather, it is a systemic relation. As I shall argue in later chapters, power and resistance are inherent components of a complex state apparatus that incorporates local political difference.
10. I have made no attempt in this work to deal with chaos theory, which is another effort to place context within formal analysis, and thus subject to essentially the same criticisms as those developed throughout this chapter. See H. Kamminga, "What Is This Thing Called Chaos?" *New Left Review* 181 (1990):49–59.
11. P. Steinberger, *Ideology and the Urban Crisis* (Albany, N.Y.: SUNY Press, 1985).
12. R. Alford and R. Friedland, *The Powers of Theories* (Cambridge: Cambridge University Press, 1985).
13. H. Lefebvre, *The Production of Space* (1974; trans., Oxford: Blackwell, 1991), pp. 378–79.
14. C. Cockburn, *The Local State* (London: Pluto Press, 1977).
15. Cockburn's book is matched in the United States by M. Gottdiener, *The Decline of Urban Politics* (Newbury Park, Calif.: Sage, 1987), which will be mentioned again in chapter 8; for a more recent review, see also S. S. Duncan and M. Goodwin, *The Local State and Uneven Development* (Oxford: Blackwell, 1988).
16. I received a grant from the erstwhile Social Science Research Council in Britain to investigate spatial patterns of access to human services; some of this

material is summarized in A. Kirby, "Neglected Aspects of Public Services Research," *Annals of the Association of American Geographers* (1983).

17. In my case, my conclusions were prompted by a number of contingencies. The first of these was my move to the U.S., which began in 1982. While I was in Berkeley, it was hard not to be influenced strongly by Manuel Castells. Concurrently, a meeting in Washington that Paul Knox, Steven Pinch, and I organized provided the opportunity to place together researchers from sociology, political science, and geography to talk about public goods and political action. Again, the importance of looking seriously at local politics was greatly emphasized by individuals such as Susan Clarke, Max Neiman, Bryan Jones, and Roger Friedland. To a British researcher used to treating "community" as an outworn outcrop of 1950s pluralism, this was indeed revelatory. My move to the University of Colorado in 1983 also pitched me into a multidisciplinary research setting, among political scientists, such as Mike Ward, who had no knowledge of geographical research, and who had a healthy skepticism for it when it was demonstrated.

18. It should be noted that Castells's book is not without its problems, as sociologists Harvey Molotch and John Logan have noted: "Space for Social Action," *Political Geography Quarterly* 9, no. 1 (1990):85–92.

19. See P. Saunders, "On the Shoulders of Which Giant?" *Australian Studies Yearbook* (Sydney: Allen and Unwin, 1983), p. 44; also A. Giddens, *A Contemporary Critique of Historical Materialism,* 2 vols. (Berkeley and Los Angeles: University of California Press, 1981, 1985).

20. Q. Skinner, "Meaning and Understanding in the History of Ideas," *History and Theory* 8 (1969):3–53.

21. One thinks here of the efforts to identify class struggle *sensu stricto* in the feudal societies of the Mediterranean.

22. Giddens, *A Contemporary Critique.*

23. See also A. Giddens, *The Constitution of Society* (Cambridge: Polity Press, 1984).

24. Geertz, *Local Knowledge.* F. Braudel, *Civilization and Capitalism,* 3 vols. (New York: Harper and Row, 1981 and 1984). For a brief review of the relations between Braudel's work and other themes outlined here, see A. Kirby, "Survey: le monde Braudellien," *Environment and Planning D: Society and Space* 4, no. 2 (1986):211–19.

25. C. Tilly, *The Contentious French* (Cambridge: Belknap/Harvard University Press, 1986) and *Coercion, Capital and the European States* (Oxford: Blackwell, 1990).

26. S. Skowronek, *Building a New American State* (Cambridge: Cambridge University Press, 1982).

27. For instance, R. Harré, *Personal Being* (Cambridge: Harvard University Press, 1983); and C. Schorske, *Fin-de-Siècle Vienna* (New York: Vintage, 1983). Both are discussed in chapter 2.

28. S. Kern, *The Culture of Space and Time* (Cambridge: Harvard University Press, 1983); E. Soja, *Postmodern Geographies* (London: Verso, 1989). My remarks should not seem to imply that Soja's work is without criticism; see, for example, papers by Deutsch and Massey in *Environment and Planning D: Society and Space* (1991).

29. Allan Pred was honored by the Swedish Academy in 1990, an important and deserved distinction. An issue of the journal *Geografiska Annaler* (vol. 73, pt. 1) deals with his contribution to the study of modernity, and his work is cited at various points within the book.

30. In addition, as a further elaboration of Allan Pred's claim that we are all a product of our space-time biographies, mention should be made of the Center for

Advanced Study in the Behavioral Sciences at Stanford, where I spent the summer of 1986. The opportunity to interact with two dozen scholars from a number of different backgrounds, many of them with historical training, indicated the possibilities, and indeed the necessity, of moving away from functionalist explanations, toward narrative investigations. My debt to Jim Farr, in particular, is greater than he may suspect.

31. Though these may also cause consternation; see D. Harvey, *The Condition of Postmodernity* (Oxford: Blackwell, 1989).

1. Terrains of Discourse

1. J. Farr, "The Estate of Political Knowledge: Political Science and the State," in J. Brown J. and D. van Keuren (eds.), *The Estate of Social Knowledge* (Baltimore: Johns Hopkins University Press, 1990), p. 2.

2. See, for example, D. Freeman, *Margaret Mead and Samoa* (Cambridge: Harvard University Press, 1983). I do not suggest that the eugenics movement did not have overtones of class as well as race; the urge to develop a perpetual ruling class was not far from the minds of Galton and others. I would argue, though, that their world view, and thus their rhetoric, revolved about race.

3. This is a composite quote, the first phrase being from Geertz, the second from Enloe, and the third from Abrams; C. Geertz, *Negara: Theatre-State in Nineteenth Century Bali* (Princeton: Princeton University Press, 1980); C. Enloe, "The Growth of the State and Ethnic Mobilization," *Ethnic and Racial Studies* 4, no. 2 (1981):123–36, p. 124 (Enloe is quoted at length in chapter 4); P. Abrams, "Notes on the Difficulty of Studying the State," *Journal of Historical Sociology* 1 (1977):58–89.

4. It would be a grueling task to attempt to chart the growth of "crisis studies" in the literature; see J. O'Connor, *The Fiscal Crisis of the State* (New York: St. Martin's, 1973); J. Habermas, *Legitimation Crisis* (Boston: Beacon Press, 1975); R. E. Arcaly and D. Mermelstein, *Fiscal Crisis of American Cities* (New York: Vintage Books, 1977).

5. B. Jessop, *State Theory* (Cambridge: Polity, 1990), p. 25.

6. Farr, "The Estate of Political Knowledge," p. 2. The sociologist in question is of course Theda Skocpol; see P. Evans, D. Reuschemyer, and T. Skocpol (eds.), *Bringing the State Back In* (New York: Cambridge University Press, 1985). For a contemporary political science perspective, see T. Mitchell, "The Limits of the State," *American Political Science Review* 85, no. 1 (1991):77–96.

7. In the past five years, a flood of literature has appeared on topics such as flexible accumulation, the hypermobility of capital, and the nature of post-Fordism. Although there has been important commentary, much of this work is remarkably uncritical; see D. M. Gordon, "The Global Economy: New Edifice or Crumbling Foundations," *New Left Review* 168 (1988):24–64.

8. A. Amin and K. Robins, "The Re-emergence of Regional Economies? The Mythical Geography of Flexible Accumulation," *Environment and Planning D: Society and Space* 8, no. 1 (1990):7–34; D. W. Harvey, "Flexible Accumulation through Urbanization," *Antipode* 19 (1987):260–86; and M. Gertler, "The Limits to Flexibility," *Transactions of the Institute of British Geographers* 13, no. 4 (1988):419–32.

9. I view the trinity of economy, civil society, and state as a metaphorical rail system, with the locomotive representing the economic engine. The infrastructure and the detailed schedule of operation are the responsibility of the railroad—and ultimately the state. Extending this simplistic analogy a little further, an engine may of course speed up, slow down, or experience a change of technology. The most difficult problem is usually predicting the behavior of the passengers, who are often

less than civil. Giddens touches on a version of this metaphor in his discussion of modernity; see A. Giddens, *The Consequences of Modernity* (Stanford: Stanford University Press, 1990), p. 139. See also J. Urry, *The Anatomy of Capitalist Societies* (London: Macmillan, 1981).

10. This account of changes in the space economy draws heavily on S. A. Marston and A. Kirby, "Industrialization, Urbanization and the Social Creation of a Space Economy," *Urban Geography* 9, no. 4 (1988):358–75.

11. This account is taken from M. Blewett, "Work, Gender and the Artisan Tradition in New England Shoemaking," *Journal of Social History* 17, no. 2 (1983):221–48.

12. M. Castells, *The City and the Grassroots* (London: Arnold, 1983), p. 314.

13. R. Walker, "The Geographical Organization of Production Systems," *Environment and Planning D: Society and Space* 6, no. 4 (1988):377–408, p. 394.

14. D. Harvey, *The Limits to Capital* (Oxford: Blackwell, 1982), p. 393.

15. See, for example, A. Pred, *The Spatial Dynamics of US Urban Industrial Growth, 1800–1914* (Cambridge, Mass.: MIT Press, 1966). A GM vehicle manufactured in Texas costs about $300 more than one produced in Detroit, because of the additional costs of transport of parts from the Midwest. These costs are offset by greater plant efficiency; see chapter 2, note 20.

16. The recent development of the Mexican-American border region via the *maquiladora* factory system indicates a closely knit pattern of production relations with resultant impacts upon social relations that is in some ways reminiscent of the nineteenth-century case (as we shall see in chapter 7).

17. Dual labor markets occur as firms recruit nationally for executive functions and locally for production employees: G. L. Clark, "The Employment Relation and the Spatial Division of Labor," *Annals of the Association of American Geographers* 71 (1981):412–24.

18. Walker, "The Geographical Organization of Production Systems," p. 396. He does not explain how the vast multiplicity of local jurisdictions in Greater Los Angeles contains and supports an integrated regional economic effort.

19. See E. Mingione, *Fragmented Societies: A Sociology of Market Life beyond the Economic Paradigm* (Oxford: Blackwell, 1991), p. 318; Amin and Robins, "The Re-emergence of Regional Economies?" pp. 17–19.

20. M. Storper and A. Scott, "The Geographical Foundations and Social Regulation of Flexible Production Complexes," in J. Wolch and M. J. Dear (eds.), *The Power of Geography* (Winchester: Unwin Hyman, 1989), pp. 21–40; discussed by Amin and Robins, "The Re-emergence of Regional Economies?" p. 15.

21. Amin and Robins, "The Re-emergence of Regional Economies?" p. 19.

22. J. Gaventa, *Power and Powerlessness: Quiescence and Rebellion in an Appalachian Valley* (Oxford: Oxford University Press, 1980).

23. As Walker reminds us, vis-à-vis Richmond, California, "nineteenth century explosives plants, in which only single Chinese men were employed, left a very different imprint than the twentieth century Chevron refinery and Pullman Sleeping Car plant in which white people with families were hired." Walker, "The Geographical Organization of Production Systems," p. 387.

24. P. Bachrach and A. Botwinick, *Power and Empowerment* (Philadelphia: Temple University Press, 1992), p. 12.

25. Does it require reiteration? Capitalism continues to touch relations between genders and races, the nature of leisure, the perception of time, the evolution of education and urban form, and many facets of human experience. This seems to be such a basic truth that it now explains everything, and consequently very little. Certainly for the individual, contesting capitalism is the equivalent of contesting gravity.

26. The regulationist school is perhaps the most coherent effort to link accumula-

tion and state action, although it must remain suspect in terms of the type of argument being developed here because of the functionalism that is implied (M. Aglietta, *A Theory of Capitalist Regulation* [London: Verso, 1979]; see also chapter 3). Efforts have also been made to link the actions of the local state and the changes in (post-)Fordist organization (see also chapter 5). For a full bibliography see S. Pinch, "The Restructuring Thesis and the Study of Public Services," *Environment and Planning A* 21 (1989):905–26, and J. Painter, "The Geography of Trade Union Responses to Local Government Privatization," *Transactions of the Institute of British Geographers* 16 (1991):214–26.

27. This volume pays relatively little attention to external relations, except in the case of the U.S.-Mexican border, discussed in chapter 7, but this is simply a reflection of my current priorities.

28. Mingione, *Fragmented Societies,* chapter 4. For taxonomies of state spending, see J. O'Connor, *The Fiscal Crisis of the State* (New York: St. Martin's, 1973). For a discussion of the poverty programs that began to account for a larger share of an expanding federal budget in the 1960s in the U.S., see J. Mollenkopf, *The Contested City* (Princeton: Princeton University Press, 1983).

29. Gordon Clark connects the legal power of the state to the demise of unions within the U.S. in his 1989 book *Unions and Communities under Siege* (Cambridge: Cambridge University Press).

30. The existence of these many forms contributes to what Lefebvre terms "spatial practice." H. Lefebvre, *The Production of Space* (1974; trans., Oxford: Blackwell, 1991), p. 38.

31. As Mingione has shown, the mid-century links between Fordism and welfarism have diminished in many industrial nations, as mass unemployment and underemployment have contributed to fiscal crises that make *preventive* welfare programs impossibly expensive; Mingione, *Fragmented Societies,* chapter 4.

32. M. Teitz, *Papers of the Regional Science Association* (1968), p. 36. The comment about the sexism in the original comes from a conversation with Michael Teitz.

33. The use of the terms "public" and "private" is, of course, quite problematical. From a feminist standpoint, the assumption of the private sphere represents a male sphere of influence which is uncontested; it also seems to imply the whimsical wish that the state could be appropriated, an issue that will be explored further in chapter 8. See C. A. MacKinnon, "Feminism, Marxism, Method and the State: Towards Feminist Jurisprudence," *Signs* 8, no. 4 (1983):635–58.

34. Urry, *The Anatomy of Capitalist Societies,* p. 43. It should be noted that for some commentators, the basic terrain of struggle can never change. In a quote where the misogyny is rivaled only by its butchery of language, Shapiro in a stroke turns the struggles of women workers back to the efforts of their superior male counterparts: "Cooke . . . identifies 'peripheral' workers, including women and ethnic minorities,' as groups 'demonstrating the lowest levels of solidarism.' This locates disadvantage negatively, as a failure to demonstrate solidarism, rather than positively, as the object of active organisation by male workers." D. Shapiro, "Policy, Planning and Peripheral Development," in the Lancaster Regionalism Group, *Localities, Class and Gender* (London: Pion, 1985), pp. 96–120, p. 101.

35. Urry, *The Anatomy of Capitalist Societies,* p. 127.

36. D. Harvey, *The Condition of Postmodernity* (Oxford: Blackwell, 1989), p. 46.

37. F. Parkin, *A Bourgeois Critique of Contemporary Marxism* (London: Macmillan, 1979), pp. 89–98. The example of gender differences intruding into labor strategies in Lowell has already been mentioned above.

38. These now include not only exclusive suburbs but also residential communities surrounded by gates and armed guards, plus communities attempting to reintroduce restrictive covenants to maintain racial balance; see, for example, P. L. Knox,

"The Restless Urban Landscape: Economic and Sociocultural Change and the Transformation of Metropolitan Washington DC," *Annals of the Association of American Geographers* 81, no. 2 (1991):181–209.

39. As clarification, these are of course analytical categories. Conflict *takes place* in localities, as we shall see in chapter 5.

40. Parkin, *A Bourgeois Critique,* p. 99.

41. Castells, *The City and the Grassroots.*

42. Ibid., p. 268.

43. Ibid., p. 269.

44. See H. Molotch and J. Logan, "The Space for Social Action," *Political Geography Quarterly* (1989).

45. P. Dunleavy, *Urban Political Analysis* (London: Macmillan, 1980).

46. R. J. Johnston, C. Pattie, and R. Allsopp, *A Nation Dividing?* (London: Longman, 1988).

47. Ibid.

48. D. Hodge and L. Staeheli, "Social Relations and Geographic Patterns of Urban Electoral Behavior," *Urban Geography* 13, no. 4 (1992):307–33.

49. Beyond that, it is at this juncture not necessary to venture; certainly, the larger claims that arise from Castells's work re the nature of urban social movements will not be addressed at this point.

50. It is possible that this argument may be seen solely as an attack upon Marx. That task, however, has already been undertaken with great sophistication—and minimal impact—by a number of commentators. Indeed, it is interesting that marxism now appears much rehabilitated to some in the face of postmodern politics (chapter 8).

51. J. Urry, "Localities, Regions and Social Class," *International Journal of Urban and Regional Research* (1981):471.

52. A. Giddens, *A Contemporary Critique of Historical Materialism* (London: Macmillan, 1981), p. 20.

53. For a critical perspective, see P. Saunders, *Social Theory and the Urban Question* (London: Hutchinson, 1986).

54. A. Pred, *Place, Practice and Structure* (Cambridge: Cambridge University Press, 1986), pp. 281–82.

55. M. B. Pudup, "Arguments in Regional Geography," *Progress in Human Geography* 12, no. 3 (1988):369–90.

56. M. Castells, "Crisis, Planning and the Quality of Life," *Environment and Planning D: Society and Space* 1, no. 1 (1983):3–22, p. 4.

57. Ibid., p. 7.

58. The suggestion that places interact is contentious and anthropomorphic and requires further explanation. I use the phrase to indicate that, for example, collectivities and institutions in localities may compete: chambers of commerce may compete for investment, senators compete for defense expenditure, resorts compete for guests and their dollars; see chapter 5. See also K. R. Cox and A. Mair, "Locality and Community in the Politics of Local Economic Development," *Annals of the Association of American Geographers* 78 (1988):307–25.

59. C. Bell and H. Newby, in D. Herbert and R. J. Johnston, *Social Areas in Cities* (London: Wiley, 1976), p. 190.

60. See, for instance, S. Rokkan and D. Urwin (eds.), *The Politics of Territorial Identity* (London: Sage, 1982).

61. Readers unfamiliar with the ways in which geographers—and, increasingly, sociologists—have wrestled with the problems of defining regions should consult A. Kirby, "Pseudo-random Thoughts on Space, Scale and Ideology," *Political Geogra-*

phy Quarterly 4, no. 1 (1985):5–18; N. Smith, "Geography, Difference and the Politics of Scale," 1992, in press; and Pudup, "Arguments in Regional Geography."

62. An explanation of quite why "urban" has emerged as a surrogate category for place requires what would amount to a major detour at this juncture, but much recent research has sought to address the existence of some specific urban effects. This literature does not often draw upon the structurationist perspective, but it implicitly addresses the notion of action being place-specific. Whether the focus is upon kinship, race, public goods, or housing construction, there is some underlying assumption that social behavior is, in the widest sense, different from place to place, or more specifically, from neighborhood to neighborhood or between city and countryside. See, for example, A. Sayer, "Defining the Urban," *Geoforum* (1984).

63. A. Scott, *The Urban Land Nexus and the State* (London: Pion, 1980), pp. 66–73.

64. Ruth Glass, in a review of Castells's *The Urban Question* published in *New Society* (London, 1977), could reply only by describing his work as "humbug."

65. P. Saunders, *Social Theory and the Urban Question* (London: Hutchinson, 1981), p. 257. He continues: "Social processes cannot be confined within particular locations." Conversely, the things that may be interesting about cities (in which category he includes specifically the circulation of capital) cannot be examined via sociological constructs.

66. P. Saunders, *Environment and Planning D: Society and Space* 1, no. 2 (1983):234–38, p. 237.

2. Here and the Elsewhere

1. The phrase comes from Darwin's *Descent of Man* of 1871. As will become clear throughout the book, I regard human practice to be reproduced specifically at the local scale; hence Bourdieu's concept *habitus*.

2. J. Meyrowitz, *No Sense of Place* (New York: Oxford University Press, 1985). The tendency has a long pedigree; Evelyn Waugh observed that "science annihilates distance" more than fifty years ago.

3. For a full discussion of this argument, see A. Kirby, "Context, *Common* Sense and the Reality of Place: A Critical Reading of Meyrowitz," *Journal for the Theory of Social Behavior* 18, no. 2 (1988):239–50; "A Sense of Place," *Critical Studies in Mass Communication* 6, no. 3 (1989):322–26; see also commentary by J. Meyrowitz, "The Generalized Elsewhere," *Critical Studies in Mass Communication* 6, no. 3 (1989):326–33.

4. D. DeLillo, *White Noise* (New York: Viking Penguin, 1985), p. 155. There is an apocryphal story that Toyota originally planned to launch a small vehicle with the appellation "Toyolette," which would have been as successful in the U.S. as Chevrolet's Nova in Mexico ("no va" implies "no go" in Spanish).

5. The connection between changes in the locality and modernity are discussed more explicitly, albeit in less detail, by Anthony Giddens. He argues that places have become phantasmagoric as a result of time-space compression. I do not accept such propositions, and this is discussed further both in this chapter and again in chapter 4. See A. Giddens, *The Consequences of Modernity* (Stanford: Stanford University Press, 1990), p. 19.

6. Meyrowitz, in subsequent work, has now cited a small selection of geographical work that accords with his interpretations; R. D. Sack, *Human Territoriality* (Cambridge: Cambridge University Press, 1986).

7. This is analogous to the phenomenon that Giddens refers to as time-space distanciation; A. Giddens, *The Constitution of Society* (Cambridge: Polity, 1984).

8. For a simple discussion of segregation in the medieval city, see *inter alia* A.

Kirby and D. M. Lambert, *The City* (London: Longman, 1985); H. Carter, *The Study of Urban Geography* (London: Arnold, 1985).

9. With retrospect, it seems futile to have attempted to exclude the capitalist message, coded in records, cassettes, and even clothes, from the DDR using blocks of concrete.

10. The complexities of this process are explored by Paul Knox in his paper "The Restless Urban Landscape: Economic and Sociocultural Change and the Transformation of Metropolitan Washington DC," *Annals of the Association of American Geographers* 81, no. 2 (1991):181–209.

11. D. W. Harvey, *The Condition of Postmodernity* (Oxford: Blackwell, 1989), p. 295.

12. A process which is of course not restricted to television. A novel such as Sinclair's *The Jungle* draws its impact ineluctably from its setting.

13. A contrast can be made with the situation comedy *Roseanne,* which exhibits more of the tendencies noted by Meyrowitz. The family is determinedly of no place; the opening credits show simply a tract house that could be found anywhere in the country. It is only through circumstantial evidence (debates over the use of chains versus snow tires) and occasional references to Chicago that we can guess that they inhabit some faceless town in Illinois.

14. A. Freedman, "National Firms Find That Selling to Local Tastes Is Costly, Complex," *Wall Street Journal,* February 9, 1987, p. 21.

15. Meyrowitz, "The Generalized Elsewhere," p. 327.

16. As a consequence of this confusion, we may note the ease with which one individual could shape postwar attitudes, as is revealed in George Kennan's many writings.

17. D. J. Walmsley, T. F. Saarinen, and C. L. MacCabe, "Down Under or Centre Stage?" *Australian Geographer* 21, no. 2 (1990):164–78.

18. This has been argued at great length by G. R. Sloan in his 1988 book *Geopolitics in United States Strategic Policy, 1890–1987* (New York: St. Martin's Press). He contrasts the complexity of German geopolitical thought with the vacuity of American geopolitics.

19. British sociologist Rees writes: "Only in a limited sense was the miners' strike a national one at all. . . . Not only was the form of the strike in each of the areas of the British coalfield substantially shaped by local characteristics . . . but also this differentiation was contributory to its overall outcome." G. Rees, "Regional Restructuring, Class Change and Political Action," *Environment and Planning D: Society and Space* 3, no. 4 (1985):389–406. Clark's work on the legislative control of unions in the U.S. was noted in chapter 1.

20. General Motors recently announced the closure of its Willow Run plant in Michigan, following major concessions by workers in Arlington, Texas; both plants' workers are members of the UAW. G. A. Patterson, "New Rules," *Wall Street Journal,* March 6, 1992, p. A1.

21. Although these are hardly the only issues to which the parties are unresponsive; on peace ballots, see M. Shuman, "Courts v. Local Foreign Policies," *Foreign Policy* 86 (1991):158-77.

22. On the "death of local politics," see S. E. Clarke and A. Kirby, "In Search of the Corpse: The Mysterious Case of Local Politics," *Urban Affairs Quarterly* 25, no. 3 (1990):389–412, with reply by Gottdiener, pp. 413–18, and response by Clarke and Kirby, p. 419; and S. A. Marston, *The People and the Public Sphere* (Tucson: University of Arizona Press, 1994).

23. See, for instance, J. Wolpert, "The Geography of Generosity," *Annals of the Association of American Geographers* 78, no. 4 (1988):665–79.

24. Gitlin has argued that this commodification process is nothing more than an

expression of the postmodern condition: "Postmodernist literature cultivates place names in the same way consumers flock to the latest ethnic cuisine—in the spirit of the collector, because the uniqueness of real places is actually waning." Leaving aside the presumption that there are "real" and "unreal" social relations in "real" and "unreal" places, Gitlin might contrast his remarks with similar insights offered by Sinclair Lewis, writing about *Main Street* several decades ago; this also would certainly undermine his assumptions about a postmodern connection.

25. The newest broadcasting network, Fox, is a case in point, offering only syndicated programs.

26. See, for instance, A. Kirby, "Things Fall Aapart: Risks and Hazards in Their Social Context," in *Nothing to Fear: Risks and Hazards in American Society* (Tucson: University of Arizona Press, 1990), pp. 17–38.

27. P. Berger and T. Luckmann, *The Social Construction of Reality* (New York: Doubleday, 1967), p. 26.

28. E. W. Soja, *Postmodern Geographies* (London: Verso, 1989), p. 15.

29. D. Harvey, *The Limits to Capital* (Oxford: Blackwell, 1982); see also N. Smith, *Uneven Development* (Oxford: Blackwell, 1984). Other citations include Manuel Castells's *The City and the Grassroots,* Lefebvre's *The Production of Space,* and Foucault's *Discipline and Punish.*

30. T. Gitlin, "Postmodernism Defined, At Last!" *Dissent,* Winter 1989; republished in *Utne Reader,* July 1989, pp. 52–60. For an interesting argument on the lack of a spatial imagination within political science, see R. Ashley, "The Poverty of Neorealism," *International Organization* 38, no. 2 (1984):225–85.

31. For an interesting survey, see M. Curry, "Postmodernism, Language, and the Strains of Modernism," *Annals of the Association of American Geographers* 81, no. 2 (1991):210–28.

32. A. Stephanson, "Regarding Postmodernism—A Conversation with Fredric Jameson," *Social Text* 17 (1987):29–54.

33. Soja writes of geography being "theoretically asleep"; *Postmodern Geographies,* p. 38. Thomas Glick has characterized the discipline as "middle class, Mid-Western and middle brow"; "In Search of Geography," *Isis* 74, no. 1 (1983):92–97.

34. See, for instance, J. Brown and D. van Keuren (eds.), *The Estate of Social Knowledge* (Baltimore: Johns Hopkins University Press, 1991).

35. For example, the studies of Bruno Latour, including the study *Laboratory Life: The Construction of Scientific Facts* (Princeton: Princeton University Press, 1986).

36. The Royal Geographical Society (RGS) played a central role in organizing exploration, scientific missions, and data collection, and took the initiative in the creation of various university departments of geography; D. Stoddart, *On Geography* (Oxford: Blackwell, 1986).

37. The recognition that American society has taken a different path from that of many European countries vis-à-vis the absence of socialism, although there is little reason to expect that social evolution will follow predictable paths from nation to nation.

38. G. F. Kennan, *Memoirs, 1925–50* (New York: Pantheon, 1967), p. 351. Efforts have been made to argue for a geopolitical sense within American foreign policy in this century, but it is unconvincing; Sloan, *Geopolitics in United States Strategic Policy.*

39. P. Steinberger, *Ideology and the Urban Crisis* (Albany: SUNY Press, 1985).

40. The phrase is Perry Miller's, quoted by Dorothy Ross in "Historical Consciousness in Nineteenth Century America," *American Historical Review* 89, no. 4 (1984):913.

41. A. W. Small, "The Beginnings of American Nationality," *Johns Hopkins University Studies in Historical and Political Science* 8 (1890):1–77.

42. S. Skowronek, *Building a New American State* (Cambridge: Cambridge University Press, 1982).

43. The statistics are repeated, with variations, at frequent intervals. It is to be generally assumed, for example, that within a class of college freshmen, only half will be able to identify the outline of the U.S. on a world map; see, for instance, E. Tenner, "Harvard, Bring Back Geography!" *Harvard Magazine,* May–June 1988, pp. 27–30.

44. From this perspective, it is unsurprising that political science (rather than geography or some other discipline) has a pivotal role within the American schoolroom, for it performs the key ideological function of transcending these locational differences and emphasizing encompassing republican values.

45. In contrast to the United Kingdom, where the rather complex national flag is frequently flown inadvertently upside down, without undue incident.

46. Ross, "Historical Consciousness in Nineteenth Century America," p. 912.

47. Discussion of the frontier takes us close to one of the starkest spatial images within American consciousness. At this moment, I accept the new western history that argues for the frontier-as-place, a point developed by Patricia Nelson Limerick in her 1986 book *Legacy of Conquest: The Unbroken Past of the American West* (New York: Norton).

48. As Farr has pointed out, there is also a large question mark beside Ross's assumptions concerning the late development of statist views; see his essay "The Estate of Political Knowledge: Political Science and the State," in J. Brown and D. van Keuren, *The Estate of Social Knowledge* (Baltimore: Johns Hopkins University Press, 1991), pp. 1–21.

49. P. Tompkins, "Review of *Interfaces of the Word,* by Walter J. Ong," *Philosophy and Rhetoric* 11, no. 4 (1978):282–89.

50. Geographers' scholarly interests include cartography, the manipulation of remotely sensed imagery, urbanism, the environment, and other general integrative topics which are poorly covered by other disciplines. Despite these niches, geography has not proved its indispensability. This problem has not lain in the identification of a particular turf; geographers deal with a basic material dimension—space—and thus complement historians and their responsibility for examining time. The problem has been one of language, of method, and of communication.

51. D. Meinig, *The Shaping of America* (New Haven: Yale University Press, 1986).

52. Giddens comments on the relations between time, space, and modernity in his book *The Consequences of Modernity* (Stanford: Stanford University Press, 1990). He argues that space has always been easier to partition than has time, which is, to say the least, a bold assertion, addressed further in chapter 4.

53. S. Kern, *The Culture of Time and Space, 1880–1918* (Cambridge: Harvard University Press, 1983); Harvey has also developed this theme in his recent writings.

54. Kern never fails to arrest the reader with an unexplained evocation: "the Belgian mystic writer Maurice Maeterlinck wrote like the wailing of oboes"; *The Culture of Time and Space,* p. 171.

55. Ibid., chapter 6.

56. C. Schorske, *Fin de Siècle Vienna: Politics and Culture* (New York: Vintage, 1981), p. xvii.

57. We could, with some accuracy, describe this quest not as an intellectual history but as an intellectual geography.

58. Schorske, *Fin de Siècle Vienna,* p. xxii.

59. Harvey, *The Limits to Capital,* p. 451.

60. This dichotomy is set up most clearly within scientific realism, which has had a faddish impact upon British social science—which is not to suggest that Harvey can be included in this camp, as Soja notes; *Postmodern Geographies,* chapter 2.

61. M. Stannard, *Evelyn Waugh* (London: W. W. Norton, 1986), p. 210.

62. S. Dalby, *Creating the Second Cold War: The Discourse of Politics* (London: Francis Pinter, 1990).

63. Such a discussion is offered in chapter 4.

64. See M. Foucault, *Discipline and Punish* (New York: Pantheon, 1977).

65. Negative externalities such as their pollution, garbage, or displaced homeless persons. This point is developed by various urbanists. I discussed this literature in my 1982 book, *Politics of Location* (New York: Methuen).

66. It is worth emphasizing that although this is a theoretically informed exercise, the study of localities in the UK has led to a good deal of debate which complains of an apparent "empirical turn"; see Soja, *Postmodern Geographies;* N. Smith, "Dangers of the Empirical Turn," *Antipode* 19, no. 1 (1987):59–68.

67. Much of this section is based on my reading of J. Shotter, "A Sense of Place: Vico and the Social Creation of Social Realities," *British Journal of Social Psychology* 25 (1986):199–211.

68. Ibid., p. 206.

69. It should be emphasized that I am not arguing for some environmental determinism here; the suggestion of coping is not intended to indicate a diminution of human agency.

70. It is not coincidental that Bourdieu employs the term *habitus* to describe the spaces in which people develop; P. Bourdieu, *Outline of a Theory of Practice* (Cambridge: Cambridge University Press, 1977). It should be remembered that my remarks are somewhat normative; it is common for real-estate interests to push development further and further into marginal locations, despite local knowledge which argues against such risk-taking; see chapter 5.

71. See once more S. A. Marston and A. Kirby, "Industrialization, Urbanization and the Social Creation of a Space Economy," *Urban Geography* 9, no. 4 (1988):358–75.

72. While this type of analysis can become complex, my argument here rests on the simpler assertion that in books such as Sinclair's *The Jungle* or Maupin's *Tales of the City,* place becomes an additional character. For an introduction to the discussion of place and literature, see E. Relph, *Place and Placelessness* (London: Pion, 1983). As many critics have observed, it is typical of postmodern artists to generate "placeless places" wherein contradictions can be made most markedly.

73. See R. Kelley, *The Cultural Pattern in American Politics* (New York: Knopf, 1989); D. J. Elazar, *American Federalism: The View from the States* (New York: Crowell, 1972); P. F. Nardulli (ed.), *Diversity, Conflict and State Politics* (Champaign: University of Illinois Press, 1989).

74. *Congressional Quarterly,* October 24, 1987, pp. 2581–94.

75. See P. J. Taylor, *Political Geography* (London: Longman, 1985); J. Agnew, *Place and Politics: The Geographical Mediation of Place and Society* (Boston: Allen and Unwin, 1987).

76. R. Kuttner, *Revolt of the Haves* (New York: Simon and Schuster, 1980).

77. D. D. Schmidt, *Citizen Lawmakers: The Ballot Initiative Revolution* (Philadelphia: Temple University Press, 1989).

78. Shuman, "Courts v. Local Foreign Policies," pp. 158–59.

79. M. Watts, "Struggles over Land, Struggles over Meaning: Some Thoughts on Naming, Peasant Resistance and the Politics of Place," in R. Golledge, H. Couclelis, and P. Gould (eds.), *A Ground for Common Search* (Goleta: Santa Barbara Geographical Press, 1988); J. Logan and H. Molotch, *Urban Fortunes: The Political Economy of Place* (Berkeley: University of California Press, 1987).

80. K. R. Cox, "Social Change, Turf Politics and Concepts of Turf Politics," in A.

Kirby, P. L. Knox, and S. Pinch (eds.), *Public Service Provision and Urban Development* (New York: St. Martin's, 1984), pp. 282–315.

81. Numerous local jurisdictions in the U.K. opposed central edicts, and to some significant degree successfully opposed the state (the poll tax turned out to be widely unpopular and was withdrawn). To paraphrase Hoggart, central authority to act against local politicians is not the same as a "ready willingness to do so." As he notes, it would be extremely difficult and very provocative for the state to take over the affairs of a local jurisdiction; K. Hoggart, *People, Power, Place* (London: Routledge, 1991), p. 286.

82. This position has been developed extensively: see, *inter alia*, T. R. Gurr and D. King, *The State and the City* (Chicago: University of Chicago Press, 1987); R. J. Johnston, *Residential Segregation, the State and Constitutional Conflict in American Urban Areas* (London: Academic Press, 1984).

83. This concept is borrowed from my colleague Michael Ward, and the reader is directed to his important work for a fuller elaboration of the complexities of his arguments; see M. D. Ward and L. House, "A Theory of Behavioral Power," *Journal of Conflict Resolution* 32 (1988):3–36. Salience will be considered in greater detail in chapters 5 and 6.

3. The Displacement of Power

1. C. Geertz, *Negara: Theatre-State in Nineteenth Century Bali* (Princeton: Princeton University Press, 1980), p. 121.

2. See, for instance, N. Poulantzas, *Political Power and Social Classes* (1973); L. Althusser, *For Marx* (1969); J. O'Connor, *The Fiscal Crisis of the State* (1973). This chapter has little to say about earlier structuralist studies emerging from the Parsonian functionalist school, except that the same problems of teleology are relevant; e.g., T. Parsons, *The Social System* (Glencoe, Ill.: Free Press, 1951). The quote is from R. Miliband, "State Power and Class Interests," *New Left Review* 138 (1983):57–68, p. 58.

3. B. D. Jones, "Political Geography and the Law: Banishing Space from Geography," *Political Geography Quarterly* 5, no. 3 (1986):283–87, p. 285.

4. T. Skocpol, *States and Social Revolutions* (Cambridge: Cambridge University Press, 1979); P. Anderson, *The Lineages of the Absolute State* (London: New Left Books, 1974); G. L. Clark and M. J. Dear, *State Apparatus* (Boston: George Allen and Unwin, 1984); A. Giddens, *The Nation State and Violence* (Cambridge: Polity, 1985).

5. R. Alford and R. Friedland, *Powers of Theory* (Cambridge: Cambridge University Press, 1985), p. xiii. Alford and Friedland cite Wildavsky's *The Politics of the Budgetary Process* as being representative of the pluralist perspective and Dahrendorf's *Class and Class Conflict in Industrial Society* as an example of managerialism.

6. See M. Castells, *The Urban Question* (London: Edward Arnold, 1977); R. Miliband, *The State in Capitalist Society* (London: Quartet, 1973); P. Saunders, *Urban Politics* (Harmondsworth: Penguin, 1979).

7. It would be possible to extend this situational argument almost indefinitely; consider, for instance, the work on the emergence of the modern state in Africa, which necessarily takes a perspective on state-society relations that permits incorporation of the complexities of the colonial state. See J. S. Wunsch and D. Olowu, *The Failure of the Centralized State* (Boulder: Westview, 1990).

8. Alford and Friedland, *Powers of Theory;* P. Dunleavy and D. O'Leary, *Theories of the State* (London: Macmillan, 1987).

9. M. Castells, *Economic Crisis and American Society* (Princeton: Princeton University Press, 1980).

10. Miliband, *The State in Capitalist Society.*

11. Alford and Friedland, *Powers of Theory,* pp. 202–22.

12. B. Anderson, *Imagined Communities* (London: Verso, 1983); Geertz, *Negara.*

13. B. Eccleston, "The State and Modernisation in Japan," in J. Anderson (ed.), *The Rise of the Modern State* (Brighton: Wheatsheaf Books, 1986), pp. 192–210.

14. For rare exceptions, see S. D. Krasner, "Approaches to the State: Alternative Conceptions and Historical Dynamics," *Comparative Politics* 16 (1984):223–46.

15. Geertz, *Negara.*

16. Ibid., p. 13.

17. Ibid., p. 134.

18. F. Neumann, *Behemoth* (New York: Octagon Books, 1942). See also C. Wright Mills's review of Neumann's *Behemoth* in the *Partisan Review* 4' (1942):432–36.

19. A. Söllner, "From Political Dissent to Intellectual Integration: The Frankfurt School in American Government, 1942–9," in B. Robbins (ed.), *Intellectuals: Aesthetics, Politics, Academics* (Minneapolis: University of Minnesota Press, 1990), pp. 225–43; B. Katz, *Foreign Intelligence* (Cambridge: Harvard University Press, 1989); B. F. Smith, *The Shadow Warriors* (New York: Basic Books, 1983); B. Katz, *Herbert Marcuse and the Art of Liberation* (London: Verso, 1982).

20. Giddens, *The Nation State and Violence;* P. Abrams, *Historical Society* (Ithaca, N.Y.: Cornell University Press, 1982).

21. C. A. MacKinnon, "Feminism, Marxism, Method and the State: An Agenda for Theory," *Signs* 7 (1982):515–44.

22. D. E. Smith, *The Everyday World as Problematic* (Boston: Northeastern University Press, 1987).

23. C. H. Enloe, "Feminists Thinking about War, Militarism and Peace," in B. B. Hess and M. M. Ferree (eds.), *Analyzing Gender* (Newbury Park, Calif.: Sage, 1987), pp. 526–47; C. H. Enloe, *Bananas, Beaches and Bases* (London: Pandora, 1989). Feminists are not the only ones to make this connection; those working with native peoples have come to similar conclusions. See P. Armitage, "Indigenous Homelands and the Security Requirements of Western Nation States," in A. Kirby (ed.), *The Pentagon and the Cities* (Newbury Park, Calif.: Sage, 1992), pp. 126–53.

24. S. A. Marston, "Who Are the People: Gender, Citizenship and the Making of the American Nation," *Environment and Planning D: Society and Space* 8 (1990):449–58, pp. 451–52.

25. Ibid., p. 454. The quote is from J. B. Landes, *Women and the Public Sphere in the Age of the French Revolution* (Ithaca, N.Y.: Cornell University Press, 1988).

26. S. Schama, *Citizens: A Chronicle of the French Revolution* (New York: Knopf, 1989), p. 462.

27. Ibid., p. 874.

28. A. Pred, *Place, Practice and Structure* (New York: Barnes and Noble, 1986).

29. C. Tilly, *Capital, Coercion and the European States* (Oxford: Blackwell, 1990), p. 15.

30. Ibid., p. 15.

31. Ibid., p. 64.

32. Ibid., p. 15.

33. C. Tilly, *Space for Capital, Space for States,* Working Paper no. 17, Center for Studies of Social Change, New School for Social Research, N.Y., 1985, p. 4.

34. Tilly also identifies the period from the end of the first millennium through to approximately 1400 as one of virtually endemic warfare, as ruling classes sought to maximize their ability to extract surplus from their own and any other available territory.

35. The use of this phrase is not designed to echo the work of Gurr and King, which takes a narrow, state-centered perspective on this relationship; see D. S. King and T. R. Gurr, "The State and the City," in P. M. Johnson and W. R. Thompson (eds.), *Rhythms in Politics and Economics* (New York: Praeger, 1985), pp. 1–22.

36. Peter Saunders and Manuel Castells reopened the debate about what cities are and how we are to understand their evolution; see M. Castells, *The City and the Grassroots* (London: Arnold, 1983); P. Saunders, *Social Theory and the Urban Question* (London: Hutchinson, 1986). The works cited in table 1 are W. Christaller, *Die zentrale Orte der Suddeutschland* (1933); M. Weber, *Economy and Society* (1924); A. Giddens, *A Contemporary Critique of Historical Materialism* (Berkeley: University of California Press, 1981); and M. Castells, *The Urban Question* (London: Arnold, 1977).

37. Castells, *The City and the Grassroots*, p. xviii.

38. Giddens, *A Contemporary Critique*, p. 145.

39. I want to focus on Giddens's errors with regard to state formation, but he also errs in terms of the basic questions of urbanization. For instance, the assumption of a single, dominant explanation of urban development is explicit in Giddens's discussion, which seems unrealistic; trade and consumption are important economic roles for any city, and are identified as such by Weber. Giddens, too, rejects a normative central place model, on the grounds that neoclassical economic assumptions are unrealistic in a precapitalist context; this is despite the application of CPT to class-divided societies by researchers such as Skinner (see G. W. Skinner, "Marketing and Social Structure in Rural China," *Journal of Asian Studies* 24 [1964]:3–43). Equally indicative is his indifference to Castells's work (*A Contemporary Critique*, p. 149).

40. F. Braudel, *Civilization and Capitalism*, 3 vols. (New York: Harper and Row, 1981, 1984). His study challenges several of Giddens's assertions, such as that the city in precapitalist societies dominates the countryside. Braudel provides several instances where urban development *preceded* rural development: in Siberia, in the New World, and in first-millennium Asia Minor (1981, p. 485). He also gives examples where there existed a reciprocity; it was always the case that the preindustrial city maintained its own agricultural lands, and even nineteenth-century cities had farms within their boundaries. Agricultural communities frequently displayed industrial activities, now more usually thought of as "urban" in character. As far as economic reciprocity was concerned, it was normal for urban wages to be high, and for surplus generated in the countryside to accumulate in city coffers; at particular periods, however, it was also normal for capital to flow away from cities and out into the countryside, to purchase estates and farms.

41. Ibid., p. 526.

42. Ibid., p. 556.

43. Giddens, *A Contemporary Critique*, p. 12.

44. R. Williams, *The Country and the City* (New York: Oxford University Press, 1973).

45. M. de Certeau, *The Practice of Everyday Life* (Berkeley: University of California Press, 1988).

46. A. Giddens, *The Constitition of Society* (Cambridge: Polity, 1984).

47. P. M. Hohenberg and L. H. Lees, *The Making of Urban Europe* (Cambridge: Harvard University Press, 1985).

48. I. Katznelson, *City Trenches* (Chicago: University of Chicago Press, 1981), p. 30.

49. Commodity prices in England rose by a factor of four between 1510 and 1610; wages barely doubled. A. Briggs, *A Social History of England* (New York: Viking, 1983), p. 135.

50. Anderson, *The Lineages of the Absolute State.*

51. M. Mann, *States, War and Capitalism* (Oxford: Blackwell, 1988), pp. 73–123. Unsurprisingly, capital in Britain was almost entirely tied up in overseas investment; the paid-up capital of all the companies quoted on the London Stock Exchange at that time was a mere 64 million pounds sterling. Data from Briggs, *A Social History of England*, p. 195.

52. M. Crenson, *Neighborhood Politics* (Baltimore: Johns Hopkins University Press, 1983).

53. Locke, quoted in ibid., p. 17.

54. J. G. Merquior, *Liberalism Old and New* (Boston: Twayne, 1991), p. 23.

55. C. S. Grant, *Democracy in the Connecticut Frontier Town of Kent* (New York: Norton, 1972), p. 26.

56. P. Steinberger, *Ideology and the Urban Crisis* (Albany, N.Y.: SUNY Press, 1985).

57. Katznelson, *City Trenches.*

58. See, for instance, D. Harvey, *The Urban Experience* (Baltimore: Johns Hopkins University Press, 1989).

59. This is not to suggest that consumption politics are the only examples available; Foster provides an account of the collective bargaining that was established— illegally—in Oldham, England at the beginning of the nineteenth century, and which was ended only after military occupation. J. Foster, *Class Struggle and the Industrial Revolution* (London: Methuen, 1974).

60. Quoted in Briggs, *A Social History of England*, p. 194.

61. See, for example, N. Smith, *Uneven Development* (Oxford: Blackwell, 1984).

62. C. Tilly, *The Contentious French* (Cambridge: Belknap/Harvard University Press, 1986), pp. 50–61.

4. A Spatial Theory of the State

1. F. Neumann, *Behemoth* (New York: Octagon, 1942), p. vii. The quote is, in full, "*Behemoth* depicts a non-state, a chaos, a situation of lawlessness, disorder and anarchy."

2. The creation of new capital cities is endemic. In recent years, Brazil, Pakistan, Nigeria, and Argentina have all relocated some or all of their central bureaucracies.

3. R. Miliband, *The State in Capitalist Society* (London: Quartet, 1973).

4. See P. Gould, *The Geographer at Work* (London: Routledge, 1985), chapter 8.

5. Both South Africa and Israel have computer surveillance systems to monitor their "other" populations—black migrant workers and Palestinians respectively. Not surprisingly, these systems are supplied by U.S. manufacturers: P. Elmer-Dewitt, "Peddling Big Brother," *Time*, June 24, 1991, p. 62.

6. M. Foucault, *Surveiller et punir: naissance de la prison* (Paris: Gallimard, 1975).

7. At the time this book was completed, the repercussions of the King beating had not exhausted themselves, but it is clear that the initial acquittal of the four LAPD officers in April 1992 caused such reactions of disgust around the country precisely because of the immediacy of the visible record.

8. One of the more interesting myths that have emerged in modern America is that there is a shadow state that operates both within the U.S. and abroad—if it is indeed a myth. Glimpses of this subterranean apparatus are revealed most clearly with regard to covert operations in Central America and in the Golden Triangle of Southeast Asia. It seems to be widely accepted that the complexities of the modern international order demand such secret forces and dirty-tricks departments within

government, as the public indifference toward Oliver North's revelations indicates. For further discussion on these themes, see H. B. Franklin, *MIA or Mythmaking in America* (Westport, Conn.: Lawrence Hill, 1992).

9. C. Enloe, "The Growth of the State and Ethnic Mobilization," *Ethnic and Racial Studies* 4, no. 2 (1981):123–36, p. 124.

10. Giddens discusses this in *The Nation State and Violence* (Cambridge: Polity Press, 1985), chapter 2. As Michael Mann points out, the premodern army could march at the most 100 miles without then requiring large amounts of supplies, which would have to be taken by force or by negotiation; Mann, *States, War and Capitalism* (Oxford: Blackwell, 1988), p. 23. On Vienna, see F. Morton, *A Nervous Splendor* (Harmondsworth: Penguin, 1979). On contemporary frontier garrisons—such as those in the BRD before reunification—see G. J. Ashworth, *War and the City* (London: Routledge, 1991), pp. 70–71.

11. R. D. Sack, *Human Territoriality* (Cambridge: Cambridge University Press, 1986), p. 107.

12. Although it should be noted that there were much earlier examples of banishment to another place, such as the leper colony; see A. Kirby, "Things Fall Apart," in A. M. Kirby (ed.), *Nothing to Fear: Risks and Hazards in American Society* (Tucson: University of Arizona Press, 1990), pp. 17–38.

13. M. Foucault, "Questions on Geography," in *Power/Knowledge: Selected Interviews and Other Writings, 1972–77,* ed. C. Gordon (Brighton: Harvester Press, 1980), pp. 63–77, p. 72. It is more usual to translate "panoptism" as "panopticism."

14. Both words can be traced back to seventeenth-century European political theory; see, for instance, G. Rosen, *From Medical Police to Social Medicine: Essays on the History of Health Care* (New York: Science History Publications, 1974), pp. 124–54.

15. M. Foucault, "Space, Knowledge and Power," in H. Rabinow, *The Foucault Reader* (New York: Pantheon, 1984), p. 243.

16. C. Tilly, *The Contentious French* (Cambridge: Belknap/Harvard University Press, 1986), p. 288.

17. Mann, *States, War and Capitalism,* chapter 1.

18. E. Rice, *Captain Sir Richard Francis Burton* (New York: Scribners, 1990). Mansfield Parkyns (1823–94) was termed "the gentleman savage" for the same reason; D. Cumming, *The Gentleman Savage* (London: Century, 1987).

19. A. Giddens, *The Consequences of Modernity* (Stanford: Stanford University Press, 1990), pp. 17–21.

20. The plaque reads "Origen de las Carretaras Radiales, Km. O."

21. C. E. Stephens, *Inventing Standard Time* (Washington, D.C.: Smithsonian Institution, 1983). It remains the case that local opposition to "foreign time" remains intense. Several counties in Indiana, for instance, have long resisted being shifted from Central to Eastern time. Arizona, in contrast, shifts back and forth between Mountain and Pacific time each year.

22. Harambee! is an exhortation for citizens to bootstrap themselves to prosperity; see G. Hyden, "Reciprocity and Governance in Africa," in J. Wunsch and D. Oluwu (eds.), *The Failure of the Centralized State* (Boulder: Westview, 1990), pp. 245–69.

23. One of the best treatments of this topic is that by Felix Driver in his paper "Power, Space and the Body," *Environment and Planning D: Society and Space* 3, no. 4 (1985):425–46.

24. A. de Swaan, *In Care of the State* (Cambridge: Polity, 1988), pp. 34–35.

25. J. R. Poynter, *Society and Pauperism* (London: RKP, 1969), p. 6.

26. De Swaan, *In Care of the State,* p. 35, translation from M. Foucault, *Histoire de la folie a l'âge classique* (Paris: Gallimard, 1972).

27. J. Acland, *A Plan for Rendering the Poor Independent of Public Contribution* (1786), quoted in Poynter, *Society and Pauperism,* p. 37; see also note 33.

28. J. Bentham, *Pauper Management Improved* (1812), pp. 21–22; reproduced in Poynter, *Society and Pauperism,* p. 133.

29. Bentham, *Pauper Management Improved.*

30. M. Foucault, "Prison Talk," in *Power/Knowledge,* pp. 37–54.

31. E. Hobsbawm, *Bandits* (New York: Pantheon, 1981).

32. With the proviso, of course, that the offender cannot escape and return to usual society; this then generates the near-mythic status of prisons such as Alcatraz and Colditz, a point discussed further below.

33. "There once was a Jewish Jehova's Witness as a race defiler with penal colony dot and escape target"; E. J. Haeberle, "Swastika, Pink Triangle and Yellow Star," in *Hidden from History: Reclaiming the Gay and Lesbian Past* (New York: Penguin, 1989), pp. 365–82, p. 377. In keeping with the discussion of the capillary system of power, it is important to note that non-Jewish guards have never been prosecuted in Israel simply for serving in the camps; those charged have always been accused of voluntaristic acts of individual cruelty.

34. Foucault, "Prison Talk."

35. The process of exiling political opponents was underway in Russia by the middle of the nineteenth century, and a relative of George F. Kennan (chapter 2) wrote on the issue in 1891: George Kennan, *Siberia and the Exile System* (New York: Century Company, 1891). For a more recent commentary, see R. L. Tŏkés, "Dissent," in H. W. Morton and R. L. Tŏkés (eds.), *Soviet Politics and Society in the 1970s* (New York: Free Press, 1984), pp. 3–59.

36. M. Foucault, "Power and Sex," in L. D. Kritzman (ed.), *Politics, Philosophy, Culture* (London: Routledge, 1988), pp. 110–24, p. 122. In an earlier version, he noted that "this resistance is never in a position of exteriority in relation to power"; *History of Sexuality* (New York: Random House, 1978), p. 95. See also N. Hartsock, "Postmodernism and Political Change," *Cultural Critique,* Winter 1990, pp. 15–33. As Bob Jessop observes in his excellent discussion of Poulantzas and Foucault, the latter was active in prison reform, gay liberation, and the anti-psychiatry movement—a broad catalogue of the practical applications of resistance; *State Theory* (Cambridge: Polity, 1990), chapter 8.

37. As he pointed out in an interview, the relationship that he emphasized was knowledge/power, not knowledge = power, a very different supposition.

38. As Jessop also notes, there may be a basic logic with regard to the micropowers and the form of struggle engendered, but this does not seem in any way reductionist to me; *State Theory,* p. 231.

39. Much of this discussion is drawn from the analysis of R. Sheppard, *On Kafka's Castle* (London: Croom Helm, 1973).

40. Recounted in Katznelson's *City Trenches.*

41. Text from F. Kafka, *The Castle* (Harmondsworth: Penguin, 1962), p. 227.

42. Ibid., p. 203.

43. Ibid., p. 205.

44. In many aspects, K. is the outsider who cannot comprehend the capillary system; he wants to rebel against it but faces the possibility of, in fact, destroying everything. This is a paradox that we will return to below.

45. S. M. Evans, *Born for Liberty* (New York: Free Press, 1989), p. 127.

46. R. Hoggart, *The Uses of Literacy* (Harmondsworth: Penguin, 1957).

47. One of the explicit subthemes of the book is the presentation of the reminiscences of an author who has risen, as a "scholarship boy," out of the very community that he describes. The book was used in my high school, in the 1960s, as an ethnography of the neighborhoods that many of our parents had only recently left.

48. Hoggart, *The Uses of Literacy,* p. 225.

49. Ibid., p. 226.

50. Ibid., p. 230.

51. Ibid., chapter 4.

52. Throughout the 1950s and 1960s, newspaper cartoons commented ruefully on the changes taking place within working-class life; a particularly easy target was always the Americanization of young people in terms of dress, language, and music.

53. D. Harvey, *The Condition of Postmodernity* (Oxford: Blackwell, 1989).

54. R. Williams, *Culture and Society* (London: NLB, 1979), p. 315. Much of my interpretation of Williams follows A. O'Connor, *Raymond Williams* (Oxford: Blackwell, 1989).

55. S. A. Marston, "Adopted Citizens: Discourse and the Production of Meaning among Nineteenth Century American Urban Immigrants," *Transactions of the Institute of British Geographers* 14 (1989):435–45.

56. G. Marcus, *Lipstick Traces: A Secret History of the Twentieth Century* (Cambridge: Harvard University Press, 1986).

57. Warhol's Factory was part club, part moveable feast, part cultural seminar, and part design corporation; see J. Carroll, *Forced Entries* (New York: Penguin, 1987). Jennie Livingston's movie *Paris Is Burning* portrays the formalized world of drag balls in New York, where the after-hours participants both re-create and thus dismantle the stereotypes of hetero culture.

58. I agree with Michael Warner when he writes that "much social theory could be usefully revised by taking gay politics as a starting point"; "Introduction: Fear of a Queer Planet," *Social Text* 29 (1991):3–17, p. 3; see also note 72.

59. One study of the classical period argues retrospectively for a distinction to be made between sexuality (i.e., heterosexuality) and pseudo-sexuality (i.e., homosexuality); K. J. Dover, *Greek Homosexuality* (Cambridge: Harvard University Press, 1978), p. vii.

60. M. Foucault, *History of Sexuality,* vol. 1 (New York: Random House, 1978), p. 147.

61. Ibid., p. 43.

62. Ibid., p. 39. Note that homosexuality was on the American Medical Association's mental disorders list until 1973.

63. L. Faderman, *Surpassing the Love of Men* (New York: William Morrow, 1981).

64. J. Steakley, "Iconography of a Scandal: Political Cartoons and the Eulenburg Affair in Wilhelmin Germany," in *Hidden from History: Reclaiming the Gay and Lesbian Past* (New York: Penguin, 1989), pp. 233–65.

65. J. Lahr, *Prick Up Your Ears* (Harmondsworth: Penguin, 1987).

66. S. Timmons, *The Trouble with Harry Hay* (Boston: Alyson Publications, 1990).

67. S. Adler and J. Brenner, "Gender and Space: Lesbians and Gay Men in the City," *International Journal of Urban and Regional Research* 16, no. 1 (1992):24–34, p. 24.

68. J. D'Emilio, "Gay Politics and Community in San Francisco since World War II," in *Hidden from History: Reclaiming the Gay and Lesbian Past* (New York: Penguin, 1989), pp. 456–76; M. Castells, *The City and the Grassroots* (London: Arnold, 1983).

69. N. Miller, *In Search of Gay America* (New York: Harper and Row, 1989).

70. P. Jackson, *Maps of Meaning* (London: Unwin Hyman, 1989).

71. On the strands of misogyny and homophobia within Marx and Engels, and their legacies, see A. Parker, "Unthinking Sex: Marx, Engels and the Scene of Writing," *Social Text* 29 (1991):28–45.

72. When I had completed this argument, I was fortunate to find Michael Warner's arguments on queer theory, which provided a much more powerful base to my

narrative. He, for example, turns around my critique of Jackson, by demanding that left social theory make a place for gay theory; he writes that "another blockage against sexual politics in the marxist tradition . . . is the close connection between consumer culture and the most visible spaces of gay culture. . . . In this most visible mode [it] is anything but external to advanced capitalism and to precisely those features of advanced capitalism that many on the left are most eager to disavow. Post-Stonewall gay men reek of the commodity. We give off the smell of capitalism in rut, and therefore demand of theory a more dialectical view of capitalism than many people have the imagination for"; Warner, "Introduction: Fear of a Queer Planet," p. 17.

73. Residence of only three days' duration makes the individual eligible for assistance—a reversal of the usual prohibitions that were discussed above with regard to vagrants.

74. Miller, *In Search of Gay America.*

75. Foucault, in Kritzman, *Politics, Philosophy, Culture,* p. 289.

76. Clause 28 has become the codeword for the British state's attack on local government support for gay and lesbian issues; for a discussion of the Labour Party's "pusillanimous" response, see A. Tobin, "Lesbianism and the Labour Party: The GLC Experience," *Feminist Review* 34 (1990):56–66, p. 66.

77. Elsewhere, I have used the example of the first discussions about public health related to HIV transmission to show just how different the readings of a risk calculus are likely to be. In San Francisco in 1984, there was intense pressure to close the bathhouses, on "common sense" public health grounds. But the gay community had an entirely different common sense—namely, how could a disease attack only homosexual men? Employing this reasonable logic, they saw another homophobic attack on their cultural landscape, and resisted the closures; Kirby, "Things Fall Apart."

78. It would be incorrect for me to imply that Jackson is the only critic to develop this line of argument; very similar views are developed by L. Knopp, "Some Theoretical Implications of Gay Involvement in an Urban Land Market," *Political Geography Quarterly* 9, no. 4 (1990):337–52. For an account that addresses coalitions, sexuality, and class, see S. Tucker, "Radical Feminism and Gay Male Porn," in S. Kimmel (ed.), *Men Confront Pornography* (New York: Crown, 1990), pp. 263–76.

79. A. Kopkind, "Once upon a Time in the West," *The Nation* 240, no. 21 (1985):657, 672–75.

80. H. Lefebvre, *The Production of Space* (1974; trans., Oxford: Blackwell, 1991); the passage concludes, "Not that hope should be placed, after the fashion of the American liberals, in pluralism *per se,* but it is not unreasonable to place some hope in things that pluralism lets by," p. 379.

5. Local States as Social Constructions

1. W. Magnusson, "Bourgeois Theories of Local Government," *Political Studies* 34 (1986):1–18, p. 1.

2. J. Nogue i Font, *Els Nacionalismes i el Territori* (Barcelona: El Llamp, 1991), p. 69.

3. S. Rokkan and D. Urwin (eds.), *The Politics of Territorial Identity* (London: Sage, 1982).

4. J. Gifreu, "From Communication Policy to Reconstruction of Cultural Identity: Prospects for Catalonia," *European Journal of Communication* 1 (1986):463–76, p. 466.

5. C. E. Diaz Lopez, "The Politicization of Galician Cleavages," in Rokkan and Urwin, *The Politics of Territorial Identity,* pp. 389–424.

6. G. Orwell, *Homage to Catalonia* (San Diego, Calif.: Harvest, 1952, 1980), p. 131.

7. I discuss these histories more closely in my *The Inner City: Causes and Effects* (Corbridge: RPA Books, 1978).

8. P. Hall, *The Inner City in Context* (London: Allen and Unwin, 1981).

9. A. Kirby, "Review of Hall's *The Inner City in Context*," *Environment and Planning A* 14, no. 12 (1982):1686–87; M. Boddy, "Center-Local Relations," *Political Geography Quarterly* 2 (1983):119–38.

10. All of these analyses revealed consistent results. However, their conclusions were unwelcome at a time when broad inferences were being emphasized within European social science. An emphasis upon structural factors left little room for detailed interpretations of local conditions and differences. Consequently, explanations emerged based upon the tenets of naturalism or realism—a simple procedure that allows one to distinguish between necessary conditions, e.g., the mode of production, and contingencies, such as place. This realism is not to be confused with the use of the term by political scientists in their realist and neorealist studies of the world order. This realist tradition is derived from Bhaskar; see A. Sayer, *Method in the Social Sciences* (London: Hutchinson, 1984).

11. For a recent review see R. Fincher, "Space, Class and Political Processes," *Progress in Human Geography* 11 (1987):496–515.

12. Contrast, for example, the arguments of D. Harvey, *The Limits to Capital* (Oxford: Blackwell, 1982), with his comments in the paper "Three Myths in Search of a Reality in Urban Studies," *Environment and Planning D: Society and Space* 2 (1987):367–76.

13. S. Duncan and M. Savage, "New Perspectives on the Locality Debate," *Environment and Planning A* 23, no. 2 (1991):155–308, p. 157.

14. It is not uncommon to find mention of "temporal processes" and "spatial processes," but these are equally impossible to imagine. There are processes that have identifiable outcomes across time and/or space, but that does not qualify them as "spatial" or "temporal."

15. C. Cockburn, *The Local State* (London: Pluto, 1977), pp. 46–47.

16. J. O'Connor, *The Fiscal Crisis of the State* (New York: St. Martin's, 1973). For a full review of this literature, see G. L. Clark and M. J. Dear, *State Apparatus* (Boston: Allen and Unwin, 1984).

17. Boddy, "Central-Local Relations."

18. S. S. Duncan and M. Goodwin, "The Local State," *Political Geography Quarterly* 1 (1982):77–96, p. 78.

19. P. Saunders, "Urban Politics," *Political Geography Quarterly* 1 (1982):181–92, p. 186.

20. Duncan and Goodwin, "The Local State," p. 90.

21. D. Massey, "The Political Place of Locality Studies," *Environment and Planning A* 23, no. 2 (1991):267–83, p. 269.

22. See, for instance, P. Cooke, *Localities* (London: Unwin and Hyman, 1989); N. Smith, "The Danger of the Empirical Turn," *Antipode* (1987); Duncan and Savage, "New Perspectives on the Locality Debate."

23. Massey, "The Political Place of Locality Studies"; see also Harvey, "Three Myths."

24. D. Harvey, *The Condition of Postmodernity* (Oxford: Blackwell, 1989), pp. 217–18. See also Massey, "The Political Place of Locality Studies," pp. 274–76.

25. Massey, "The Political Place of Locality Studies," p. 277; emphasis added.

26. Ibid.

27. R. Barff, "Living by the Sword and Dying by the Sword? Defense Spending

and New England's Economy in Retrospect and Prospect," in A. Kirby, *The Pentagon and the Cities* (Newbury Park, Calif.: Sage, 1992).

28. D. Massey and L. McDowell, "A Woman's Place?" in *Geography Matters!* (Cambridge: Cambridge University Press, 1984), pp. 128–47.

29. J. R. Logan and H. R. Molotch, *Urban Fortunes: The Political Economy of Place* (Berkeley and Los Angeles: University of California Press, 1987).

30. K. Cox and A. Mair, "From Localised Social Structure to Localities as Agents," *Environment and Planning A* 23, no. 2 (1991):197–214, p. 202.

31. D. Hodge and L. Staeheli, "Social Relations and Geographic Patterns of Urban Electoral Behavior," *Urban Geography* 13, no. 4 (1992):307–33.

32. Report from the Environmental Protection Agency dated October 30, 1991. A total of 98 cities was noted, including San Diego, New York, Milwaukee, Phoenix, and Baltimore.

33. E.g., tripling the cost of gasoline and parking fees, a $1,000 second-car tax, mandatory no-drive days, and a four-day week would reduce the hydrocarbon level in L.A. by a grand total of 8 percent from the 1983 base by 2010; data from M. Russell, "Tropospheric Ozone and Vehicular Emissions," in M. Waterstone (ed.), *Risk and Society* (Dordrecht: Kluwer, 1992).

34. R. E. Parker and J. R. Feagin, "Military Spending in Free Enterprise Cities: The Military-Industrial Complex in Houston and Las Vegas," in Kirby, *The Pentagon and the Cities;* M. Davis, *City of Quartz* (London: Verso, 1990).

35. See, for example, I. Preston, "A Strike Diary, Brookhouse, S. Yorkshire," in R. Sommel et al. (eds.), *The Enemy Within* (Andover: RKP, 1986), pp. 100–18. The example of the racist attack on Rodney King in Los Angeles has already been used; see J. G. Dunne, "Law and Disorder in Los Angeles," *New York Review of Books* 38, no. 15 (1991):23–29, and *Christopher Report, the Independent Commission on the Los Angeles Police Department* (1991).

36. Personal Interconnections in Tucson and Pima County

Helen Gilmartin Justice of the Peace	Two sons, Sheriff's Department; daughter-in-law, Justice Court
John Bernal Director of Transportation	Sister, City Magistrate; brother and brother-in-law, Transportation; brother, School District
Dan Eckstrom County Supervisor	Brother, head of Jobs Training Partnership Act Program
Greg Lunn County Supervisor	Brother, Labor Union Services (county contract); father-in-law, Constable William Allen
Raul Grijalva County Supervisor	Wife, Tucson-Pima County Library system
Ed Moore County Supervisor	Son, formerly County Recorder's Office
Peter Ronstadt Police Chief	Brother, director of City Parks
Sheriff Clarence Dupnik	Brother, County Transportation Department; stepson, Health Department
Presiding Superior Court Judge Thomas Meehan	Daughter-in-law, office of the Superior Court

Superior Court Judge William Scholl	Wife, Sheriff's Department
Superior Court Judge Lawrence Fleischman	Wife, office of Judge Nichols
County Attorney Stephen D. Neeley	Wife, private attorney under state contract; formerly City Public Defender
Immigration and Naturalization Service, Tucson Manager William Johnston	Wife, office of the County Recorder
Tucson City Clerk Kathy Detrick	Husband, Deputy City Attorney; brother-in-law, head of City Consumer Affairs Division

37. See, for instance, a study of economic development in Cambridge, England: P. Crang and R. L. Martin, "Mrs. Thatcher's Vision of the 'New Britain' and the Other Sides of the 'Cambridge Phenomenon,'" *Environment and Planning D: Society and Space* 9, no. 1 (1991):91–116.

38. This extensive summary is taken with permission of the author from S. A. Marston, "Citizens in Conflict," Working Paper no. 88–6, Department of Geography and Regional Development, University of Arizona, 1989. The issue is developed at greater length in her *The People and the Public Sphere* (Tucson: University of Arizona Press, 1994).

39. Logan and Molotch, *Urban Fortunes*, p. 292.

40. S. S. Duncan and M. Goodwin, *The Local State and Uneven Development* (Oxford: Blackwell, 1988).

41. See, for example, Clark and Dear, *State Apparatus;* Duncan and Goodwin, *The Local State and Uneven Development*.

42. M. J. Dear and J. Wolch, *Landscapes of Despair* (Princeton: Princeton University Press, 1987).

43. I do not suggest that these economic development strategies are costless; they depend, in some measure, on the recommodification of places such as Baltimore, New Orleans, and Detroit as tourist or convention centers, with predictable consequences in terms of urban renewal and population displacement. See L. Knopp, "Some Theoretical Implications of Gay Involvement in an Urban Land Market," *Political Geography Quarterly* 9, no. 4 (1990):337–52.

44. That is to say, externalities such as noise associated with road construction; see A. Kirby, "The External Relations of the Local State in Britain," in K. Cox and R. J. Johnston (eds.), *Conflict, Politics and the Urban Scene* (London: Longman, 1982), pp. 88–104.

45. K. A. Owens, "Just How Much Power Should These States Have?" *Arizona Daily Star*, August 14, 1991, p. A11. The author continues with the allusion: "Going from New York to New Hampshire could be like going from Hong Kong to the Congo." This is revealing in terms of the assumptions about current uniformity in the U.S. versus "those wacky foreigners"; it also implies that without central control, New Hampshire could easily become as savage or othered as Africa.

46. R. J. Johnston and C. Pattie, "People, Attitudes, Milieux and Votes," *Transactions of the Institute of British Geographers* 13, no. 3 (1988):303–23.

47. J. Agnew, "Better Thieves Than Red?" *Political Geography Quarterly* 7 (1988):307–21.

48. For example, *Report of the Anti-Defamation League of B'nai B'rith*, Fall 1991, pp. 1–2, Phoenix, Arizona.

49. See chapter 2, note 77; also M. H. Shuman, "Courts v. Local Foreign Policies," *Foreign Policy* 86 (1991):158–77.

50. On political cultures, see Elazar.

51. Such as the work of O'Connor, for example.

52. A recent review is offered by G. Boyne and M. Powell, "Territorial Justice: A Review of Theory and Evidence," *Political Geography Quarterly* 10, no. 3 (1991):263–81.

53. Many of the quantitative studies have been unsuccessful, probably because of the coarse scale on which they have been undertaken. There is, though, a mass of reliable anecdotal evidence; see *Congressional Quarterly,* October 24, 1987, pp. 2581–94.

54. The phrase is discussed in M. Waterstone and A. Kirby, "Escaping the Conceptual Box: Ideological and Economic Conversion," in Kirby, *The Pentagon and the Cities.*

55. Such as New Mexico or Nevada.

56. In 1990, 72 bases were candidates for closure. Over 90 percent of the bases chosen by the Secretary of Defense were in House Democratic districts, with 41,000 civilian jobs at stake. Only 499 jobs were threatened at bases in House Republican districts.

57. I discuss these kinds of cases in Kirby, "The External Relations of the Local State in Britain."

58. See note 76 below.

59. 108 S. Ct. 1355 (1988), reh'g denied, 108 S. Ct. 2837 (1988); 469 US 528 (1985), reh'g denied 471 US 1049 (1985).

60. *Baker,* 108 S. Ct. 1361.

61. Foreign commentators, used to national curricula, are often shocked by the fact that education is controlled locally in the U.S., and that in consequence, local officials and parents decide what shall be taught. Fawcett and Thomas comment in some amazement on Texas governor James Ferguson, who once stated, "If English was good enough for Jesus, it's good enough for the schoolchildren of Texas." Lyndon Johnson used to tell a story of a would-be teacher who was told that there was a difference in the community over geography: "Do you teach that the world is round or do you teach that the world is flat?" "I can teach it either way," was the inevitable reply. E. Fawcett and T. Thomas, *America and the Americans* (London: Fontana, 1983), p. 298. Census data indicate that 43 percent of African Americans in the Northeastern region of the U.S. attend schools that are 95 percent nonwhite.

62. See G. L. Clark and N. Blomley, "Law, Theory and Geography," *Urban Geography* 11, no. 5 (1990):433–46.

63. R. H. Freilich, S. M. Connet, and J. E. Walters, "Federalism in Transition: The Emergence of New State and Local Strategies in the Face of the Vanishing Tenth Amendment," *The Urban Lawyer* 20 (1988):863–967.

64. This definition comes from the best work on this topic, G. L. Clark, *Judges and the Cities* (Chicago: University of Chicago Press, 1985).

65. Magnusson, "Bourgeois Theories of Local Government," p. 2.

66. R. J. Johnston, "Local Government and the State," in M. Pacione (ed.), *Progress in Political Geography* (London: Croom Helm, 1985), pp. 152–76.

67. A good deal has been written about localities with revolutionary tendencies—for example, the "Moscows" and "Soviets" that have grown up intermittently throughout Europe. A very early example was the illegal establishment of collective bargaining in Oldham, England at the beginning of the nineteenth century, which was ended after military occupation; see Duncan and Goodwin, *The Local State and Uneven Development,* and J. Foster, *Class Struggle and the Industrial Revolution* (London: Methuen, 1974). For an overview of center-local relations in the U.K., see K. Hoggart, *People, Power, and Place* (London: Routledge, 1991).

68. Magnusson, "Bourgeois Theories of Local Government."

69. Duncan and Goodwin, *The Local State and Uneven Development;* J. R.

Wolch, *The Shadow State* (New York: The Foundation Center, 1990). Representing as it did several million voters, the GLC was not typical of the local states that we have considered above. Given its size and geographical extent, it is unsurprising that the GLC was governed less like a local state and more like a regional government, with its own foreign policy, arts policy, and so on.

70. A. Kirby, "A Public City: Concepts of Space and the Local State," *Urban Geography* 4, no. 3 (1983):191–202.

71. The sheer weight of the state's response indicates a perception of the political threat to the state by a local unit. To paraphrase Hoggart, the state stoops dangerously low when it attacks the local jurisdiction; nor have social movements ceased in London, a recognition that local politics emerge from long-standing social practice, and do not depend explicitly upon forms of local government for shape or vigor; *People, Power, and Place.*

72. Duncan and Goodwin, *The Local State and Uneven Development*, p. 269.

73. M. D. Ward and L. House, "A Theory of Behavioral Power," *Journal of Conflict Resolution* 32 (1988):3–36.

74. These simplistic allusions are mine.

75. This is discussed further by R. Siverson and H. Starr, *The Diffusion of War* (Ann Arbor: University of Michigan Press, 1991).

76. No. 85–1199 *First English Evangelical Lutheran Church of Glendale v. County of Los Angeles, California,* Ct. App. Cal., 2d App. Dist. and No. 86–133 *Nollan Et. Ux v. California Coastal Commission,* 177 Cal. App. 3d. 719, 223 Cal. Rptr 28.

77. Shuman, "Courts v. Local Foreign Policies."

78. Not the least advantage is that the dispersal of the groups has made it impossible for judges and the IRS to seize Operation Rescue's assets.

79. Giddens, *The Nation State and Violence* (Cambridge: Polity Press, 1985), p. 21.

80. See T. M. Knox's 1952 translation of Hegel's *Philosophy of Right* (Oxford: Oxford University Press), for instance, pp. 122–23 and paragraph 288. This line of reasoning is also developed with great elegance by Magnusson, "Bourgeois Theories of Local Government."

81. See L. A. Mulholland, "Hegel and Marx on the Human Individual," in W. Desmond (ed.), *Hegel and His Critics* (Albany: SUNY Press, 1989), pp. 56–71.

82. For a broader interpretation of the return to Hegel, see K. Surin, "Marxism and 'The Withering Away of the State,'" *Social Text* 9, no. 3 (1990):35–54.

6. Ordnance and Ordinance

1. Charles Dickens, *Martin Chuzzlewit* (1842); see J. Anderson, "Packing Heat," *New Republic,* February 25, 1985, pp. 38–39.

2. See, for additional information, P. Rossi and J. D. Wright, *Under the Gun* (New York: Aldine, 1983).

3. J. D. Wright, "Second Thoughts about Gun Control," *The Public Interest* 91, no. 3 (1988):23–39.

4. Notable here is the 1968 Gun Control Act, which was a significantly timed response to the assassinations of that year.

5. Wright, "Second Thoughts about Gun Control."

6. In 1987, 16 people were shot in one incident in Palm Bay, Florida; in 1988, 16 were shot in two incidents in Illinois and South Carolina, and 7 were killed in Sunnyvale, California; in 1989, 35 children were wounded in Stockton, California.

7. The vote on October 17, 1991 removed a clause from an anti-crime bill dealing with assault weapons and large ammunition clips; the vote was 247–177. A

clause allowing the use of improper search warrants was passed by virtually the same margin.

8. Executive Director's Report "Special Issue: Guns and Violence—A National Tragedy," *The Police Chief,* March 1988, p. 8.

9. M. K. Beard and K. M. Rand, "The Handgun Battle," *Bill of Rights Journal* 20 (1987):13–16.

10. It is not the intention of this chapter to explore the motives of the NRA and its 3 million members in resisting gun control. There is no question, though, that arms manufacture is big business, and it is not unusual for industries which produce controversial products (alcohol, tobacco) to maintain extensive lobbying efforts. This is explored further in the North Carolina case, below.

11. Beard and Rand, "The Handgun Battle."

12. While individual owners and pro-gun interests have challenged Morton Grove (and similar ordinances) from the standpoint of the Second Amendment, it is also easy to see the roots of conflict between localities and the States over this issue. The irony of the Second Amendment for residents in localities passing gun-control ordinances is that while it does not guarantee *individual* rights, it does apply explic-itly to the rights of the States: the Supreme Court ruled in 1886, in a judgement involving Illinois, that States could indeed regulate the private holding of firearms in any way that they chose; ibid., p. 14.

13. L. D. Cress, "An Armed Community: The Origins and Meaning of the Right to Bear Arms," *Journal of American History* 71 (1984):22–42; see also a response by R. E. Shalhope, pp. 587–92.

14. The Morton Grove resolution begins as follows:

Whereas: thousands of Americans are felled by handguns annually; whereas the vast majority of police officers killed in the line of duty were felled by handguns; whereas the use of handguns for sporting or recreational purposes does not require the keeping of handguns in private homes; and whereas the US Supreme Court ruled in 1939 that firearms regulation is not unconstitutional unless it impairs the effectiveness of the State militia; and whereas the Village of Morton Grove, Cook County Illinois has recently adopted ordinances prohibiting the sale and possession of handguns. . . .

15. L. Schey and G. R. Rossler, "The Morton Grove Ordinance," *Police Chief* 50, no. 2 (1983):22.

16. *Wall Street Journal,* 1987, p. 21.

17. *New York Times,* May 13, 1987, p. 17; *Wall Street Journal,* September 3, 1987, p. 21; compare with chapter 5, note 45.

18. T. Lattanzio, "Florida Gun Owners and Lawmen Stand Together," *American Rifleman* 135, no. 5 (1987):42–43.

19. M. Tucker, "The Consequences of Liberalizing Gun Laws," *Police Chief* 55 (1988):68–69.

20. Lattanzio, "Florida Gun Owners and Lawmen," p. 88.

21. Ibid.

22. Ibid.

23. G. L. Clark, *Judges and the Cities* (Chicago: University of Chicago Press, 1985), p. 161.

24. The specifically local interests in this case are the concerns of Maryland residents over the spillover of drug-related gang violence from Washington, D.C. *Wall Street Journal,* October 22, 1988; *Guns and Ammo,* March 1989, pp. 28–31. In contrast, the NRA's national agenda has included $2.7 million worth of support for the 1986 McClure/Volker amendments (HR 4332) to the 1968 Gun Control Act, which *inter alia* overrode local legislation concerning the interstate transport of weapons.

25. This discussion is taken from G. R. Jacob and A. Kirby, "On the Road to

Ruin: The Transportation of Deadly Cargoes," in J. Birks and A. Ehrlich (eds.), *The Environmental Consequences of Preparing for War* (San Francisco: Sierra Books, 1990), pp. 71–95.

26. General Preamble to Inconsistency Rulings IR7 through IR15, 49 *Federal Register* 46, 632, 1984.

27. T. Wallace, "Preemption of Local Laws by the Hazardous Materials Transportation Act," *University of Chicago Law Review* 53 (1986):654–81, p. 661.

28. Lattanzio, "Florida Gun Owners and Lawmen," p. 43.

29. Indeed, the unthinkable is already occurring. North Carolina legislators discussed increasing taxes on tobacco in 1991 because of budget shortfalls, a tactic they had never dared try before; *Wall Street Journal,* June 17, 1991, p. A12.

30. *New York Times,* November 11, 1989, p. 13.

31. All of these concerns are discussed in greater detail in my chapter "The Pentagon *versus* the Cities?" in A. Kirby (ed.), *The Pentagon and the Cities* (Newbury Park, Calif.: Sage, 1992), pp. 1–22.

32. See S. Tucker, "Gender, Fucking and Utopia: An Essay in Response to John Stoltenberg's *Refusing to Be a Man,*" *Social Text* 9, no. 2 (1990):1–34.

33. P. Weiss, "Forbidden Pleasures," in M. S. Kimmel (ed.), *Men Confront Pornography* (New York: Crown, 1990), pp. 91–98.

34. S. Tucker, "Radical Feminism and Gay Male Porn," in ibid., pp. 263–76.

35. This has been explained in terms of the Tiebout hypothesis, a neoclassical game in which residents circulate until they find a jurisdiction which has the bundle of services they require at the lowest price. Such a view sees a perpetual sorting and segregation of residents into units that are very different, even when they are close by. See my paper "Pseudo-random Thoughts on Space, Scale and Ideology in Political Geography," *Political Geography Quarterly* 4, no. 1 (1985):5–18, and J. Whiteman, "Deconstructing the Tiebout Hypothesis," *Environment and Planning D: Society and Space* 1 (1983):339–53. It should be noted that while this perspective is clearly based on the whimsy of rational choice models, similar interpretations were made by Fabian socialists such as Sidney Webb, who wrote that "in the State of Tomorrow . . . those who did not like the arrangements of Hampstead would always be able to move to Highgate"; quoted in W. Magnusson, "Bourgeois Theories of Local Government," *Political Studies* 34 (1986):1–18, p. 13.

36. *Los Angeles Times,* November 7, 1991, p. A41.

37. For a detailed examination of aboriginal land claims issues and resistance in Newfoundland, see P. Armitage, "Indigenous Homelands and the Security Requirements of Western Nation States: Innu Opposition to Military Flight Training in Eastern Quebec and Labrador," in A. Kirby (ed.), *The Pentagon and the Cities* (Newbury Park, Calif.: Sage, 1991), pp. 126–53.

38. For press reports, see *Insight,* September 10, 1990, pp. 36–38.

39. In the spring of 1992, the FBI raided several Indian reservations where gambling was taking place without State approval.

7. New Places, New Politics

1. W. H. Auden, "In Praise of Limestone," in *Nones* (New York: Random House, 1952).

2. This chapter is an extension of a conference paper written by the author in November 1990, based on discussions with colleagues at the University of Arizona. That paper, "On the Edge of All Possibilities: Political-Economic Change Where Core Meets Semi-periphery," by Andrew Kirby with Helen Ingram, Melinda Laituri, and Barbara Morehouse, was prepared for a meeting on Urban Planning and Government Reorganization in Poland ("Polish Needs, U.S. Lessons") which took place at

Rutgers University. The influence and assistance of colleagues at, and financial support from, the Udall Center for Studies in Public Policy are noted with thanks.

3. See, for instance, D. Gordon, "Global Economy: New Edifice or Crumbling Foundation?" *New Left Review* 168 (1988):24–65. This critique is reviewed—and somewhat summarily dismissed—by D. Harvey, *The Condition of Postmodernity* (Oxford: Blackwell, 1989), p. 191.

4. E. Mingione, *Fragmented Societies* (Oxford: Blackwell, 1991), p. 433.

5. Naturally enough, these definitions are still grounded in the more certain context of *historical* meanings, such as those that resurfaced around the fiftieth anniversary of the attack on Pearl Harbor in 1991. In communities in Arizona, Japanese vehicles were banned from commemorative parades—and just for good measure, *German* vehicles were also excluded.

6. Mingione, *Fragmented Societies,* p. 434.

7. By way of reminder, this interpretation rests upon a critique of the new industrial geography, which claims a localization trend that forms the base for a new class politics; see, for instance, A. Amin and K. Robins, *Environment and Planning D: Society and Space* 8, no. 1 (1990):7–34; Lefebvre, cited in ibid., p. 26.

8. This emphasis upon scale is consistent with, though not necessarily in agreement with, the formulations of world systems theory and its variations; for a recent summary, see P. Taylor, "Political Geography within World-Systems Analysis," *Review* 14, no. 3 (1991):387–402.

9. Watts quotes Gomez-Pena, who asks, "Who are we exactly? The off-spring of the synthesis, the victims of the fragmentation; the victims of double colonialism or the bearers of a new vision?" M. Watts, "Mapped Meaning, Denoting Difference, Imaging Identity: Dialectical Images and Postmodern Geographies," *Geografiska Annaler* 73B (1991):7–16, p. 11.

10. In this regard, the vulnerability of the peso is revealed; in McDonald's restaurants inside the Canadian border, transactions can be undertaken directly in either Canadian or U.S. dollars.

11. Literally "halfbreed." I have borrowed this word from the writings of Gloria Anzaldua; see *Borderlands = La Frontera* (San Francisco: Spinsters/Aunt Lute, 1987).

12. L. Cattan, "TV en espanol ofrece calidad cuestionable," *Arizona Daily Star,* November 13, 1991.

13. J. Carrillo, "The De-ideologizing of Studies on Maquiladoras," *Journal of Borderlands Studies* 5, no. 1 (1990):10–14, p. 13.

14. J. B. Anderson, "Maquiladoras and Border Industrialization: Impact on Economic Development in Mexico," *Journal of Borderlands Studies* 5, no. 1 (1990):5–9, p. 7; L. Sklair, *Assembling for Development: The Maquila Industry in Mexico and the United States* (Boston: Unwin Hyman, 1989).

15. See Mingione, *Fragmented Societies,* chapter 6. Development of the Mezzogiorno was based upon wholesale migration of families from rural areas, the maintenance of localized crafts, and the consequent development of small-scale industries. The situation in northern Mexico is very different, as we see there seasonal migration, few if any skills being transplanted to urban areas, and little indigenous capitalization.

16. J. Carrillo, *Mercados de Trabajo en la Industria Maquiladora de Exportacion* (Tijuana: COLEF, 1991).

17. B. Tomaso and R. Alm, "Economy vs. Ecology: Mexico's Drive for Growth Eclipses Concerns about Toxic Waste from Border Plants," *Transboundary Resources Report* 4, no. 1 (1990):1–3.

18. See, for example, M. Castells, *The City and the Grassroots* (London: Arnold, 1983). The El Paso Interreligious Sponsoring Organization (EPISO) and San Anto-

nio's Communities Organized for Public Service (COPS) have both sponsored political activism along the Texas border in recent years; see G. Towers, "Alinsky Organizing in El Paso and San Antonio," paper presented to the Western Social Science Organization, Reno, 1991.

19. The taxonomy of core, periphery, and semi-periphery is, of course, taken from the world-systems literature. By the core, we are identifying economically developed capitalist nation states (U.S., BRD, France). In the periphery, we can place the many dozen LDCs that are burdened with massive foreign debts, rising populations, shrinking export returns, and falling standards of living. Somewhere between the two extremes lie the nations of the semi-periphery; many of them are planned economies that have undergone some economic transformations, extensive urbanization, and industrialization, but which have failed to escape the whirlwind of the international debt crisis. Mexico would be a candidate for inclusion in the semi-periphery; see R. Ross and D. Trachte, *Global Capitalism: The New Leviathan* (New York: SUNY Press, 1990).

20. I use the term "frontier" deliberately, in order to give a sense of administrative discontinuity between states, even though Giddens rejects the term as archaic; A. Giddens, *The Nation State and Violence* (Cambridge: Polity Press, 1985), p. 52.

21. See ibid., chapters 2–4.

22. The authority figure from elsewhere is a stock character in many novels, such as Gabriel Chevalier's *Clochmerle,* or indeed many of Kafka's stories. Along the *frontera,* this figure is now typically a member of the U.S. Border Patrol, an agency whose oversight is divided between the FBI, the Office of the Inspector General, the Justice Department, and the U.S. Attorney's Office. In consequence, it has been described as "the most uncontrolled, unsupervised and undisciplined law-enforcement agency in the country." W. Langewische, "The Border," *The Atlantic* 269, no. 5 (1992):53–92, p. 70.

23. L. Herzog, *Where North Meets South: Cities, Space, and Politics on the U.S. Mexico Border* (Austin, Tex.: CMAS, 1990).

24. For a successful piece of work, see J. W. House, *Frontier on the Rio Grande* (Oxford: Clarendon, 1982).

25. M. de Certeau, *The Practice of Everyday Life* (Berkeley: University of California Press, 1984), p. 127.

26. In the fall of 1991, Mexico removed all its uniformed frontier officers overnight, and reassigned them to other duties. They were replaced by a new cohort, dressed not in uniform but in dark blue suits. The move took place amidst intense discussions over free trade, and was designed to overcome the corruption among border personnel that slows down cross-border traffic. New checkpoints to facilitate faster processing of trucks and private vehicles are also under construction along the border.

27. Hundreds of millions of dollars of personal capital find their way out of Mexico every year and are placed in U.S. bank accounts.

28. O. Martinez, "Transnational Frontizeros: Cross Border Linkages in Mexican Border Society," *Journal of Borderlands Studies* 5, no. 1 (1990):79–94.

29. As Newman also points out, this has had an unexpected consequence: while it has made Palestinians easier to control, it has also allowed car bombers to retaliate against Israeli drivers. D. Newman, "Civilian and Military Presence as Strategies of Territorial Control," *Political Geography Quarterly* 8, no. 3 (1989):215–28. Mexico's *frontizeros* also display different license plates, and share an ability with U.S. residents to drive freely within the border zone. On the frictions generated by the militarization of a border region, see J. P. Augelli, "Nationalization of Dominican Borderlands," *Geographical Review* 70, no. 1 (1980):19–35; R. Strassoldo, "Regional Development and National Defense: A Conflict of Values and Power in a

Frontier Region," in R. Strassoldo (ed.), *Confini e Regioni* (Trieste: Edizioni LINT, 1973).

30. Despite a climate of attrition in the defense sector, Congress approved appropriations of $20.5 million for new facilities in southern Arizona, both for the National Guard and at Fort Huachuca, site of an extensive remote-sensing operation directed against drug imports.

31. There are many reasons why this new "enemy" has been attacked at this time, and the need by military leaders to create new tasks is an important one; see M. Waterstone and A. Kirby, "Escaping the Conceptual Box: Ideological and Economic Conversion," in A. Kirby (ed.), *The Pentagon and the Cities* (Newbury Park, Calif.: Sage, 1992).

32. Direct quotes taken from unpublished briefing material distributed to JTF-Six personnel, 1990.

33. Other flows—such as the smuggling of firearms and automobiles into Mexico—are rarely addressed in the U.S.

34. S. Harding, "Aerostat!" *Soldiers* (1990):14–20.

35. C. Duarte, "Tucson Border Patrol Sector Is No. 1 in Seizures for Fiscal '91," *Arizona Daily Star,* November 14, 1991, p. B2.

36. M. Williams, "INS Plans to Use More Soldiers in Control of the Border," *Arizona Daily Star,* October 25, 1990. There has also been increased cooperation between local police officers, in an apparent effort by the United States to generate greater legitimacy for the Mexican authorities.

37. Indeed, a diplomatic note was issued by the Mexican ambassador in Washington, and heightened tensions were observed in negotiations between national representatives; see *New York Times,* February 18, 1990: "Sovereignty and suspicion hinder U.S./Mexico drug alliance." During 1991, these fears subsided, primarily as a result of Mexico's urgency to ratify the FTA, and both countries signed a Mutual Legal Assistance Treaty. This permits U.S. law enforcers greater latitude in investigating drug and auto theft cases in Mexico.

38. Recent calls to monitor the U.S. Border Patrol, generated by a citizens' task force in San Diego County, also emphasized the importance of participation by Mexican citizens; "Citizens' Review Panel Urged for Border Patrol," *Arizona Daily Star,* May 24, 1992.

39. San Diego would be an important exception to this argument, although much of its economic development was predicated on its military infrastructure.

40. H. M. Ingram, "State Government Officials' Role in U.S./Mexico Transboundary Resource Issues," *Natural Resources Journal* 28 (1988):431–49.

41. See, for example, M. H. Shuman, *Building Municipal Foreign Policies* (Irvine, Calif.: Center for Innovative Diplomacy, 1987).

42. Ngugi wa Thiong'o, *Petals of Blood* (London: Heinemann).

43. The Border Trade Alliance is a corporate group that attempts to link the needs of investors and producers in both countries. The Border Governors' Conference is a forum that attracts gubernatorial representatives from both Mexico and the U.S. The 1991 meeting attracted ten governors, who discussed trade, investment, health, and the environment. The Organization for Free Trade and Development is a newer group dedicated to providing research information to corporations wanting to take advantage of NAFTA.

44. A. M. Kirby and K. A. Lynch, "A Ghost in the Growth Machine: The Aftermath of Rapid Population Growth in Houston," *Urban Studies* 24, no. 6 (1987):587–96; J. Logan and H. Molotch, *Urban Fortunes* (Berkeley: University of California Press, 1987).

45. It is not uncommon to see a hose thrown over the international fence in

Nogales, connecting a water truck that serves the unsupplied *colonias* to a hydrant in Arizona.

46. J. Juffer, "Dump at the Border," *The Progressive,* October 1988, pp. 24–29. As Tomaso and Alm comment, the trade in 55-gallon drums also points to the lax controls exerted on the disposal of toxics; "Economy vs. Ecology," p. 2.

47. A. Tecle, *Multicriterion Modeling of Wastewater Management* (Tucson: Department of Hydrology, University of Arizona, 1986). Water represents a fundamental resource in a semi-arid region such as the Southwest, and social conflicts and coalitions have arisen over the questions of water supply, use, and quality. Within Ambos Nogales, the topographic layout of the area imposes a particular pattern of river flow and aquifer access which dictates that residents and industrial users on both sides of the border are in direct competition for water. The flow of the Santa Cruz also decrees that wastewater—much of it untreated—flows from Sonora to Arizona. We can interpret these conflicts as examples of real political struggles and as metaphors for the wider processes of social change within the locality.

48. D. Solis and S. L. Nazario, "U.S., Mexico Take On Border Pollution," *Wall Street Journal,* February 25, 1992, p. B1.

49. EPA/SEDUE, *Integrated Environmental Plan for the Mexico/U.S. Border Area* (1991). Sections of the report cite the *Encyclopedia Britannica,* and population data are hopelessly out of date; B. Hawkins, "Botched Rescue," *Tucson Weekly,* November 6, 1991, pp. 12–15.

50. Subsequent reports commit the U.S. to less financial support than Mexico, despite its vastly superior economy; *Wall Street Journal,* February 25, 1992, p. B1.

51. As NAFTA came closer to reality during 1991, a number of federal infrastructural projects were announced, including the improvement of bridges and other border crossings. In Nogales, Arizona, federal funds were sought to construct a new access road for a large shopping mall. The Mexican government also indicated a willingness to improve roads leading to border crossings.

52. See, for instance, the remarks of Duke in the newsletter of his National Association for the Advancement of White People; E. Langer, "The American Neo-Nazi Movement Today," *The Nation,* July 16–23, 1990, p. 95.

53. There is an irony to Bentsen's comments, given his opposition to Free Trade, for Mexico has begun to move rapidly toward tougher implementation since NAFTA talks began; see M. McIntosh, *Doing Business in Mexico* (Albuquerque: International Transboundary Resources Center, 1992), p. 22.

54. Statements reported in K. Hickox, "Border Alert," *Arizona Daily Star,* August 20, 1991, p. A9.

8. Empowerment within the Local State

1. R. Williams, *Towards 2000* (Harmondsworth: Penguin, 1985), p. 268.

2. For example, a number of American and European magazines, including *Spy, Actuel,* and *Face,* provided lists of telephone numbers attached to government fax machines throughout China, so that their readers could protest the events of Tiananmen Square in 1989.

3. See K. Surin, "Marxism and 'The Withering Away of the State,'" *Social Text* 9, no. 3 (1990):35–54.

4. This observation follows Daniel Bell; A. Giddens, *The Consequences of Modernity* (Stanford: Stanford University Press, 1990), p. 65.

5. Gayatri Spivak writes of capital being "sublated into the speed of light" in "The Political Economy of Women as Seen by a Literary Critic," in E. Meed (ed.), *Coming to Terms* (London: Routledge, 1989), pp. 218–29.

6. There was, for example, a long and sterile literature in the 1970s exploring the question of an optimum *city* size.

7. The U.S. Border Patrol budget increased 77 percent between 1986 and 1991.

8. P. Kennedy, "The (Relative) Decline of America," *Atlantic Monthly,* August 1987, pp. 29–38.

9. N. Hartsock, "Postmodernism and Political Change: Issues for Feminist Theory," *Cultural Critique* 14 (1990):15–34.

10. As a critic of the state and of the psychiatric establishment, Foucault was a combatant in a number of critical political struggles; as a homosexual who died of AIDS, he had a personal life that was also symbolic of struggle. D. Eribon, *Michel Foucault* (Cambridge: Harvard University Press, 1991).

11. D. Harvey, *The Condition of Postmodernity* (Oxford: Blackwell, 1989), p. 46.

12. Ibid., p. 239.

13. Iris Murdoch, *The Sovereignty of Good* (Cambridge: Cambridge University Press, 1967), p. 72; quoted in B. T. Wilkins, *Hegel's Philosophy of History* (Ithaca: Cornell University Press, 1974), p. 143.

14. D. Harvey, "Reconsidering Social Theory: A Debate," *Environment and Planning D: Society and Space* 5, no. 4 (1987):367–76, p. 373.

15. P. Bachrach and A. Botwinick, *Power and Empowerment* (Philadelphia: Temple University Press, 1992).

16. Ibid, p. 168.

17. M. Gottdiener, *The Decline of Urban Politics* (Newbury Park, Calif.: Sage, 1987).

18. Harvey, *The Condition of Postmodernity,* pp. 238–39; A. Pred, *Making Histories and Constructing Human Geographies* (Boulder: Westview, 1990), p. 232.

19. M. H. Shuman, "Courts v. Local Foreign Policies," *Foreign Policy* 86 (1992):158–77, p. 167, citing law theorist J. N. Moore. Young attributes the same sentiment to Jeane Kirkpatrick, arguing that "foreign policy cannot be made by the citizenry"; I. M. Young, *Justice and the Politics of Difference* (Princeton: Princeton University Press, 1990), p. 84. See also C. F. Alger's excellent review "The World Relations of Cities," *International Studies Quarterly* 34 (1990):493–518.

20. M. Glassner, *Neptune's Domain* (London: Unwin Hyman, 1990).

21. A. Ross, "Is Global Culture Warming Up?" *Social Text* 28 (1991):3–30.

22. I write that there "appear to" be globalization processes, for this is a contested assertion in some fields. For instance, Gordon has tried to show that we are not in a different phase of capital transfer at present; see chapter 1. In terms of popular culture, we see phenomena such as "world music," but this is a misleading conceit that is simply the haphazard repackaging of folk and classical music from various local cultures, without any effort at synthesis or integration.

23. R. B. J. Walker, "Sovereignty, Identity, Community," in R. B. J. Walker and S. H. Mendlovitz (eds.), *Contending Sovereignties* (Boulder: Lynne Rienner, 1990), pp. 159–86.

24. I am indebted to Jim Farr for clarifying that Hobbes, too, alongside Locke, recognized natural law.

25. Although the state typically acts to control labor unions, we should note Miliband's inclusion of the latter in the institutions of the state, insofar as they act to control and standardize workplace action. R. Miliband, *The State in Capitalist Society* (London: Quartet, 1973) (see chapter 3).

26. The *Citizen's Charter,* White Paper Cm 1599 (London: Government Cabinet Office, 1991).

27. A. Kearns, "Active Citizenship and Urban Governance," *Transactions of the Institute of British Geographers* 17, no. 1 (1992):20–34.

28. The Kettering Foundation, *Citizens and Politics: A View from Main Street America* (Dayton, Ohio, 1991).

29. Ibid., p. 8.

30. Young, for example, dismisses community life as "utopian," on the grounds that it does not deal with the interactions of individuals within locales or interactions across the borders of localities; Young, *Justice and the Politics of Difference,* pp. 233–34.

31. B. J. Eckstein, *The Language of Fiction in a World of Pain: Reading Politics as Paradox* (Philadelphia: University of Pennsylvania Press, 1990).

32. Bachrach and Botwinick, *Power and Empowerment,* chapter 7.

33. See Riet Delsing's use of Foucault in her analysis of women's struggles in Chile, "Sovereign and Disciplinary Power," in K. Davis, M. Leijenaar, and J. Oldersma, *The Gender of Power* (Newbury Park, Calif.: Sage, 1991), pp. 129–53. She writes, "Foucault takes issue with the practice of posing a hierarchy of 'real issues' when he states that 'nothing in society will be changed if the mechanisms of power that function outside, below and alongside the state apparatuses, on a much more minute and everyday level, are not also changed' (Foucault, 1980, 60)." The examples of Eastern Europe are instructive in this context, for there citizens are faced with the challenge of rehabilitating thousands of individuals who were placed in the secret police, the universities, and other institutions by the state prior to 1990.

34. M. Foucault, "The Masked Philosopher," in S. Lotringer (ed.), *Foucault Live* (New York: Semiotexte, 1989), p. 202.

INDEX

ANDREW KIRBY is Associate Dean of Social and Behavioral Sciences at the University of Arizona, where he is also Professor of Geography and Regional Development. He edits the series Advanced Area Studies for Routledge and Society, Environment, and Place for the University of Arizona Press. He has written or edited more than a dozen books, including *Nothing to Fear: Risks and Hazards in American Society* and *The Pentagon and the Cities*.